Connell   423 So. Rampart
Los Angeles
SWELL PHOTOGRAPHER

George Herriman in a cabinet portrait, c. 1940. Courtesy of and thanks to Philippe Ghielmetti.

KRAZY & IGNATZ.

by George Herriman.

"He Nods in Quiescent Siesta."

Completing the Full-Page Comic Strips.

1943-44.

Edited by Bill Blackbeard
with Contributions by Jeet Heer and Michael Tisserand.

Fantagraphics Books, SEATTLE.

Published by Fantagraphics Books.
7563 Lake City Way North East,
Seattle, Washington, 98115, United States of America.

Edited by Bill Blackbeard.
Except where noted, all research materials appear courtesy of the San Francisco Academy of Cartoon Art.
Additional research by Jeet Heer.
Design, decoration, and occasional cutlines by Chris Ware.
Production assistance and scanning by Paul Baresh.
Promoted by Eric Reynolds.
Published by Gary Groth and Kim Thompson.

First Fantagraphics Books edition: July 2008.

ISBN: 978-1-56097-932-6.

Printed in Korea through Print Vision.

Special thanks to Derya Ataker, Arnold Blumberg, Dee Cox, Claudine Dixon, Craig Englund,
Andrew Farago, John Fawcett, Steve Geppi, Philippe Ghielmetti, Glen David Gold, Hal Hagy, Andy
Hershberger, Harvey Leake, Peter Maresca, Rick Marschall, Dan McConnell, Craig McCracken, Patrick
McDonnell, Ulrich Merkl, Peter Merolo, Joe Moore, Mark Newgarden, Rob Stolzer, Catherine
Ternaux & the CNBDI, Michael Tisserand, and Malcolm and Karen Whyte.

KRAZY & IGNATZ.

George Herriman's last Sunday page, original drawing, 1944. Courtesy of Geppi's Entertainment Museum.

THE TRAGEDY OF A MAN WITH AN ABSENT MIND.

By Bill Blackbeard.

*"I want **me**."*
—*Isaac Asimov on his death bed*

When the ravages of a disease like George Herriman's deadly cirrhosis of 1944 have taken their toll on a once active intellect, what remains may be the mere breathing hull of a departed persona where a mentality has simply shut down for good. Poe put it well: "Broken is the golden bowl, the spirit, from forever." It is a kind of death in seeming life, the saddest exit a human being can take from creative self-awareness in art and life.

In Herriman's case, the shutdown of self can be (all too painfully) tracked in the first of his final four Sunday *Kat* tabs, presumably drawn in April, the month of his death, for release in June of 1944. (Apparently he had been drawing these in monthly groups of four or five for syndicate delivery, having been encouraged to adhere to this routine by his doctor as worthwhile therapy.) It is clear that the Herriman we have read in prior work is irretrievably gone: The page design is fine, as usual, as are the color, layout, and background art, but the character action, viewed in terms of Coconino reality, is simply Mad Hatter.

Why, in the first of the group (June 4), is Ignatz residing underground with a brick on his head? Why is Ignatz's commentary reduced to "uh-h, ah-h"? Why does Offisa Pupp echo this monosyllable with an "Ah-h" of his own, while seeking bricks in a gutter with a suddenly extensible divining stick?

Similar mysteries cloud the lovely design of the page for June 11, 1944. The stunted Krazy of the first panel can be accounted for by the grueling pain Herriman's disease caused him when drawing, also leading to storylines utilizing a minimum of characters in the very last two *Kat* pages. In this episode, we do have two charming touches of the now largely lost artist in his allotting a "k" in spelling "crow" only to Krazy's dialogue, and in his little drawing of a "scaremouse" in the bottom panel. Elsewhere, all is enigma. Is the upright stick in the next to last panel supposed to suggest Ignatz's earthy domicile, complete with brick, waiting for a puppset cop to strike? And why the long winding and very empty road to nowhere? The debate over the scarecrow goes nowhere, with Ignatz shown uncharacteristically throwing away an unused brick for no apparent reason.

In the weird aquatics of the last two June *Kats* we find Krazy (referred to as "him" in the first of the two) apparently as bent on submerging herself in multi-colored pools of water as Ignatz was in burying himself in soil.

And yet... It could be argued that the images of interment and submersion (and even more so the final two panels, which show Krazy first paralyzed and then floating), unmoored from any apparent point or premise within the strips' storylines, represent Herriman grappling with his own impending death. In which case this quartet of strips comprises a sad, eerie, and yet in some ways fitting conclusion to Herriman's insuperable run on what has often been called the greatest comic strip ever drawn — more oblique in its wistfulness than Charles Schulz's famous final Sunday-page farewell to his *Peanuts* characters, yet similarly affecting and definitive.

This volume concludes the reprinting of the second, decade-long, group of color *Krazy Kat* Sunday pages (1935-1944). The first, from 1919, will appear when Fantagraphics reprints the first nine years of mostly black and white Sundays originally released in book form by Eclipse Comics, projected as a series of three fat volumes. Also in queue are collections of the komplete (insofar as they can be gathered) *Krazy Kat* dailies, the full *Stumble Inn* daily-and-Sunday run, more short-lived strips such as the little-seen 1930s Sunday-only domestic comedy *Us Husbands*, and the complete *Baron Bean*. In these pages Herriman lives on, and we hope you will continue to join us in our celebration of his work.

—Bill Blackbeard, Watsonville, May 2008

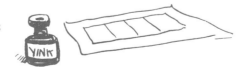

Herriman
2217 Maravilla [St]
Hollywood
Calif.

LOS ANGELES AUG 6 3:30 PM 1938 CALIF.

UNITED STATES POSTAGE 3 CENTS HOLLYWOO[D]

LOUISE S. SWINNERTON
409 LINCOLN
"PALO ALTO"
CALIFORNIA

I was just a lad of 42 —
a fine, upstanding bucko,
full of a fine bottle of
rheumatism — sore feet,
and a bent lock bone —
— T'was a jaunty journey
Sweet loss — the memory
lingers —
Here am I, writing —
which I dislike as much
as I do, taking a bath —
— God forgive me —
y' lured me — asking me
to send you last — this
picture — I'm a weakling —!

Yours' too true comrade —
one friend — ~~too~~ one woman,
and one undershirt —
there is the glory —

P.S. and one
Kidney!

"Ole man" HERRIMAN

"Louise — my dear —
Aye, my good woman
I do indeed deem it
a comical picture —
I've had many a
sweet laugh at it
— and others — of that
trip — which I still
have — what a
gruant aggregation —
what a fine body
of men — —
— that you two
ladies should so
perpetuate yourselves
— Have ye no shame?
My birth day was
celebrated at that
time — I still
have, the "paper"
signed by all
in the "botty" —
Yours among them —

Letter to Louise Swinnerton, August 6th, 1939. Herriman apparently wrote it to her in the bathtub.
Collection C. Ware.

HERRIMAN'S LAST DAYS.

(or, All Kats are Gray in the Dark.)

By Jeet Heer & Michael Tisserand.

In the end, almost the only thing George Herriman had left was Krazy Kat. While other successful cartoonists of his era tended to take early retirements, still signing their strips but leaving the actual writing and drawing to apprentices, Herriman remained ever the artist and in his last years threw himself more and more into his work. As Herriman's admirer Charles Schulz would do with *Peanuts*, Krazy Kat's creator basically died with his strip, continuing to keep his deadlines until the end, leaving behind two months' worth of strips, including a fascinating unfinished week's worth of dailies.

Although he wasn't an old man when he died in 1944 of non-alcoholic cirrhosis of the liver, only 63 in fact so not even eligible for legal retirement, he had suffered more than his share of the ravages of age, especially with the loss of loved ones. In September of 1931, his wife Mabel was killed in a car accident, as she swerved to avoid hitting another vehicle. It was a young death: she was only 49 and hadn't even seen her two daughters, Toodles and Barbara, both in their twenties at the time, start their own families and be well launched in their careers (both daughters had inherited their father's aesthetic inclinations and worked as artists).

Death often leads to regrouping within families and this certainly happened with the Herrimans. Half a year after the car accident, in March 1932, the 23-year-old Barbara became engaged to Ernest Pascal, who was English-born, 35-year-old and an accomplished novelist, screenwriter and playwright. Pascal was married at the time of the engagement but got a quick Reno divorce in time for a May wedding. The year he married Barbara, Pascal authored a play called *Husband's Holiday*, and he would go on to win lasting success in Hollywood writing scripts for well-known films as *The Hound of the Baskervilles* and serve as the President of the Screen Writers Guild from 1935 to 1937.

In 1934, Barbara and Ernest Pascal had their only child together, daughter Dinah (Dee for short). That same year Barbara's older sister, the 31-year-old Toodles (also known as Toots), then working as an artist, hopped on a plane to Yuma, Arizona where she married Jack Wagner, a 42-year-old screen writer who was as much a Hollywood

fixture as his new brother-in-law Pascal. Newspapers described the wedding as an "aerial elopement." Wagner had started his career as an assistant cameraman to D.W. Griffith and during his early years of married life wrote movies like *Annapolis Farewell* (1935) and *Dancing Pirate* (1936). The two Herriman weddings were strikingly parallel with both daughters rather speedily marrying screenwriters roughly a decade their senior.

Although Herriman was a young widower, just entering into his fifth decade when his wife died, he showed no inclinations to remarry. He did carry on a flirty friendship and correspondence with Louise Swinnerton, the ex-wife of Jimmy Swinnerton, a fellow cartoonist and close Herriman friend. In her earlier life, Louise had dealt with her share of roughneck men not just during her marriage to the hard-drinking and fast-living Jimmy but also in her career as a Hearst journalist, so she appreciated Herriman's gentleness, his reserved soft-spoken ways. But throughout their relationship Louise was the more active and interested party.

Why did Herriman retreat so much from active life in his last years? His health might have been a factor: he underwent a major kidney operation in 1938. During these years, his hands became creaky with arthritis, making drawing difficult, although he stoically kept up his craft. In a late-life letter to Jack Kent, a comics fan who would become a cartoonist himself, Herriman complained that "my old brain has lost its cunning and my old fingers are stiff – and won't go where I want them to."

Since Herriman lived in the Hollywood Hills, loved movies, and had many friends in the film industry, he could take comfort in the fact that his growing family was staying so close to him, both geographically and artistically. But just as the sudden death of Mabel opened the 1930s, another unexpected death closed the decade. In late 1939, Barbara, who suffered from epilepsy, died during an operation, leaving behind her husband and a 5-year-old daughter.

Barbara's daughter, Dee Cox, is now 74 years old and offers us the best glimpse we can get of her grandfather's last years. In Tucson, Arizona, on the southern end of the state where her grandfather set all his *Krazy Kat* strips, Cox keeps a home that's filled with memorabilia from Herriman's life and career, including a Navajo rug bearing the cartoonist's name. Her grandfather, she admits, is her 'favorite subject.'

"I was 9 years old when he died," she remembers. "When I knew him, he was a recluse. His daughter – my mother – had died, and his wife had died. Then he had a Japanese houseboy who got hauled off to the internment camps. The only person left for him was my Aunt Toots." (As with the death of Mabel, Barbara's sudden passing led to a family regrouping, and Toots seems to have become the glue that held them together. She not only took a maternal interest in her niece but also kept in touch with her brother-in-law, helping to produce one of Ernest Pascal's plays in the 1940s.)

Cox's aunt would take the young girl along to visit the cartoonist, who at that time was working at a drawing table in 'a pretty house in the hills,' she recalls. "He used to sit in the living room, wearing his Stetson and chain-smoking Bull Durhams. He had five Scotties, and he would say, 'Now, I have to go down and buy a leg of lamb for the dogs.'"

By the end of grandfather's life, she says, he retreated more and more into his work. "Coconino County and that strip was his reality. He was totally immersed into this world that he created."

Cox's collection of her grandfather's work includes hand-drawn cards she received from him on birthdays. She adores the *Krazy Kat* strips, especially those with her favorite character, Joe Stork. She even took a trip to New Orleans with her daughter, to see the place that George Herriman and his family left more than a century ago. "All my kids have been raised hearing about Krazy Kat," she says.

Her family was a Hollywood family and everyone was an artist in some fashion, says Dee. Her father's work as a screenwriter is still remembered and Cox is eager to emphasize that her mother, Barbara, was also an artist who painted and drew cartoons. In fact, George Herriman considered Barbara to be a budding cartoonist, Cox says. Also typical for Hollywood, the family was liberal in both personal and political matters. "The family was completely liberal," Cox says. "Religion was never mentioned in my household as a child, and race was never an issue."

In fact, Cox says, she heard that her grandmother had promised her grandfather's parents that the children would be raised Catholic. "But it didn't happen," she says.

Despite their liberal outlook, the family's own race was never discussed openly. "That was a family secret," Cox says. "I was certainly never told about it." Looking back, she recalls her aunt frequently going out to get her hair straightened (an act mimicked by Krazy Kat, who gets a straightened tail in one strip), and that her dad used to joke that her grandfather always wore his Stetson to cover his hair. "In another milieu one could have figured it out, but it was so unthinkable in those days."

In fact, it wasn't until Herriman's birth certificate was uncovered in the early 1970s that Cox herself learned of the family's Creole roots. Having just lived in Africa for several years with her husband and children, she was delighted at the news of her own mixed blood. And having just witnessed apartheid first-hand, she believed she understood why her great-grandparents decided to move to California. "We saw where blacks couldn't sit on benches, couldn't eat in restaurants,

couldn't go to the doctor. So I saw the reason why my grandfather's family left New Orleans."

Cox's memories of her grandfather mesh very nicely with the strips he drew in his last years. These are very much the work of an artist who is immersed in his fictional world. One Sunday shows Ignatz standing at a cliff, surveying the landscape of Coconino and proudly proclaiming "Isolation, 'sweet isolation' – in all it's poetic beauty – And I do plot a plan by which to render this superb solitude into a tangible to-do." This might have been Herriman's credo: using the isolation of his life to plot out ever-fresh scenarios of brick-throwing and legal retribution amid the sublime beauty of his version of the Southwest.

Although wrapped up in his strip, Herriman didn't totally ignore the outside world. The last few years of *Krazy Kat* feature many topical references. Zoot suits, a fashion rage among African-Americans and

Original drawing, for the 40th birthday of Herriman's daughter, Toots, May 1943.
This page: the envelope; opposite: the letter. Courtesy of the Cartoon Art Museum of San Francisco, with special thanks to Andrew Farago. — *J.H.*

Hispanics in the mid-1940s, are mentioned in *Krazy Kat*. The Second World War, which led to the internment of his houseboy, is also felt strongly in the strip, with the characters growing victory gardens, saving electricity with planned blackouts, and talking about the need for patriotic rationing.

Despite the patriotism of these wartime strips, Herriman didn't go in for the blind jingoism found in rival features like *Terry and the Pirates*, where the war effort was uncritically celebrated. The strip of August 2nd, 1942 contained an unusually pointed bit of political satire on wartime censorship, with Offisa Pupp making this contradictory argument: "Justice, decency, liberty – whatever offend them ... must suffer 'censorment'. Law." On April 25, 1943, Krazy Kat sees some "royal" birds, a King Fisher and his queenly wife. This intrusion of monarchy might be related to the fact that during the WWII some European crowned heads were exiled to the United States. This strip contains some subtle political humor with the other characters upbraiding Krazy's royalist sympathies. "And here we're all equal, almost," Mrs. Kwakk Wakk lectures. That "almost" is a nice touch.

Racial identity, a thread that runs through Herriman's life and work, was clearly on his mind in his last weeks of his life. On May 21st, 1944, Offisa Pupp and Krazy talk about how some animals are more valued if they're white rather than brown. The strip starts like this:

Offisa Pupp: "Mr. W. Weasel," the insurance co. consider him a poor risk – when he's brown.

Krazy: Fency a color makin' a difference in its value.

Offisa Pupp: He must be "white" to have a high rate of value – that makes him an "ermine."

Krazy: But how does he get "white"?

Later in the strip, the poor weasel does, like many other Coconino residents before him, figure out how to pass as white, with a little help

from Ignatz and a beauty parlor. (The beauty parlor calls to mind the salons where Herriman's daughters got their hair straightened). This strip, a reflection on the economic and social barriers that make passing necessary, was perhaps Herriman's final word on his racial identity. Interestingly, while passing is justified in the strip, it is also implicitly described as weaselly behavior.

What spiritual thoughts, if any, did Herriman have in his last years? While his family's inherited Catholicism might have fallen into abeyance, the education he received at St. Vincent's Academy as a teenager clearly left a lasting mark, as can be seen not just in the language of sin and forgiveness that permeates *Krazy Kat* but also in Herriman's many allusions to Biblical language and Latin (the language of the traditional Mass, which the cartoonist studied as a schoolboy). Herriman's last unfinished dailies are built around a Latin pun, showing a drunkard hick-upping these words: "hic haec hoc" (all declensions of the pronoun "this," frequently taught in introductory Latin classes).

Beyond his boyhood Catholicism, Herriman's spiritual interests roamed widely. Exotic religions flourished in Hollywood in the early 20th century and Herriman was familiar enough with them to gently chide séances, yogis, and gurus in his comic strip. More seriously, Herriman was fascinated by the spiritual beliefs of the Navaho Indians,

especially their ideas about reincarnation. He once told his friend Gilbert Seldes that he wanted to be reborn as an Indian. Reincarnation shows up occasionally as a plot device in *Krazy Kat*, with a suggestion that the Ignatz/Krazy relationship goes back to ancient Egypt, if not farther. In a deeper structural way as well, *Krazy Kat* is all about reincarnation with the characters re-enacting their destiny day after day, each fresh dawn a new occasion for brick throwing and Mouse jailing, followed by tomorrow's return to the status quo ante.

Although the characters go through the motions of their destined triangle again and again, there is very little (if any) tiredness in *Krazy Kat*. What's striking in the last strips is how zestful Herriman's work remained, how inventive especially in his sense of design. Herriman's arthritis did hinder his art slightly: the figures he drew became stiffer and his line scratchier and less fluid. But perhaps to compensate, he grew increasingly daring in his compositional sense and bold in colors. The strip of April 23, 1944 is a particularly good example of this trend, displaying the title "Krazy Kat" centered like a red sun surrounded by trapezoid panels that shoot out like rays.

Comic strip characters usually don't age, aside from anomalies like the casts of *Gasoline Alley* and *For Better or For Worse*, but Herriman did allow a slight indication that his characters were getting older after more than three decades in the funny pages. Take a look at the way Krazy, Ignatz and Pupp are drawn in 1944 and compare them to their younger incarnations (say in 1918 or 1930). In their youth these characters were leaner, sprightlier, and more angular. In their last few years, they've become pudgier and rounder as if they had gained weight, with Krazy carrying a noticeable belly. In his old age, Offisa's Pupp's face is more sewn in and pinched. Again, the parallel with Charles Schulz suggests itself: in his last decade, Schulz often had his characters hunch forward slightly or sink themselves into chairs, as if they were senior citizens. For both Herriman and Schulz, the private worlds they created in their comic strips was so personal that they couldn't totally preserve their characters from the encroachment of old age.

Herriman's last dailies and Sundays are potent with meaning. In his unfinished dailies we get rare clues about his working method. He would pencil in a rough sense of where the characters would stand along with an initial notation of the dialogue; then he would ink in the figures and polish the words. For him the drawings came first, and the finished dialogue was developed as an organic part of the process of finishing the strip. This procedure is very different than that followed by younger cartoonists like Harold Gray, who would first write out nearly complete dialogue in a notebook, have it transcribed into the strip, and then add in the figures. For Gray, speech came first and pictures were secondary. Herriman operated from the opposite assumptions, seeing art and dialogue as inextricably linked.

The last two Sundays are surprisingly melancholy. In the penultimate strip Offisa Pupp and Ignatz dive into the water to save Krazy from drowning, a bit of heroics that turns out to be unnecessary. In the final strip, Offisa Pupp first ignores evidence that Krazy is drowning, thinking it a practical joke, but then realizes his mistake and rescues the cat, who is rendered completely and uncharacteristically silent by the trauma. Given all the wonderful words Krazy uttered during his (or her) life, the muteness of the last panel is eerie and evocative. The show is over and there is nothing left to be said.

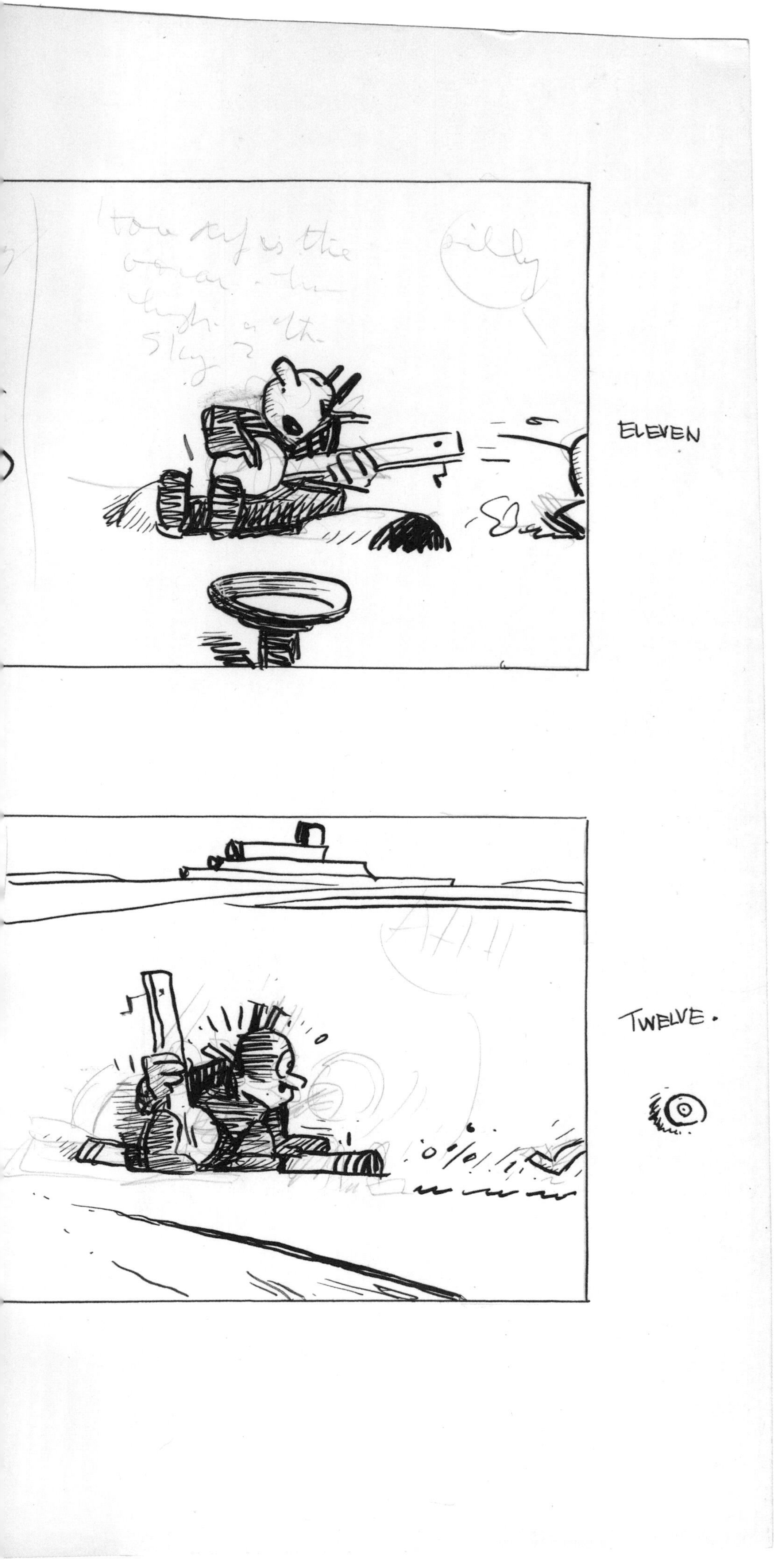
ELEVEN
TWELVE.

Original drawing, left unfinished on Herriman's drawing table at the time of his death. These are the last two daily strips that Herriman ever drew. Collection C. Ware and Tim Samuelson.

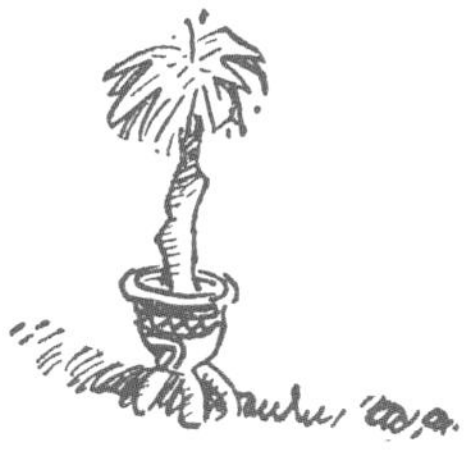

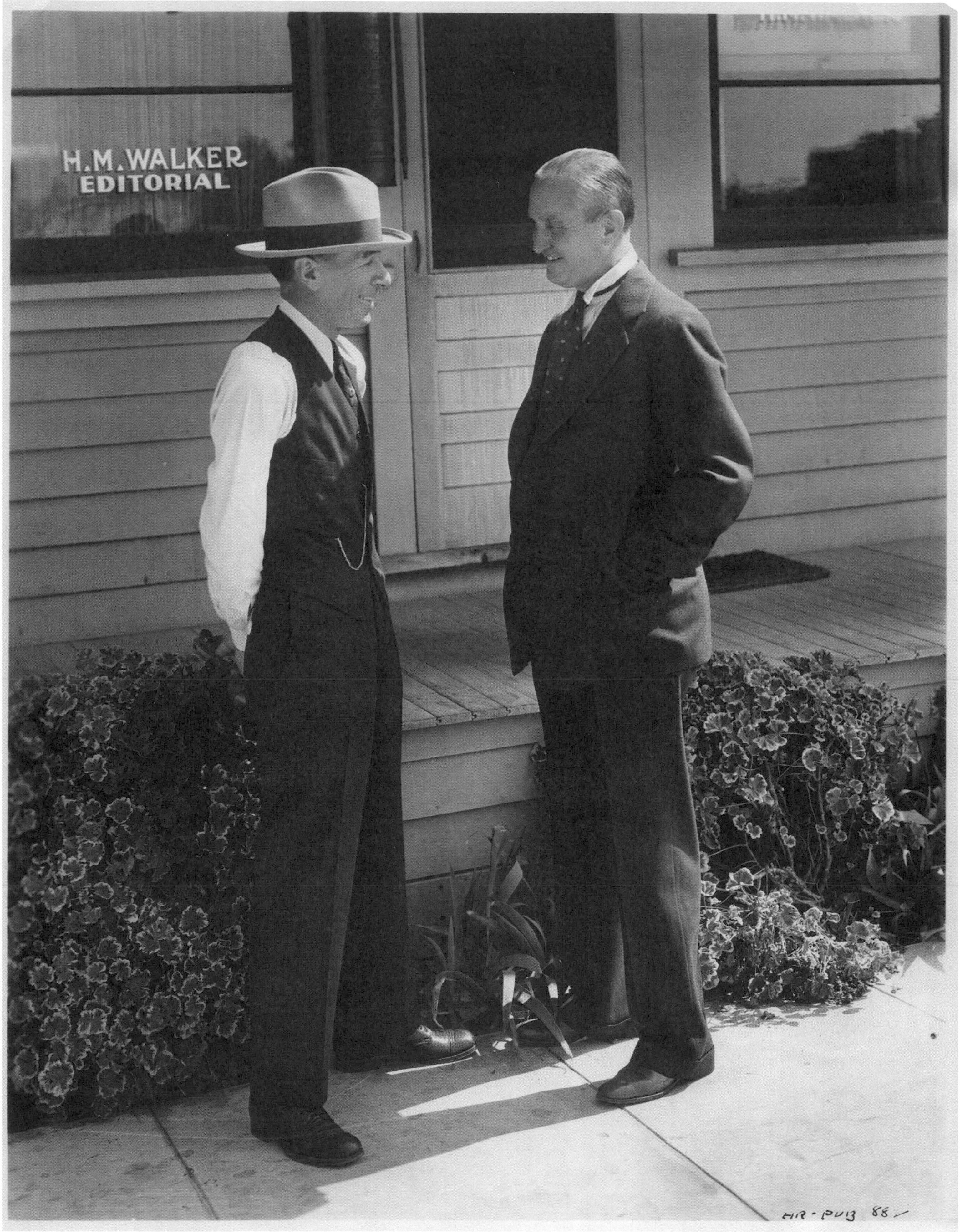
H.M. WALKER
EDITORIAL
HR-PUB 88

George Herriman and Beanie Walker, writer for the Hal Roach "Our Gang" comedies, and reportedly Herriman's closest friend. Herriman enjoyed working on his strips on the Roach Studio lot. Along with Tom McNamara, Walker had once been in the newspaper business but later moved on to motion pictures. Opposite, top: Herriman and Walker in a less posed portrait. Both photographs courtesy of Rob Stolzer.

Left: Presentation drawing for Beanie Walker and his wife for their wedding anniversary, 1929. Note Walker's apparently love of fine clothing. Original size, 12" square. Courtesy of John Fawcett of the Maine Antique Toy and Art Museum.

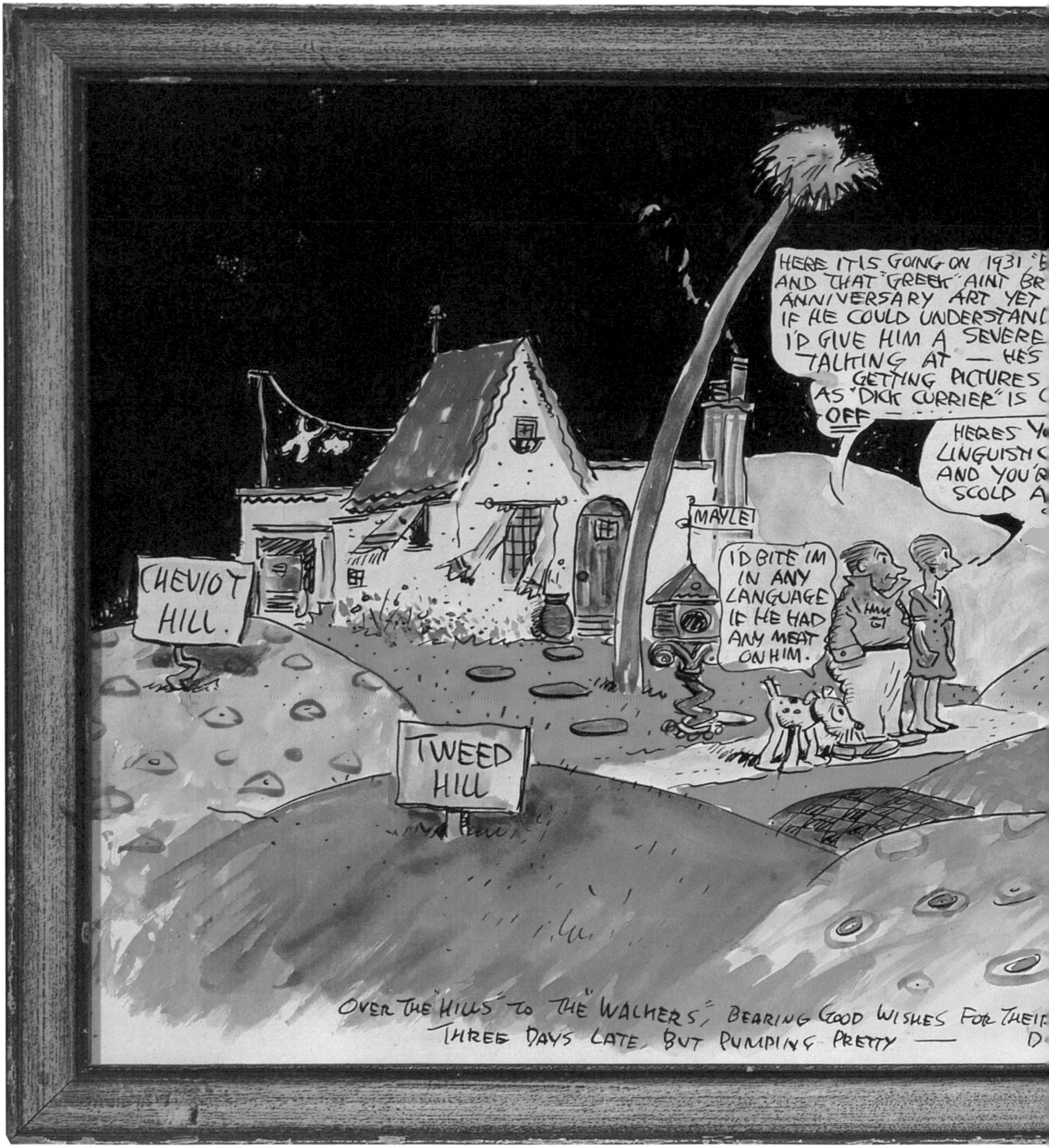
HERE IT IS GOING ON 1931 AND THAT "GREEK" AINT ANNIVERSARY ART YET IF HE COULD I'D GIVE HIM A SEVERE TALKING AT — HE'S GETTING PICTURES AS "DICK CURRIER" IS OFF —
MAYLE
I'D BITE IM IN ANY LANGUAGE IF HE HAD ANY MEAT ON HIM.
CHEVIOT HILL.
TWEED HILL
OVER THE "HILLS" TO THE "WALKERS", BEARING GOOD WISHES FOR
THREE DAYS LATE BUT PUMPING PRETTY —

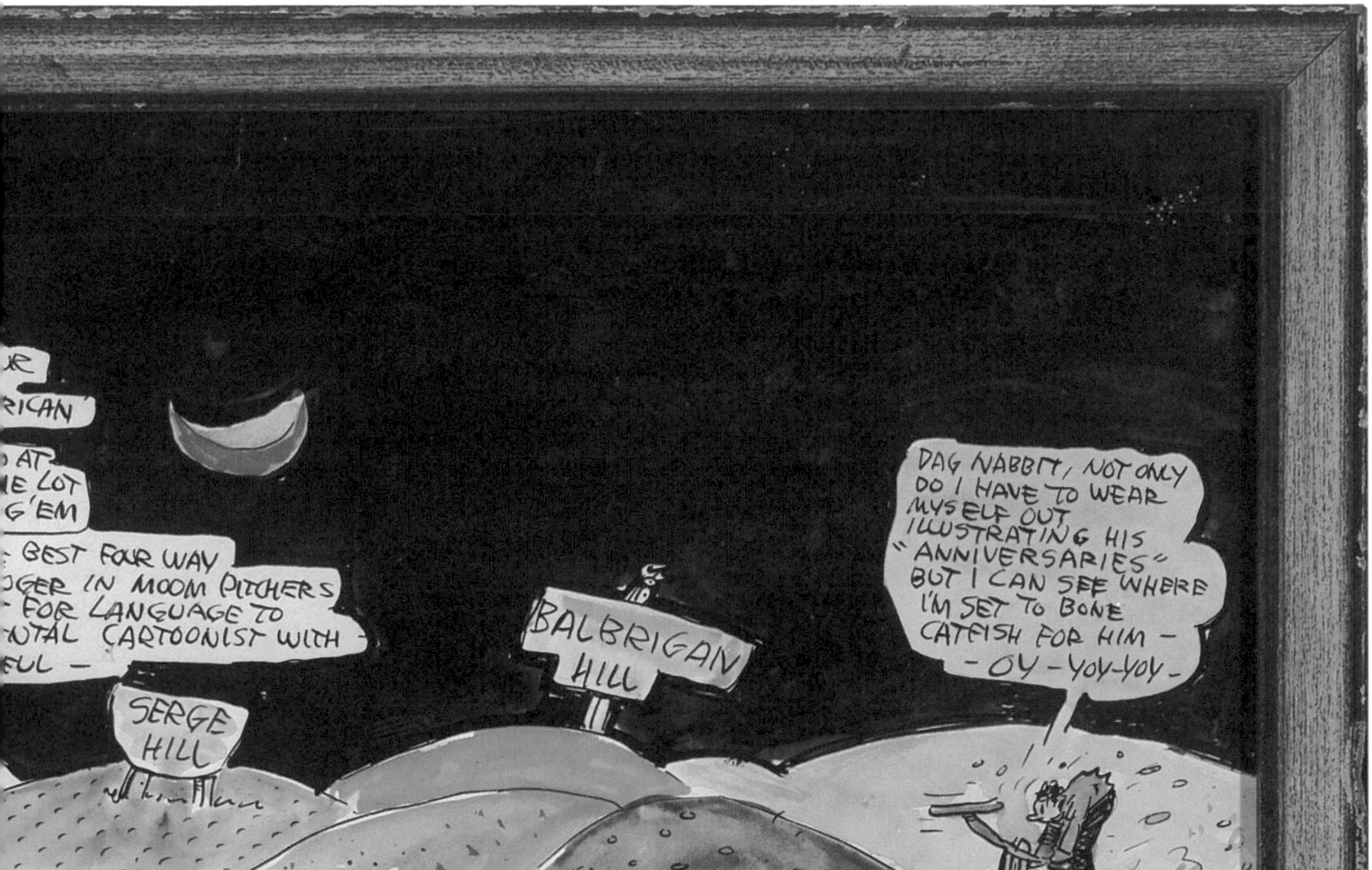
DAG NABBIT, NOT ONLY DO I HAVE TO WEAR MYSELF OUT ILLUSTRATING HIS "ANNIVERSARIES" BUT I CAN SEE WHERE I'M SET TO BONE CATFISH FOR HIM - OY-YOY-YOY -
BALBRIGAN HILL
SERGE HILL
WORSTED HILL
BEST FOUR WAY
IN MOOM PITCHERS
FOR LANGUAGE TO
CARTOONIST WITH
ANNIVERSARY" — IN ART FORM —
14 — ARRIVING SEPT 17 — 1930.
OLE MAN "HERRIMAN"

Presentation drawing for Beanie Walker and his wife for their 1930 wedding anniversary, making a joke of Walker's love of elegant clothing and fabrics. Note Herriman self-portrait pumping the railroad handcar. Courtesy of John Fawcett of the Maine Antique Toy and Art Museum.

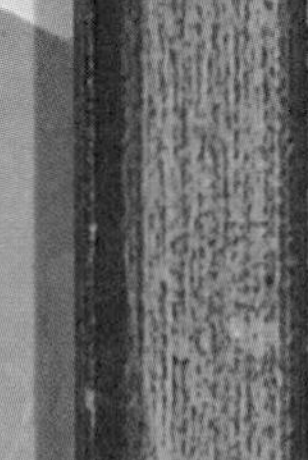

"JOE TORK"
PURVEYOR OF PROGENY TO PRINCE & PROLETARIAN WINGS HIS WAY FROM HIS ROOST ON THE CREST OF THE "ENCHANTED MESA" BEARING. A BUNDLE.

and. MRS. KWAKK WAKK FOR THE FIRST TIME OPENS HER UMBRELLA.

and. "KRAZY KAT" SEALS HIS CHIMNEY FOR A MOMENT, OR MORE.

and. "WALTER CEPHUS" AUSTRIDGE EFFACES HIMSELF.

and. "OFFICER PUPP" TAKES UMBRAGE IN THE SECLUSION OF HIS KLINK.

TO IGNATZ MOUSE'S HOGAN, A "SPECIAL DELIVERY"

THERE IS KURIOSITY IN KOKONINO.

THE RECIPIENT EMERGES, AMPLE WITH ATTITUDE.

HERRIMAN

"MR. KOOWING DUVV, THAT PASSIONATE PACIFIST HAVING GIVEN TO THAT ROUGH RAUCOUS AND REPTILIAN REGION OF CUCONINO AN UNCTUOUS AND OLEAGINOUS AMPLITUDE OF PEACE. DEPARTS — CREDITED WITH THE REGENERATION OF ITS TOUGHEST CITIZEN = IGNATZ MOUSE IS BEING MEASURED FOR A HALO. AND IS SPROUTING PINFEATHERS OF ANGEL HOOD.

SUCCESS.

"KRAZY KAT" IS SMITTEN BY THE STING OF HIS CALM HE TOSSES NO "BRICKS"

"KOLIN KELLY" FEELS THE BRUNT HIS PACIFICISM HE BUYS NO "BRICKS"

OFFICER PUPP ACHES WITH THE INERTIA OF HIS TRANQUILITY HE FILL NO KLINK.

"MRS. KWAKK WAKK" BOILS IN THE STEW OF HIS AMIABLE AMITY. HE SUPPLIES NO GOSSIP.

IT'S THAT "DOVE" WHO STARTED IT — IT'S HIS FAULT

MY FAULT?

YES, YOUR FAULT !!!

IT'S ALL YOUR FAULT !!!

MY FAULT?

POW

YES YOUR FAULT !!!

IT'S ALL YOUR FAULT !!!

HOO-RAY !!!

POW

ZIP

HERRIMAN

Previous spread: two pages drawn for *Vanity Fair*, August, 1930. Courtesy of Derya Ataker.

Above: Presentation drawing for Boyden Sparkes in hand-decorated matte and frame, 22" x 24", 1937.
Courtesy of The International Museum of Cartoon Art, photo by Steven Barnes of *Photographic Solutions*.

Opposite: Dated April 12, 1921, this original Herriman watercolor drawing was a gift to a couple of his acquaintance, the Wellingtons, commemorating a traumatic event (albeit with a happy ending). Late one night Mrs. Wellington had surprised a burglar, who assaulted her — but the couple's Scottie, Mike, attacked the intruder and drove him off. The drawing duly commends Mike for his heroism. Whereas some elements of the crest on the bottom are easy to decode ("IN LEGGUS MIKUS BITUM YEGGUS" — the last word appending a faux Latin-us to the then-popular phrase "yegg," meaning a tough or a thug), one needs to know Latin to figure out that "Kave Kanem" is a Herrimanized version of "Cave Canem" (Beware of Dog). As for "Sic stoze"... well, can you figure that one out? If not, the answer is in the DeBaffler on page 118!
Reproduced with the kind permission of, and art provided by, Peter Merolo and Glen David Gold. —K.T.

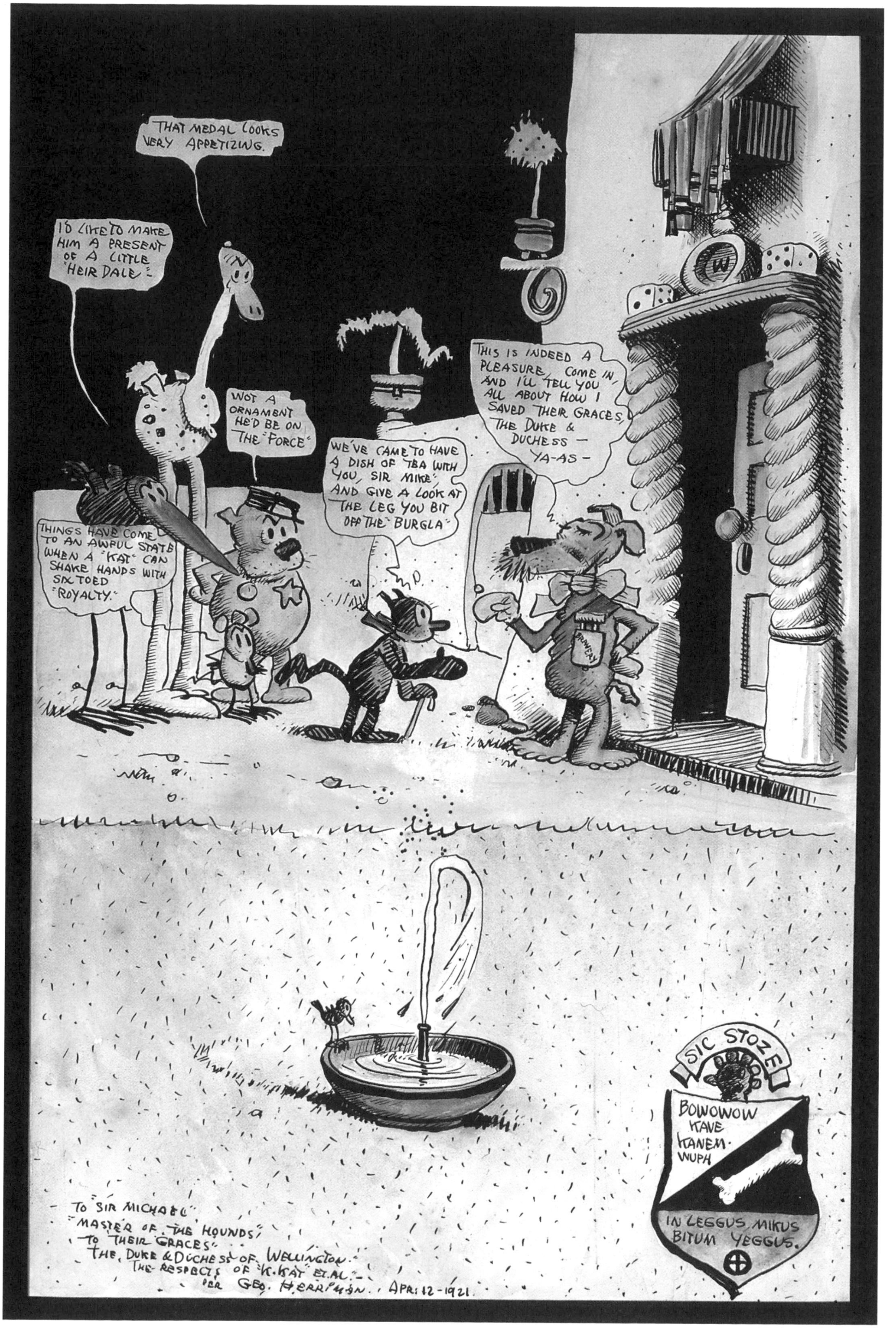
THAT MEDAL LOOKS VERY APPETIZING.
I'D LIKE TO MAKE HIM A PRESENT OF A LITTLE "HEIR DALE"
WOT A ORNAMENT HE'D BE ON THE "FORCE"
THINGS HAVE COME TO AN AWFUL STATE WHEN A "KAT" CAN SHAKE HANDS WITH SIX TOED "ROYALTY."
WE'VE CAME TO HAVE A DISH OF TEA WITH YOU, SIR MIKE AND GIVE A LOOK AT THE LEG YOU BIT OFF THE "BURGLA"
THIS IS INDEED A PLEASURE, COME IN, AND I'LL TELL YOU ALL ABOUT HOW I SAVED THEIR GRACES, THE DUKE & DUCHESS — YA-AS —
W
SIC STOZE
BOWOWOW KAVE KANEM WUPH
IN LEGGUS MIKUS BITUM YEGGUS.
TO SIR MICHAEL
MASTER OF THE HOUNDS
TO THEIR GRACES
THE DUKE & DUCHESS OF WELLINGTON.
THE RESPECTS OF K. KAT ET. AL.
PER GEO. HERRIMAN. APR: 12-1921.

The largest piece of Herriman original artwork known to exist, this 36" x 48" piece was actually (see the pull cord below) a bona fide working windowshade. Created by Herriman for his goddaughter, it spent over 40 years rolled up until it was purchased by John Fawcett of the John Fawcett Maine Antique Toy and Art Museum, who kindly provided it to us for its first public appearance here. Photograph by Hal Hagy. —K.T.

Title page from a copy of Clare Briggs's *When a Feller Needs a Friend*, decorated by Herriman as a gift to Jack Wright in 1917. "From the Tribe Of Herriman," reads the dedication; "May you always have a friend — and may you never need a friend." Courtesy of Malcolm and Karen Whyte collection.

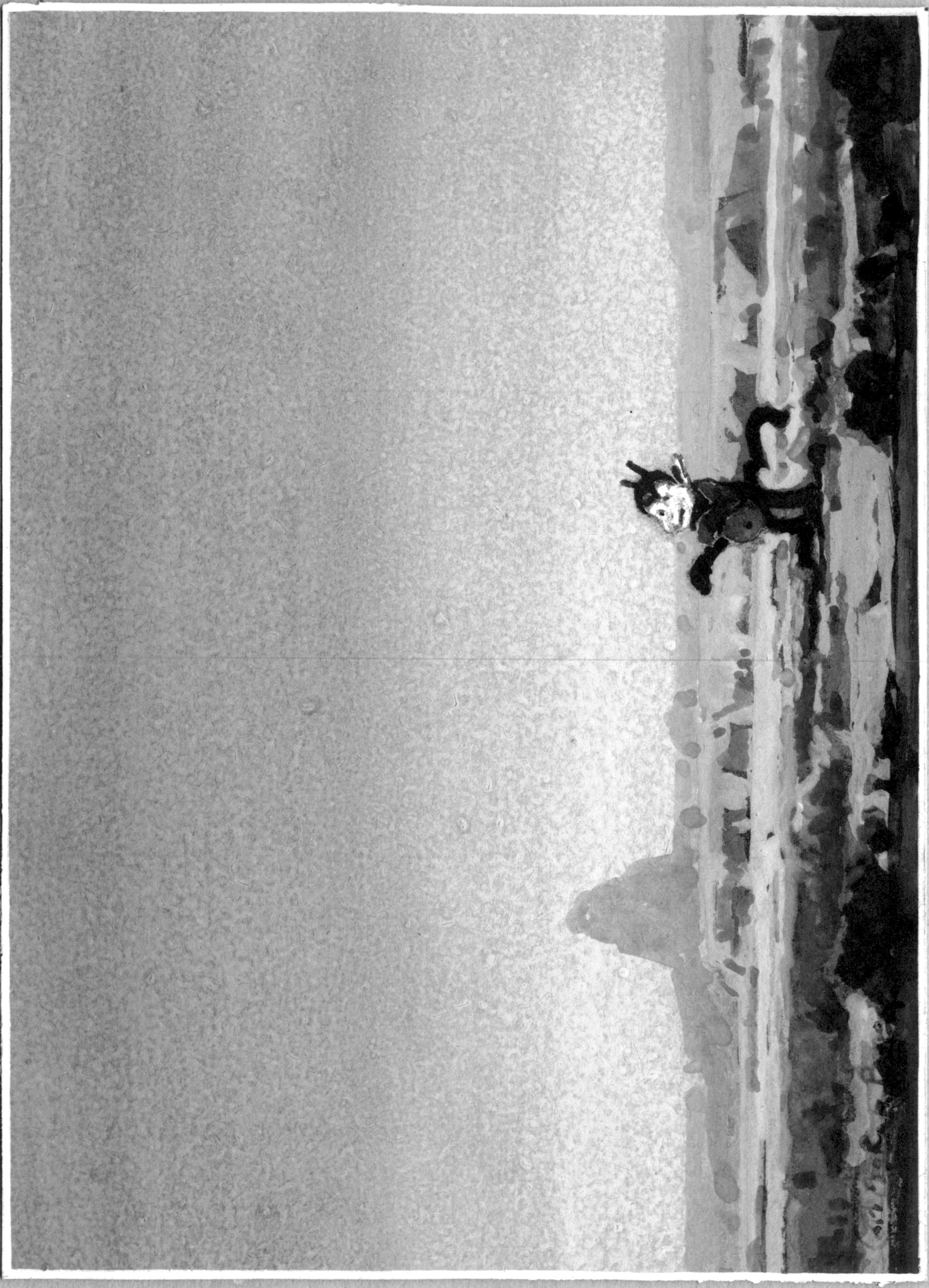

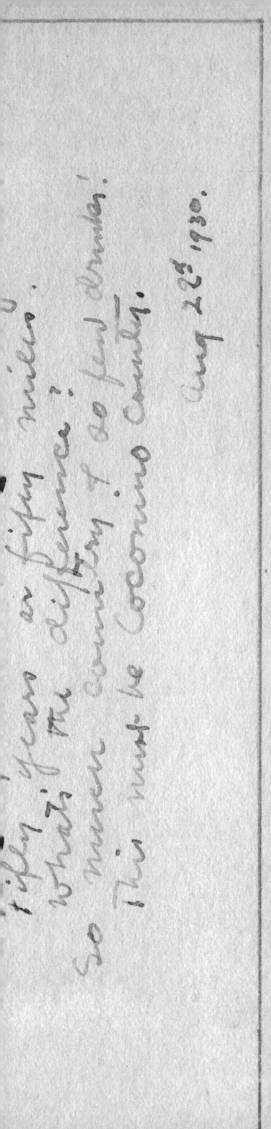

Above: Presentation drawing, possibly for John Wetherill in Kayenta, Arizona, who ran something of a tourist resort which Herriman, Jimmy Swinnerton, Frank King and other cartoonists visited in the 1920s and 1930s. "Toots" would have been Herriman's daughter Mabel, and "Tom" likely Tom McNamara. Courtesy of Harvey Leake.

Opposite: George Herriman, watercolor on board, August 22, 1930. The inscription reads:

What mysterious surroundings!
Fifty years or fifty miles.
What's the difference?
So much country and so few drinks! (?)
This must be Coconino county.
Aug 22nd 1930.

Courtesy of the Cartoon Art Museum of San Francisco, with special thanks to Andrew Farago.

The Adventures of Krazy Kat in Kokoland, an odd attempt to play to the juvenile market by Saalfield publishing in the "Big-Little book" format, 1936. Though the interior artwork is culled from daily strips, the cover is clearly not by Herriman. Collection C. Ware.

Above: Krazy Kat Comic Club money, Premium play money, c.1930s. Krazy Kat was the lowest denomination in the set, and Popeye was the highest. Courtesy of Mark Newgarden.

Right: "Carnival slum" doll featuring the animated cartoon design, 1930s. Marked "KRAZY KAT ©KFS" on ear. Courtesy of Mark Newgarden.

Unlicensed novelty package from Portland Oregon, 1930s. Courtesy of Mark Newgarden. Following page: Newspaper advertisement for the early Hearst-produced Krazy Kat animated cartoons, 1916.

"KRAZY KAT" and "IGNATZ MOUSE"

Famous little characters created by George Herriman and appearing daily in the CHICAGO EVENING AMERICAN, will come to life on the screen and appear regularly in the

HEARST-VITAGRAPH NEWS PICTORIAL

Beginning To-Day. Shown at All Leading Motion Picture Houses.

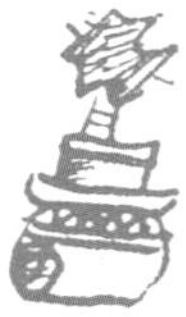

1943.

Readers, please note: an Ignatz "dingbat" placed below a strip indicates a relevant or related footnote at the volume's end for that particular selection, all to be found in the "Ignatz Debaffler" section.

IT WILL BLOOM INTO A BEAUTIFIL "BLOTSOM" — A SPRING "BLOTSOM" —
IN THIS SORT OF TIME, YOU PLANT A SPRING FLOWER — SHAME — SHAME ON YOU — YOU SHOULD PLANT A FRUIT, A VEGETABLE, A PEA, A BEAN, A-A-
"KRAZY KAT"
Registered U. S. Patent Office
AN' YOU IS SHOE IT WOULD BE MO' "PETTI YOTTIC MO' HONNIBIL MO' ON THE "NUPP & NUPP" — AN'
NO DOUBT ABOUT IT "KAT," YOU HAND ME THAT USELESS NO-ACCOUNT SPRING FLOWER, AND I WILL HAND YOU THIS LITTLE BEAN BUSH WHICH WILL IN TIME YIELD A SWEET AMPLITUDE OF NUTRITION AND SUSTENANCE —
I WILL HAVE A SWEET-SMELLING SPRING FLOWER — HE WILL HAVE A CROP OF JUMPING BEANS — JUMPING ALL OVER THE MAP —
HAA HAA HAA
HAA HAA
LIL' DOLLIN', HIS NOBIL SOUL SHOWED ME THE ERRA OF MY WAY, — SNIFF, IS ALL I COULD DO WIT' A SPRING FLOWA — — BUT NOW, WIT' THIS LIL' "BINN BUTCH" — I-I-I —
PLANTING JUMPING BEANS, SHAME ON YOU, YOU FRIVOLOUS WRETCH — — —
?
AND FOR THAT SWEET SPRING FLOWER, HE GIVES THAT SIMPLE "KAT" A POTTED JUMPING BEAN VINE —
AND TO THINK THAT I CANT ARREST THE RASCAL — THERE IS NO LAW AGAINST IT — — — ORDER IS POWERLESS, MAKES ME SO DERN MA-A-AD . .
OF COURSE, THERE IS ALWAYS FATE TO OVERTAKE HIM — WHO KNOWS — EH ?
ALRIGHT, WOMAN, WHO ?
Copr. 1943 King Features Syndicate, Inc., World rights reserved.
1-3

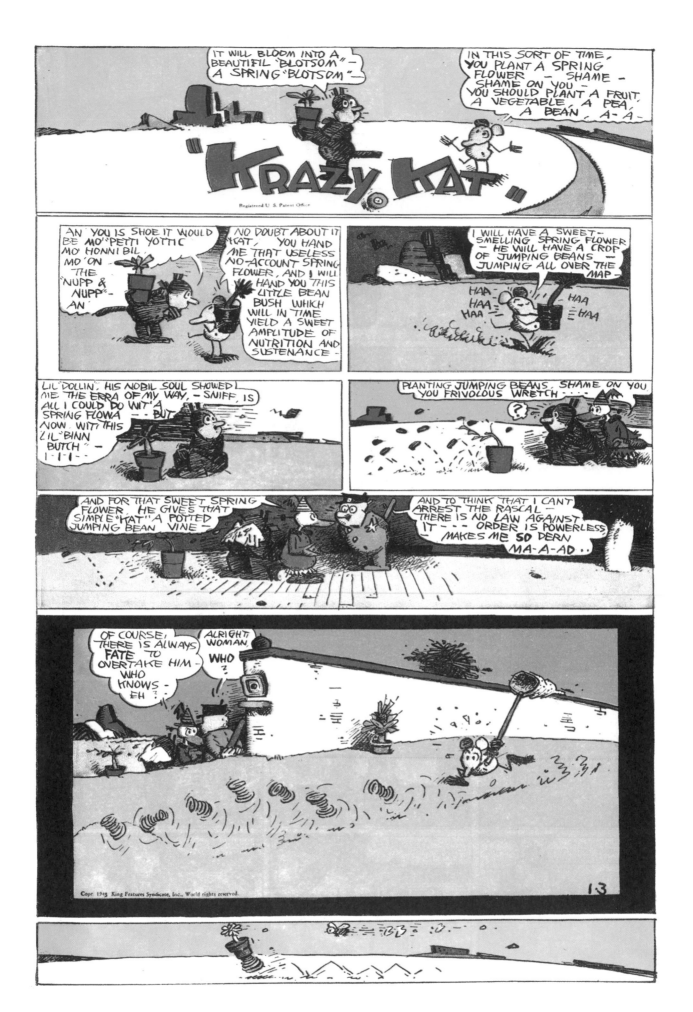

January 3rd, 1943.

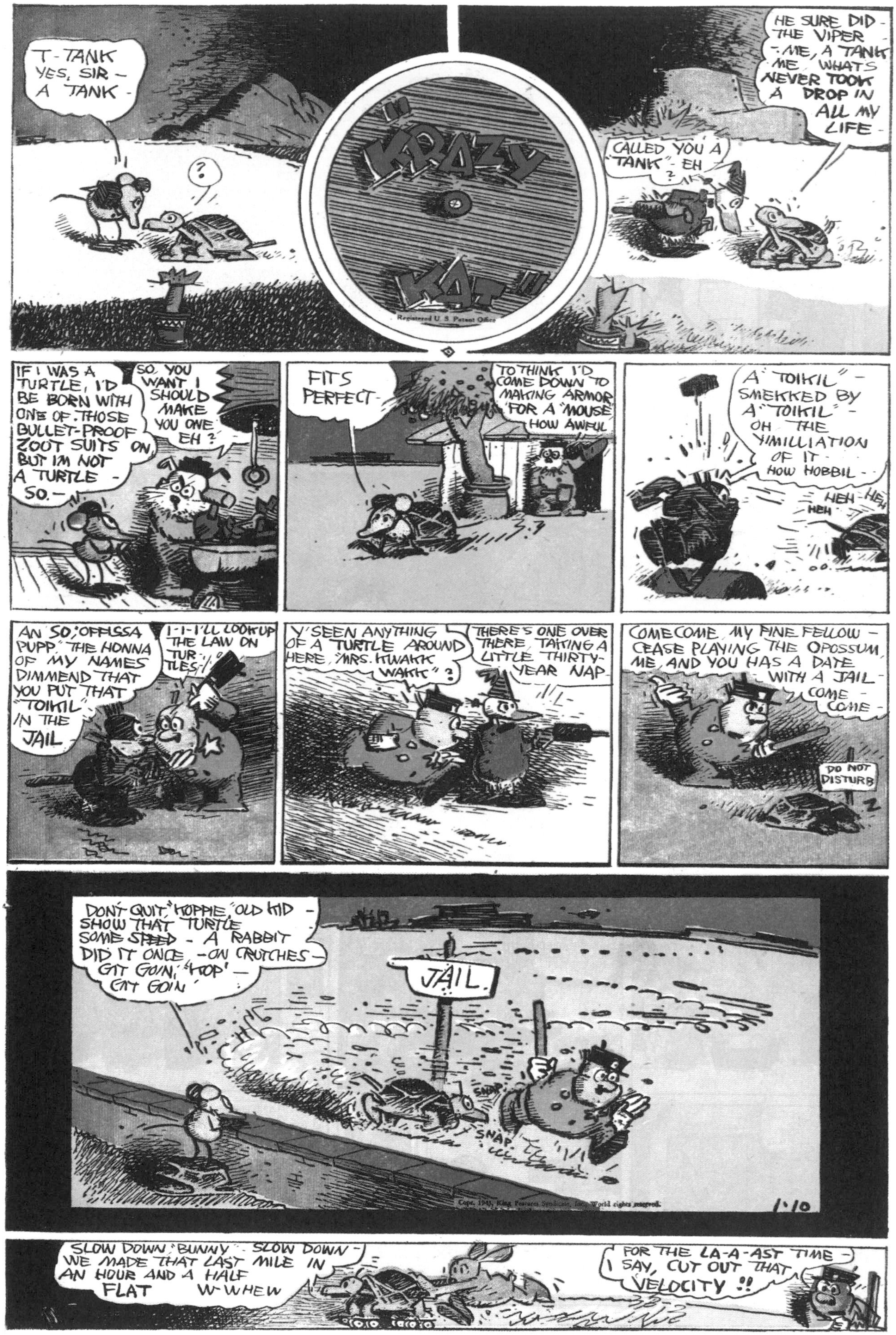
T-TANK YES, SIR - A TANK -
"KRAZY KAT"
Registered U. S. Patent Office
CALLED YOU A "TANK" - EH ?
HE SURE DID - THE VIPER - ME, A TANK - ME WHAT'S NEVER TOOK A DROP IN ALL MY LIFE -
IF I WAS A TURTLE, I'D BE BORN WITH ONE OF THOSE BULLET-PROOF ZOOT SUITS ON, BUT I'M NOT A TURTLE - SO. -
SO, YOU WANT I SHOULD MAKE YOU ONE EH ?
FITS PERFECT -
TO THINK I'D COME DOWN TO MAKING ARMOR FOR A "MOUSE" HOW AWFUL
A "TOIKIL" - SMEKKED BY A "TOIKIL" - OH THE YIMILLIATION OF IT HOW HOBBIL -
HEH HEH HEH
AN SO, "OFFISSA PUPP," THE HONNA OF MY NAMES DIMMEND THAT YOU PUT THAT "TOIKIL" IN THE JAIL
I-I-I'LL LOOK UP THE LAW ON TURTLES
Y' SEEN ANYTHING OF A TURTLE AROUND HERE, "MRS. KWAKK WAKK" ?
THERE'S ONE OVER THERE TAKING A LITTLE THIRTY-YEAR NAP -
COME COME, MY FINE FELLOW - CEASE PLAYING THE OPOSSUM, ME AND YOU HAS A DATE WITH A JAIL - COME - COME -
DO NOT DISTURB
DON'T QUIT, "HOPPIE," OLD KID - SHOW THAT TURTLE SOME SPEED - A RABBIT DID IT ONCE - ON CRUTCHES - GIT GOIN, "HOP" - GIT GOIN' -
JAIL
SNAP
SNAP
1-10
SLOW DOWN, "BUNNY" - SLOW DOWN - WE MADE THAT LAST MILE IN AN HOUR AND A HALF FLAT W-WHEW
FOR THE LA-A-AST TIME - I SAY, CUT OUT THAT VELOCITY !!

January 10th, 1943.

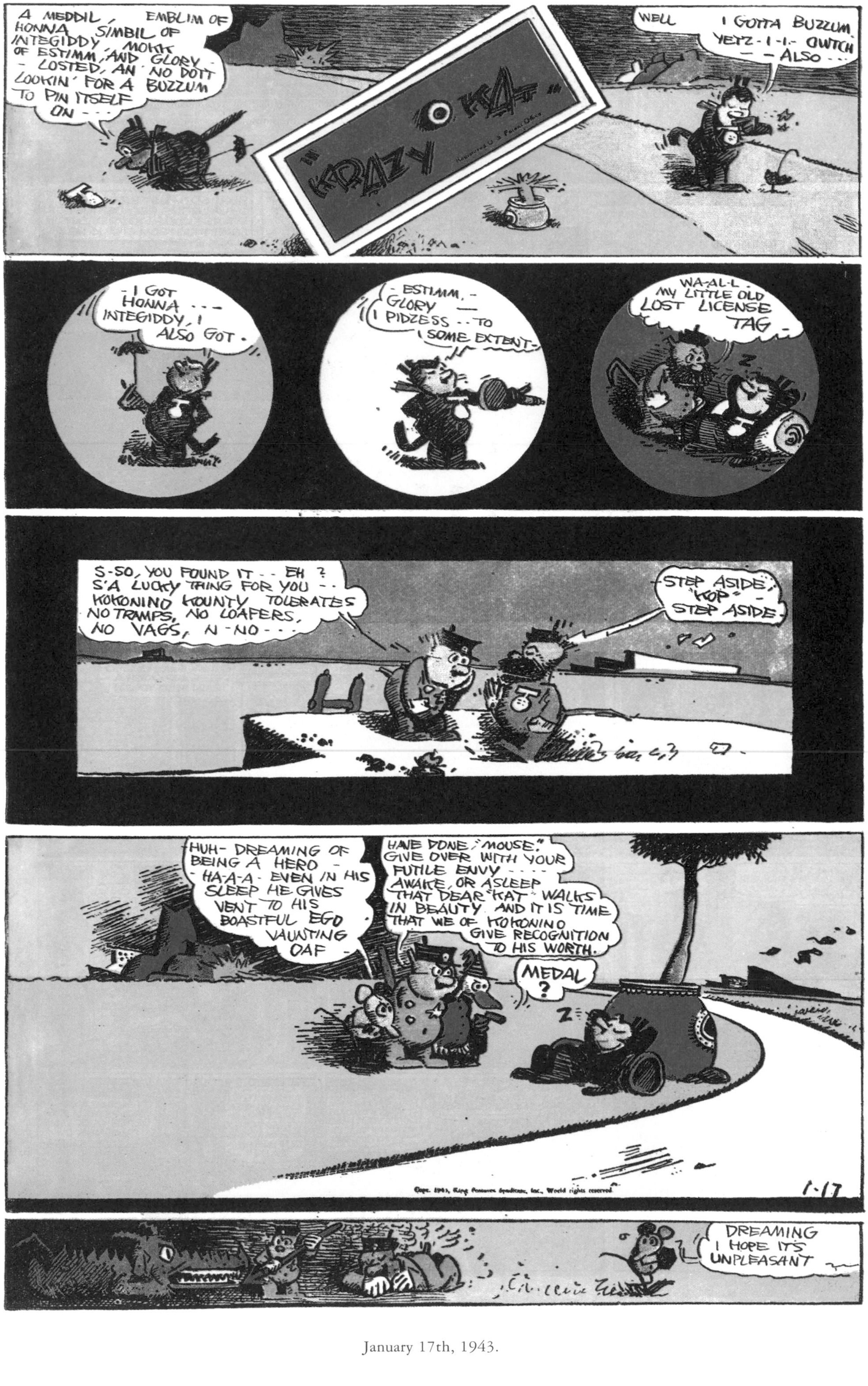
A MEDDIL, EMBLIM OF HONNA, SIMBIL OF INTEGIDDY, MOHR OF ESTIMM, AND GLORY - LOSTED, AN NO DOTT LOOKIN' FOR A BUZZUM TO PIN ITSELF ON - - -
KRAZY KAT
WELL
I GOTTA BUZZUM YETZ - I - I - OWTCH - - ALSO - - -
- I GOT HONNA - - - INTEGIDDY, I ALSO GOT -
- ESTIMM, GLORY - I PIDZESS - - TO SOME EXTENT -
WA-AL-L MY LITTLE OLD LOST LICENSE TAG -
S-SO, YOU FOUND IT - - EH ? S'A LUCKY THING FOR YOU - - KOKONINO KOUNTY TOLERATES NO TRAMPS, NO LOAFERS, NO VAGS, N - NO - - -
- STEP ASIDE, "KOP" - STEP ASIDE -
- HUH - DREAMING OF BEING A HERO - HA-A-A - EVEN IN HIS SLEEP HE GIVES VENT TO HIS BOASTFUL EGO VAUNTING OAF -
HAVE DONE, "MOUSE." GIVE OVER WITH YOUR FUTILE ENVY - - - - AWAKE, OR ASLEEP THAT DEAR "KAT" WALKS IN BEAUTY AND IT IS TIME THAT WE OF KOKONINO GIVE RECOGNITION TO HIS WORTH.
MEDAL ?
1-17
DREAMING I HOPE ITS UNPLEASANT

January 17th, 1943.

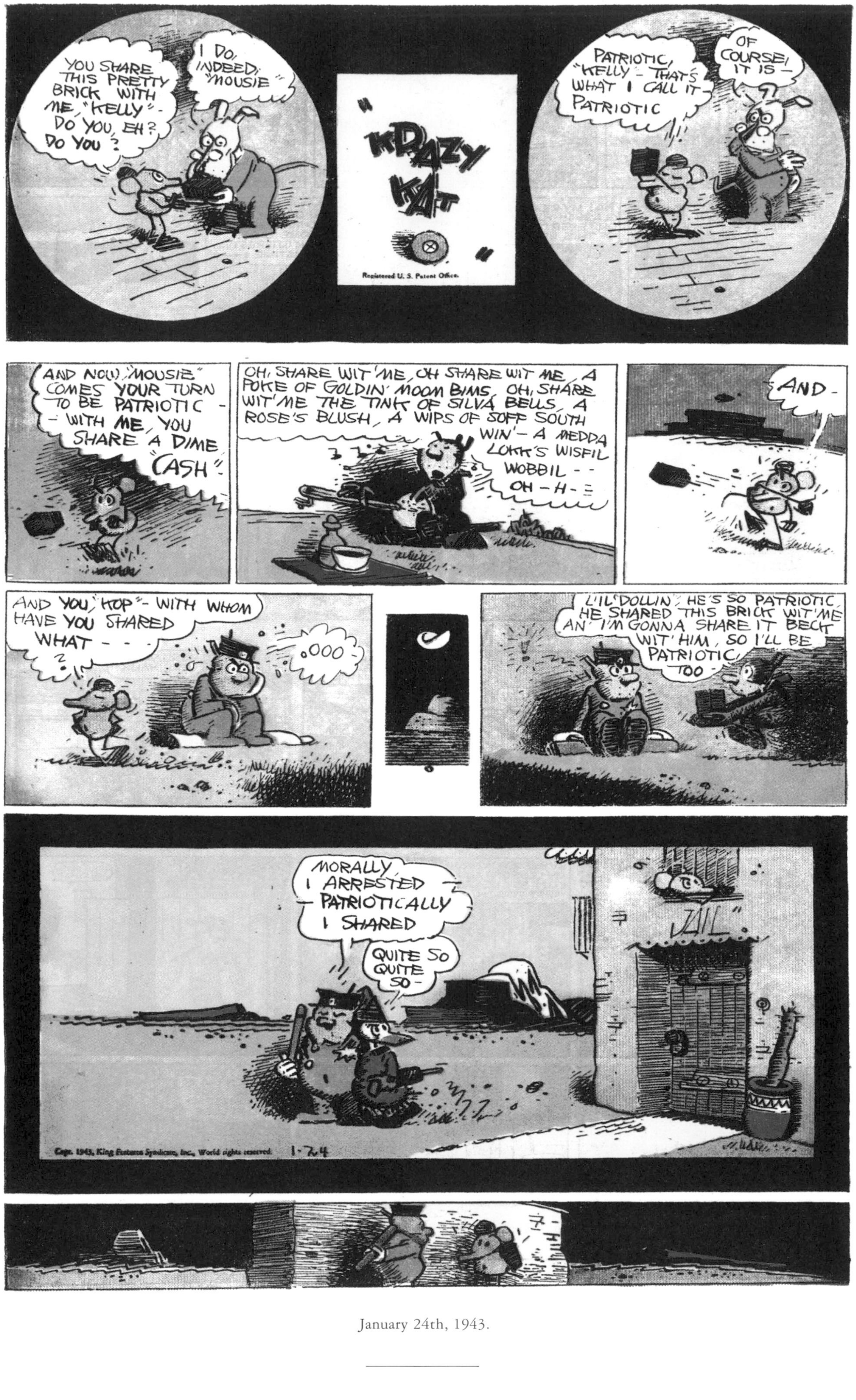
YOU SHARE THIS PRETTY BRICK WITH ME, "KELLY" - DO YOU, EH? DO YOU?
I DO, INDEED, "MOUSIE"
"KRAZY KAT"
Registered U. S. Patent Office.
PATRIOTIC, "KELLY" - THAT'S WHAT I CALL IT - PATRIOTIC
OF COURSE! IT IS -
AND NOW, "MOUSIE" COMES YOUR TURN TO BE PATRIOTIC - - WITH ME YOU SHARE A DIME CASH
OH, SHARE WIT' ME, OH SHARE WIT ME, A POKE OF GOLDIN' MOOM BIMS, OH, SHARE WIT' ME THE TINK OF SILVA BELLS, A ROSE'S BLUSH, A WIPS OF SOFF SOUTH WIN' - A MEDDA LOKK'S WISFIL WOBBIL - - OH - H -
AND -
AND YOU, "KOP" - WITH WHOM HAVE YOU SHARED WHAT - - -
OOO -
L'IL DOLLIN, HE'S SO PATRIOTIC HE SHARED THIS BRICK WIT'ME AN' I'M GONNA SHARE IT BECK WIT' HIM, SO I'LL BE PATRIOTIC TOO -
MORALLY, I ARRESTED - PATRIOTICALLY I SHARED
QUITE SO QUITE SO -
JAIL
Copr. 1943, King Features Syndicate, Inc., World rights reserved. 1-24

January 24th, 1943.

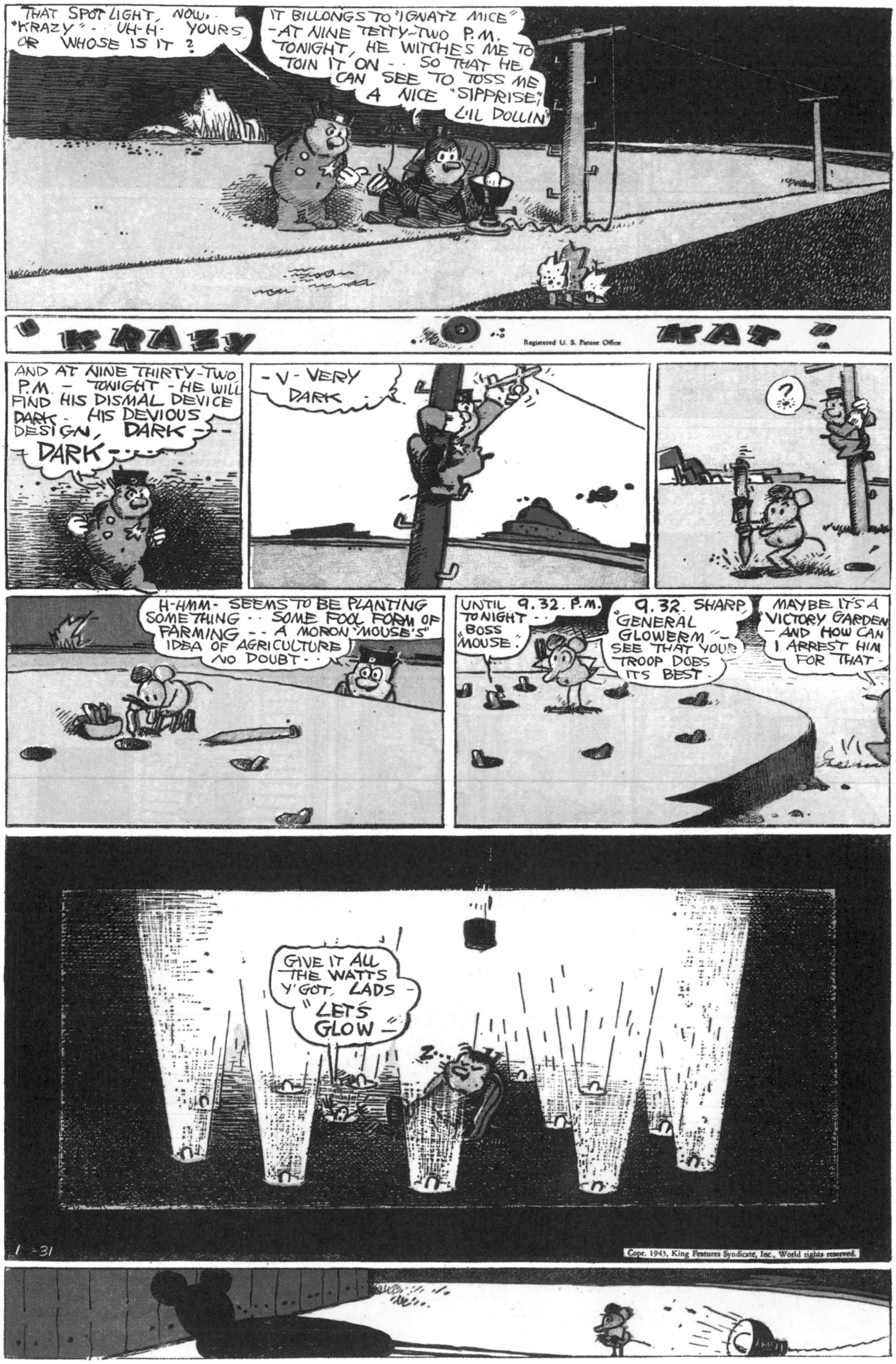
THAT SPOT LIGHT, NOW, - "KRAZY" - - UH-H- YOURS OR WHOSE IS IT ?
IT BILLONGS TO "IGNATZ MICE" - AT NINE TETTY-TWO P.M. TONIGHT, HE WITCHES ME TO TOIN IT ON - - SO THAT HE CAN SEE TO TOSS ME A NICE "SIPPRISE," L'IL DOLLIN'
KRAZY KAT
Registered U. S. Patent Office
AND AT NINE THIRTY-TWO P.M. - TONIGHT - HE WILL FIND HIS DISMAL DEVICE DARK - HIS DEVIOUS DESIGN, DARK - - - DARK - - -
- V - VERY DARK
?
H-HMM - SEEMS TO BE PLANTING SOMETHING - - SOME FOOL FORM OF FARMING - - A MORON "MOUSE'S" IDEA OF AGRICULTURE NO DOUBT - -
UNTIL 9.32. P.M. TONIGHT - - "BOSS MOUSE."
9.32. SHARP "GENERAL GLOWERM" - SEE THAT YOUR TROOP DOES ITS BEST -
MAYBE IT'S A "VICTORY GARDEN" - AND HOW CAN I ARREST HIM FOR THAT -
GIVE IT ALL THE WATTS Y'GOT, LADS - "LET'S GLOW -"
1-31
Copr. 1943, King Features Syndicate, Inc., World rights reserved.

January 31st, 1943.

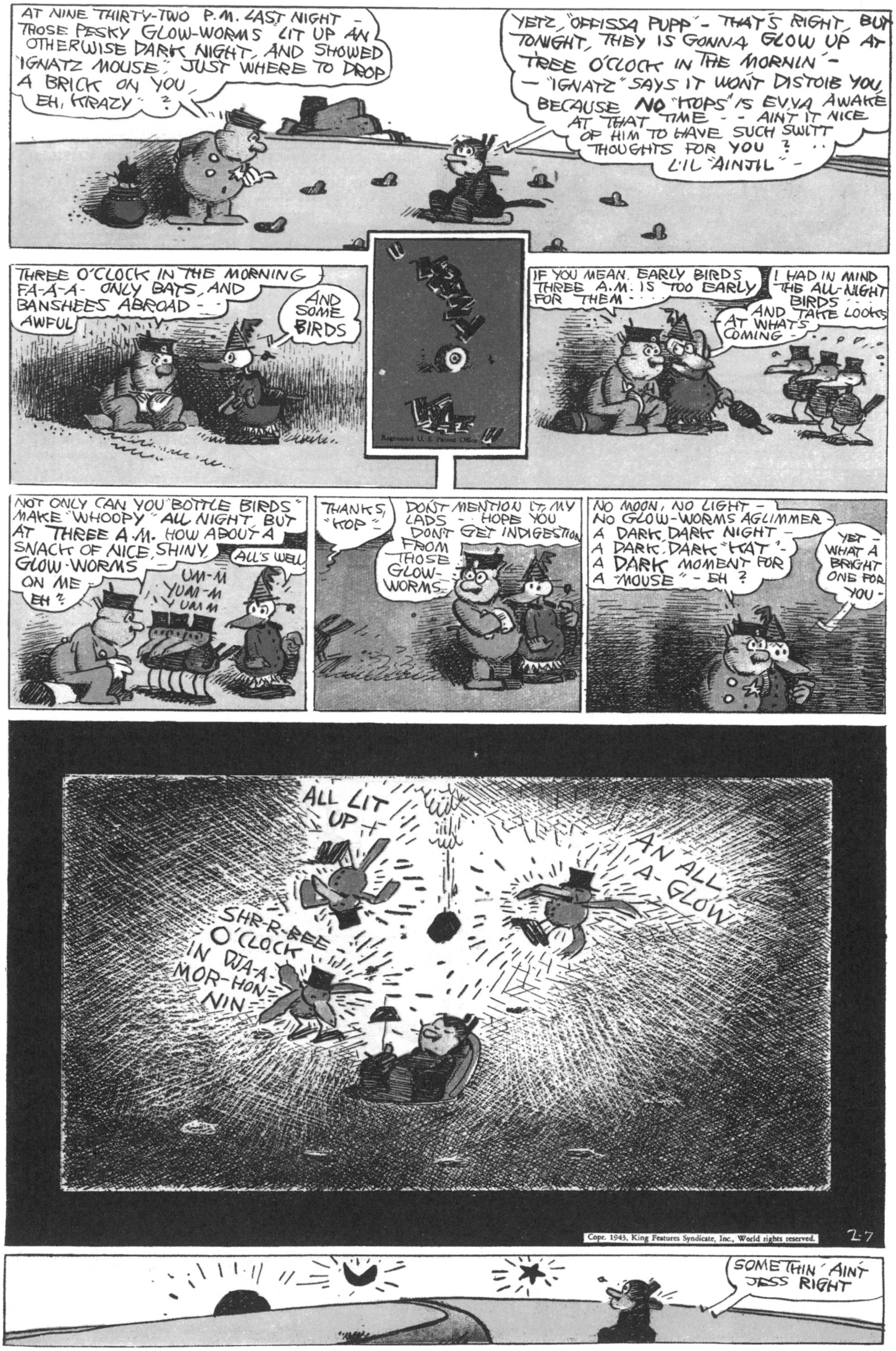
AT NINE THIRTY-TWO P.M. LAST NIGHT - THOSE PESKY GLOW-WORMS LIT UP AN OTHERWISE DARK NIGHT, AND SHOWED "IGNATZ MOUSE" JUST WHERE TO DROP A BRICK ON YOU EH, KRAZY ?
YETZ, "OFFISSA PUPP" - THAT'S RIGHT, BUT TONIGHT, THEY IS GONNA GLOW UP AT TREE O'CLOCK IN THE MORNIN' - - "IGNATZ" SAYS IT WON'T DISTOIB YOU, BECAUSE NO "KOPS" IS EV,YA AWAKE AT THAT TIME - - AIN'T IT NICE OF HIM TO HAVE SUCH SWITT THOUGHTS FOR YOU ? .. L'IL AINJIL -
Registered U.S. Patent Office
THREE O'CLOCK IN THE MORNING FA-A-A- ONLY BATS, AND BANSHEES ABROAD - AWFUL
AND SOME BIRDS
IF YOU MEAN, EARLY BIRDS THREE A.M. IS TOO EARLY FOR THEM -
I HAD IN MIND THE ALL-NIGHT BIRDS
AND TAKE LOOKS AT WHAT'S COMING -
NOT ONLY CAN YOU BOTTLE BIRDS MAKE "WHOOPY" ALL NIGHT, BUT AT THREE A.M. HOW ABOUT A SNACK OF NICE, SHINY, GLOW-WORMS - ON ME EH ?
ALL'S WELL
UM-M YUM-M YUMM
THANKS, "KOP" -
DON'T MENTION IT, MY LADS - HOPE YOU DON'T GET INDIGESTION FROM THOSE GLOW-WORMS
NO MOON, NO LIGHT - NO GLOW-WORMS AGLIMMER - A DARK, DARK NIGHT - A DARK, DARK "KAT" - A DARK MOMENT FOR A "MOUSE" - EH ?
YET - WHAT A BRIGHT ONE FOR YOU -
ALL LIT UP
AN ALL A-GLOW
SHR-R-REE O'CLOCK IN DJA-A MOR-HON NIN
Copr. 1943, King Features Syndicate, Inc., World rights reserved.
2-7
SOMETHIN' AIN'T JESS RIGHT

February 7th, 1943.

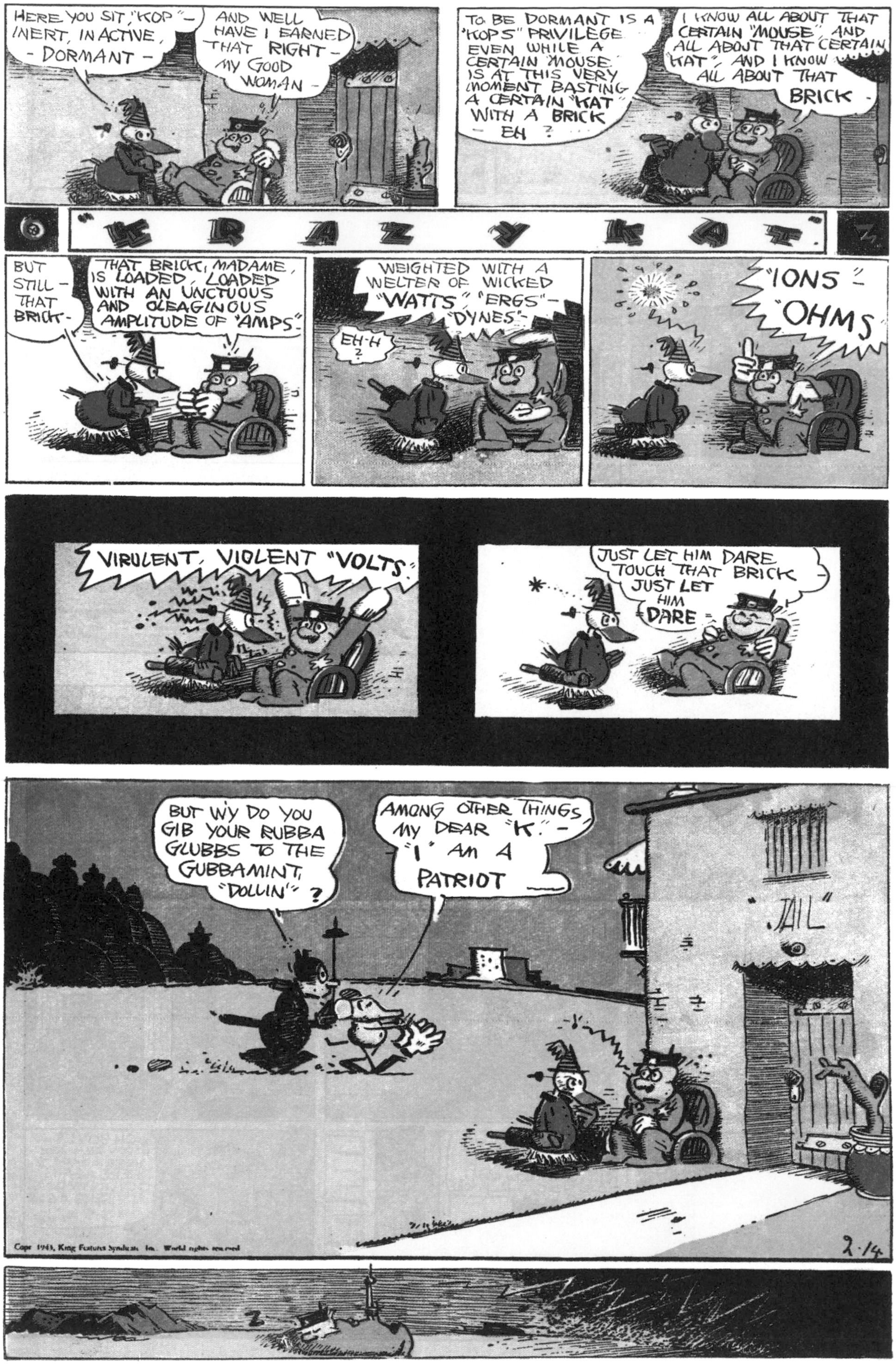

HERE YOU SIT, "KOP" — INERT, INACTIVE, — DORMANT —
AND WELL HAVE I EARNED THAT RIGHT — MY GOOD WOMAN —
TO BE DORMANT IS A "KOP'S" PRIVILEGE EVEN WHILE A CERTAIN "MOUSE" IS AT THIS VERY MOMENT BASTING A CERTAIN "KAT" WITH A BRICK — EH ?
I KNOW ALL ABOUT THAT CERTAIN "MOUSE" AND ALL ABOUT THAT CERTAIN "KAT", AND I KNOW ALL ABOUT THAT BRICK —
"KRAZY KAT"
BUT STILL — THAT BRICK —
THAT BRICK, MADAME, IS LOADED, LOADED WITH AN UNCTUOUS AND OLEAGINOUS AMPLITUDE OF "AMPS"
WEIGHTED WITH A WELTER OF WICKED "WATTS", "ERGS" — "DYNES" —
EH-H ?
"IONS" — "OHMS"
VIRULENT, VIOLENT "VOLTS"
JUST LET HIM DARE TOUCH THAT BRICK — JUST LET HIM DARE
BUT WY DO YOU GIB YOUR RUBBA GLUBBS TO THE GUBBAMINT, "DOLLIN" ?
AMONG OTHER THINGS MY DEAR "K." — "I" AM A PATRIOT
"JAIL"
2·14

February 14th, 1943.

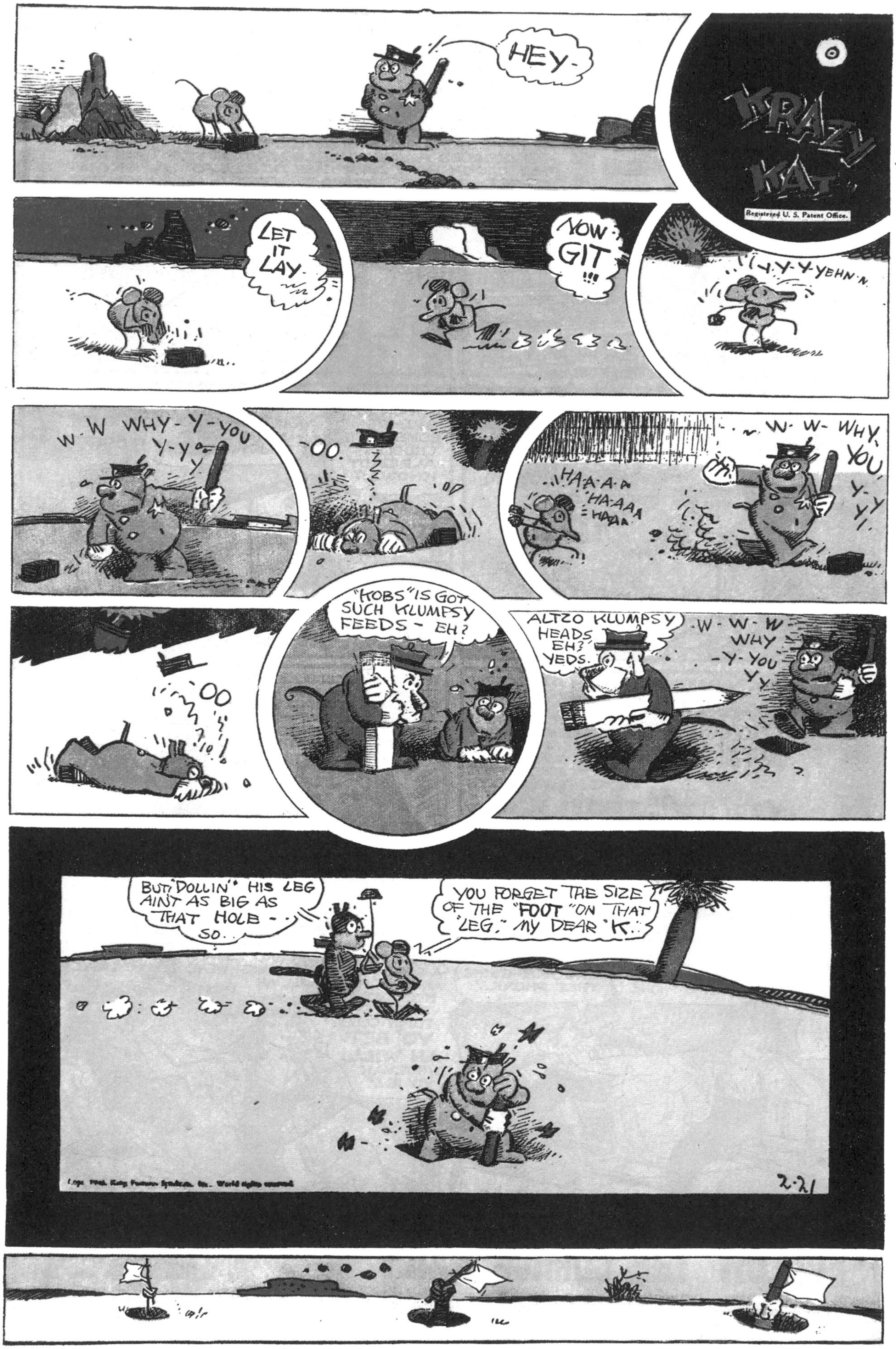
HEY-
KRAZY KAT
Registered U. S. Patent Office.
LET IT LAY
NOW GIT !!!
Y-Y-Y-YEHN-N
W-W WHY-Y-YOU Y-Y-Y
OO.
W-W-WHY, YOU Y-Y Y
HA-A-A HA-AAA HAAA
"KOBS" IS GOT SUCH KLUMPSY FEEDS - EH?
ALTZO KLUMPSY HEADS EH? YEDS.
W-W-W WHY-Y-YOU YY
BUT; "DOLLIN'" HIS LEG AINT AS BIG AS THAT HOLE -- SO.
YOU FORGET THE SIZE OF THE "FOOT" ON THAT "LEG," MY DEAR "K."
2-21

February 21st, 1943.

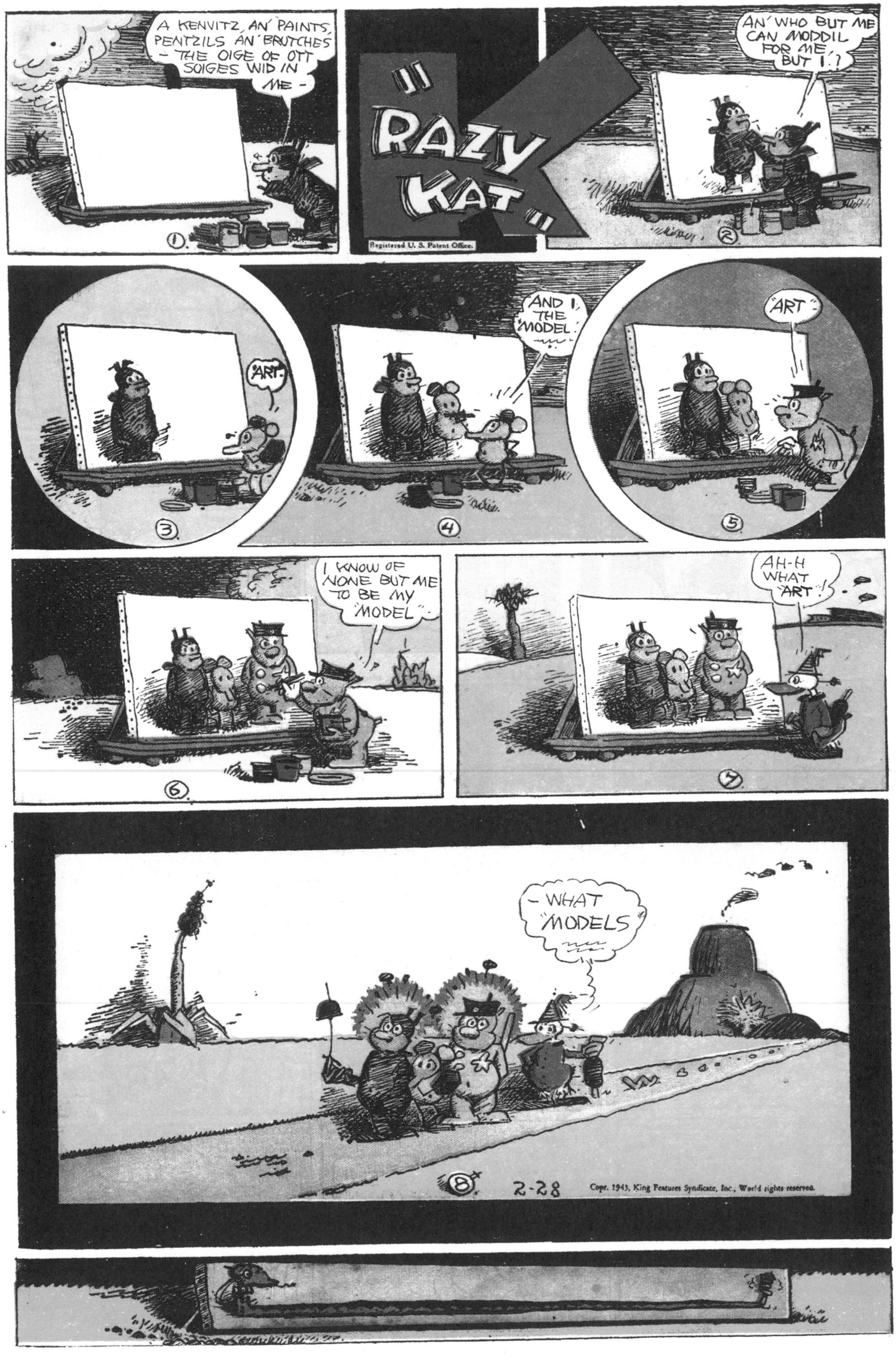
A KENVITZ, AN' PAINTS, PENTZILS AN' BRUTCHES - THE OIGE OF OTT SOIGES WID IN ME -
"KRAZY KAT"
Registered U. S. Patent Office.
AN' WHO BUT ME CAN MODDIL FOR ME, BUT I.?
"ART."
AND I, THE "MODEL."
"ART"
I KNOW OF NONE BUT ME TO BE MY "MODEL"
AH-H WHAT "ART"!
- WHAT "MODELS"
2-28
Copr. 1943, King Features Syndicate, Inc., World rights reserved.

February 28th, 1943.

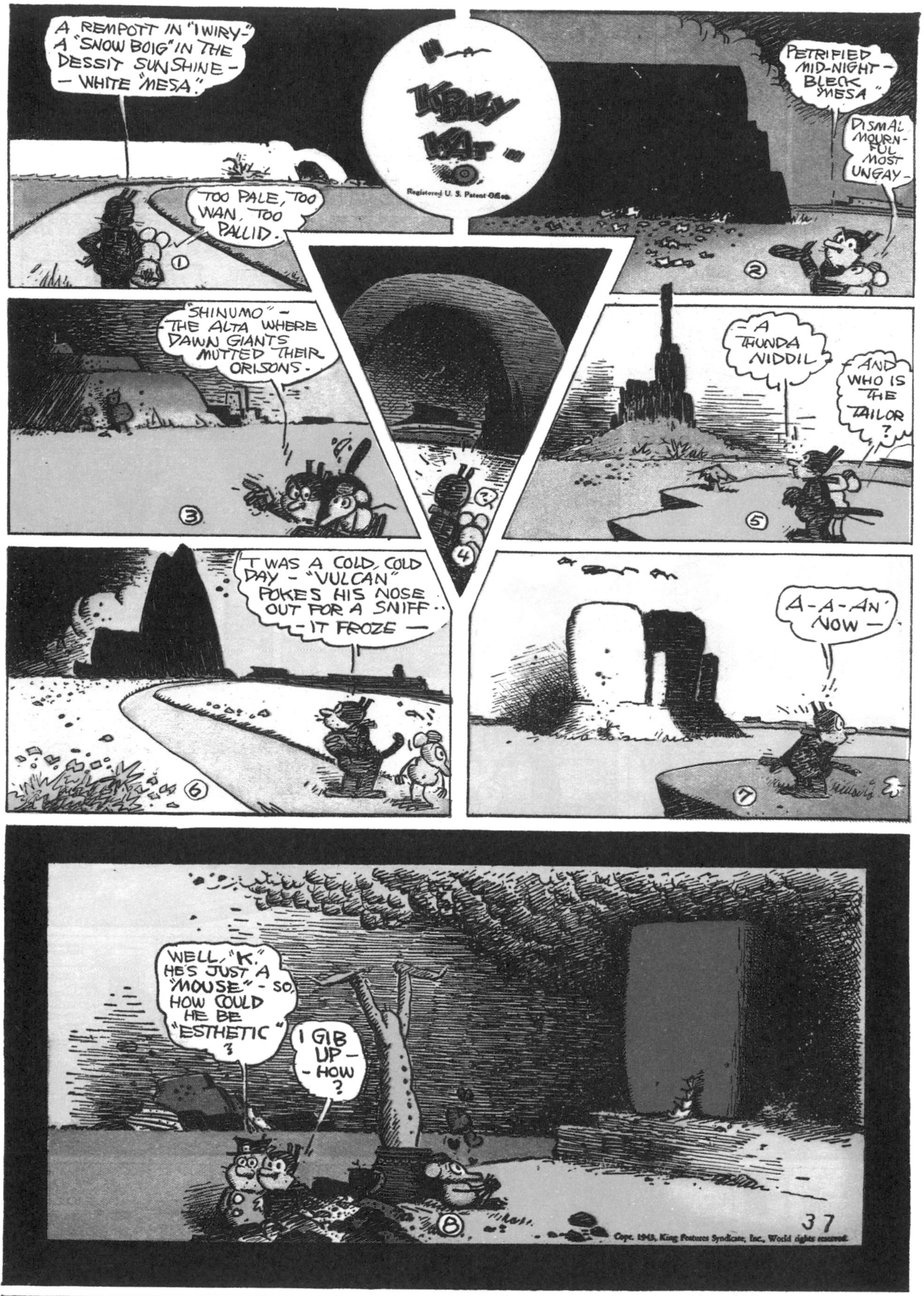
KRAZY KAT
Registered U. S. Patent Office.
A REMPOTT IN "IWIRY" - A "SNOW BOIG" IN THE DESSIT SUNSHINE - - WHITE "MESA".
TOO PALE, TOO WAN, TOO PALLID.
PETRIFIED MID-NIGHT BLECK "MESA" -
DISMAL MOURN-FUL MOST UNGAY -
"SHINUMO" - THE ALTA WHERE DAWN GIANTS MUTTED THEIR ORISONS.
?
- A THUNDA NIDDIL -
- AND WHO IS THE TAILOR ?
'T WAS A COLD, COLD DAY - "VULCAN" POKES HIS NOSE OUT FOR A SNIFF - - IT FROZE -
A-A-AN' NOW -
WELL, "K." HE'S JUST A "MOUSE" - SO, HOW COULD HE BE "ESTHETIC" ?
I GIB UP - - HOW ?
37
Copr. 1943, King Features Syndicate, Inc., World rights reserved.

March 7th, 1943.

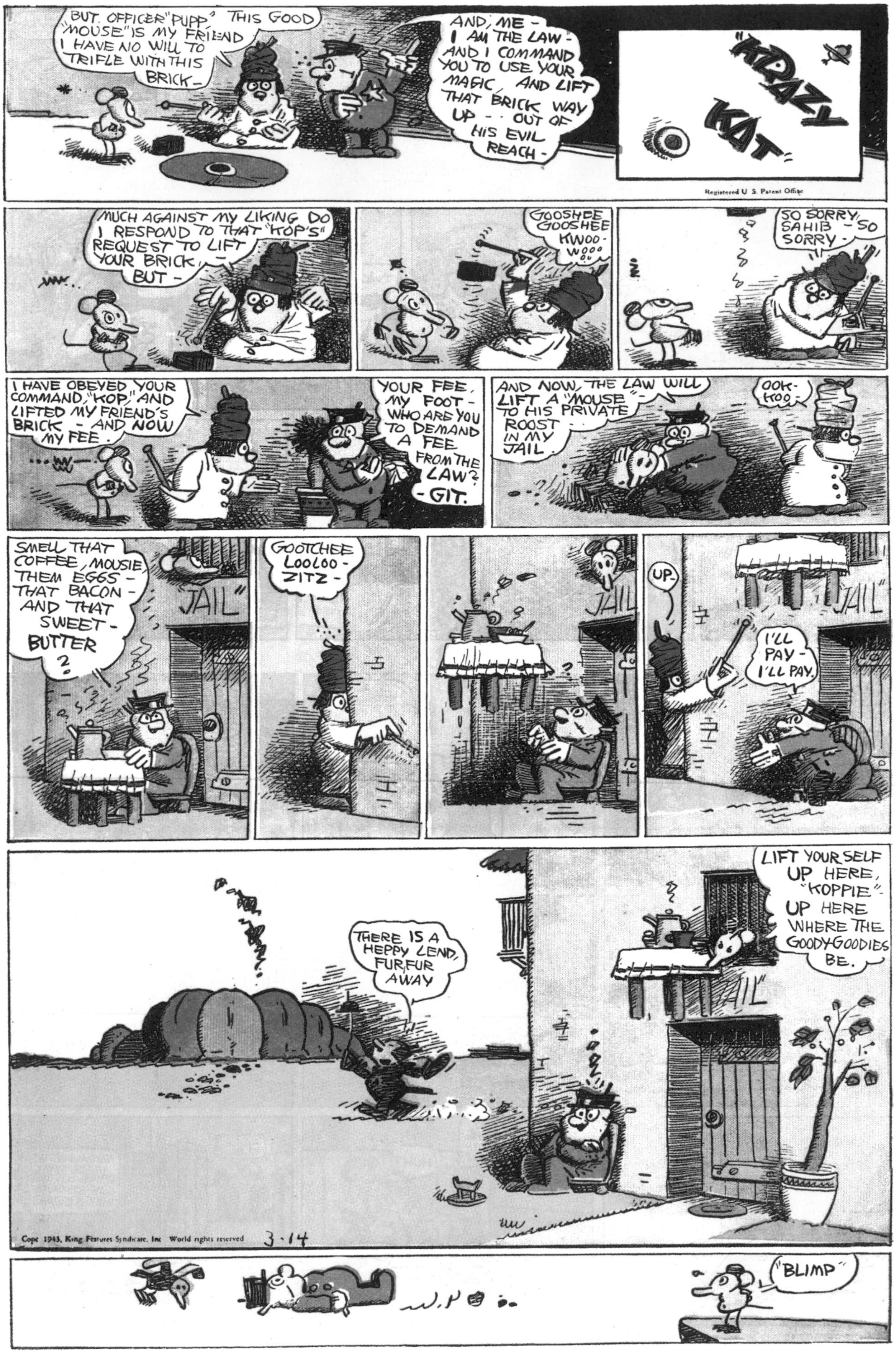
BUT, OFFICER "PUPP," THIS GOOD "MOUSE" IS MY FRIEND I HAVE NO WILL TO TRIFLE WITH THIS BRICK -
AND, ME - I AM THE LAW - AND I COMMAND YOU TO USE YOUR MAGIC, AND LIFT THAT BRICK WAY UP - - OUT OF HIS EVIL REACH -
"KRAZY KAT"
Registered U. S. Patent Office
MUCH AGAINST MY LIKING DO I RESPOND TO THAT "KOP'S" REQUEST TO LIFT YOUR BRICK, - BUT -
GOOSHEE GOOSHEE KWOO-WOOO
SO SORRY, SAHIB - SO SORRY -
I HAVE OBEYED YOUR COMMAND, "KOP," AND LIFTED MY FRIEND'S BRICK - AND NOW MY FEE.
YOUR FEE, MY FOOT - WHO ARE YOU TO DEMAND A FEE FROM THE LAW? - GIT.
AND NOW, THE LAW WILL LIFT A "MOUSE" TO HIS PRIVATE ROOST IN MY JAIL.
OOK-HOO
SMELL THAT COFFEE, MOUSIE, THEM EGGS - THAT BACON - AND THAT SWEET - BUTTER ?
"JAIL"
GOOTCHEE LOOLOO - ZITZ -
JAIL
UP.
I'LL PAY - I'LL PAY.
"JAIL"
THERE IS A HEPPY LEND, FUR, FUR AWAY
LIFT YOUR SELF UP HERE, "KOPPIE" UP HERE WHERE THE GOODY-GOODIES BE.
JAIL
Copr 1943, King Features Syndicate, Inc World rights reserved
3-14
"BLIMP"

March 14th, 1943.

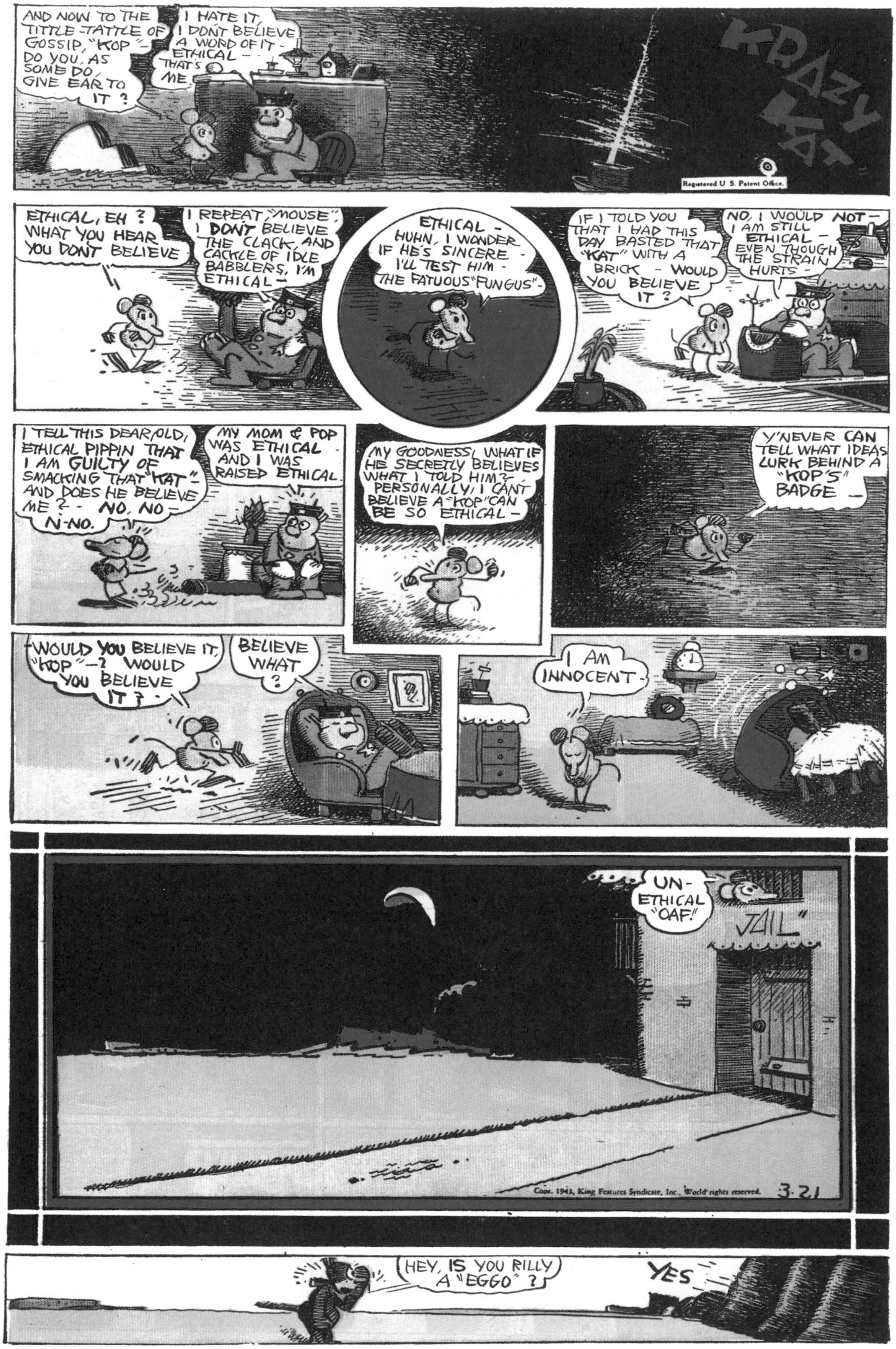
KRAZY KAT
Registered U. S. Patent Office.
AND NOW TO THE TITTLE-TATTLE OF GOSSIP, "KOP"— DO YOU, AS SOME DO, GIVE EAR TO IT ?
I HATE IT, I DON'T BELIEVE A WORD OF IT— ETHICAL— THAT'S ME.
ETHICAL, EH ? WHAT YOU HEAR YOU DON'T BELIEVE
I REPEAT, "MOUSE", I DON'T BELIEVE THE CLACK, AND CACKLE OF IDLE BABBLERS, I'M ETHICAL—
ETHICAL— HUHN, I WONDER IF HE'S SINCERE— I'LL TEST HIM— THE FATUOUS "FUNGUS"—
IF I TOLD YOU THAT I HAD THIS DAY BASTED THAT "KAT" WITH A BRICK— WOULD YOU BELIEVE IT ?
NO, I WOULD NOT— I AM STILL ETHICAL— EVEN THOUGH THE STRAIN HURTS—
I TELL THIS DEAR, OLD, ETHICAL PIPPIN THAT I AM GUILTY OF SMACKING THAT "KAT"— AND DOES HE BELIEVE ME ?— NO, NO— N-NO.
MY MOM & POP WAS ETHICAL— AND I WAS RAISED ETHICAL.
MY GOODNESS, WHAT IF HE SECRETLY BELIEVES WHAT I TOLD HIM?— PERSONALLY, I CAN'T BELIEVE A "KOP" CAN BE SO ETHICAL—
Y'NEVER CAN TELL WHAT IDEAS LURK BEHIND A "KOP'S" BADGE—
—WOULD YOU BELIEVE IT, "KOP"—? WOULD YOU BELIEVE IT ?
BELIEVE WHAT ?
I AM INNOCENT—
UN-ETHICAL "OAF."
"JAIL"
Copr. 1943, King Features Syndicate, Inc., World rights reserved.
3.21
HEY, IS YOU RILLY A "EGGO" ?
YES—

March 21st, 1943.

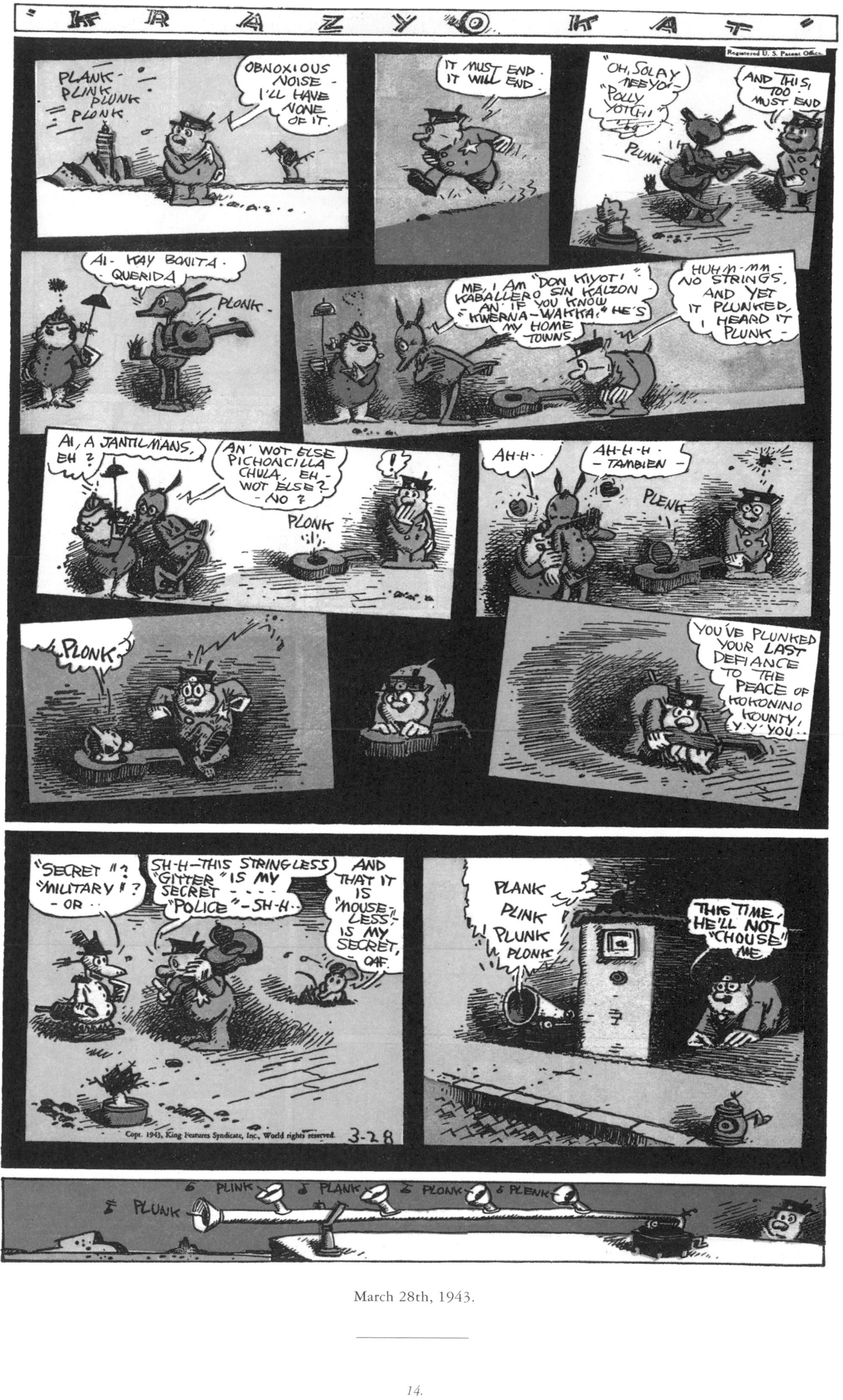
KRAZY KAT
Registered U. S. Patent Office.
PLANK - PLINK PLUNK PLONK
OBNOXIOUS NOISE - I'LL HAVE NONE OF IT.
IT MUST END - IT WILL END
"OH, SOLAY NEEYO" - "POLLY YOTCHI"
AND THIS, TOO - MUST END
PLUNK
AI - KAY BONITA - QUERIDA
PLONK -
ME, I AM "DON KIYOTI KABALLERO SIN KALZON" - AN' IF YOU KNOW "KWERNA-WAKKA" HE'S MY HOME TOWNS
HUH-M-MM - NO STRINGS, AND YET IT PLUNKED, I HEARD IT PLUNK -
AI, A JANTILMANS, EH ?
AN' WOT ELSE PICHONCILLA CHULA, EH - WOT ELSE ? - NO ?
PLONK
AH-H -
AH-H-H - TAMBIEN -
PLENK
PLONK
YOU'VE PLUNKED YOUR LAST DEFIANCE TO THE PEACE OF KOKONINO KOUNTY, Y-Y-YOU -
"SECRET" ? "MILITARY" ? - OR -
SH-H-THIS STRINGLESS "GITTER" IS MY SECRET - - - "POLICE" - SH-H -
AND THAT IT IS "MOUSE-LESS" - IS MY SECRET, OAF.
Copt. 1943, King Features Syndicate, Inc., World rights reserved.
3-28
PLANK PLINK PLUNK PLONK
THIS TIME, HE'LL NOT "CHOUSE" ME.
PLUNK
PLINK
PLANK
PLONK
PLENK

March 28th, 1943.

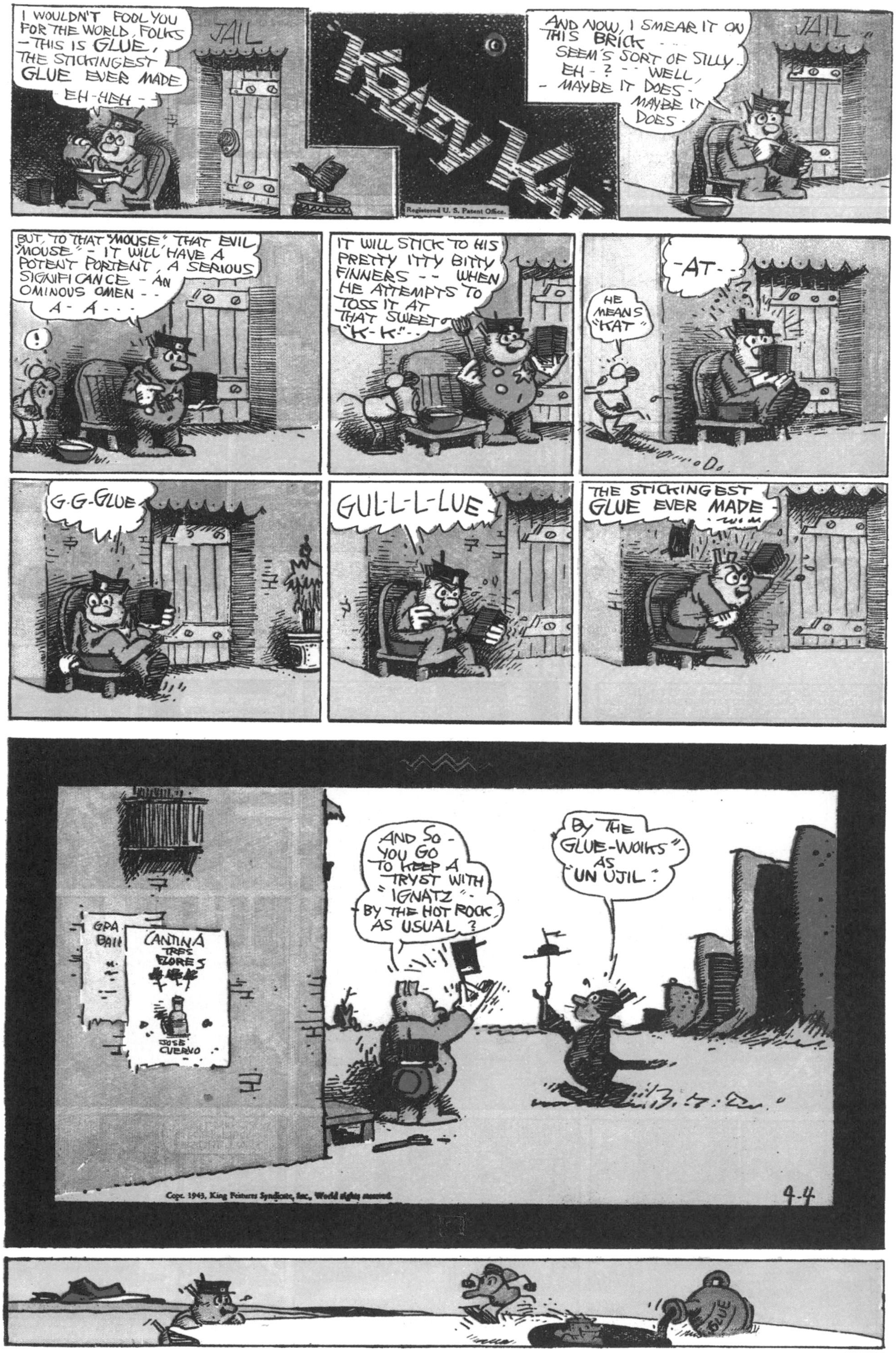
I WOULDN'T FOOL YOU FOR THE WORLD, FOLKS - THIS IS GLUE, THE STICKINGEST GLUE EVER MADE
EH-HEH --
JAIL
KRAZY KAT
Registered U. S. Patent Office.
AND NOW, I SMEAR IT ON THIS BRICK SEEM'S SORT OF SILLY.. EH - ? - - WELL, - MAYBE IT DOES - MAYBE IT DOES -
BUT, TO THAT "MOUSE," THAT EVIL "MOUSE" - IT WILL HAVE A POTENT PORTENT, A SERIOUS SIGNIFICANCE - AN OMINOUS OMEN - -
A - A - - -
!
IT WILL STICK TO HIS PRETTY ITTY BITTY FINNERS - - WHEN HE ATTEMPTS TO TOSS IT AT THAT SWEET "K-K" - -
-AT - -
HE MEANS "KAT"
G-G-GLUE
GUL-L-L-LUE -
THE STICKINGEST GLUE EVER MADE
AND SO - YOU GO TO KEEP A TRYST WITH "IGNATZ" - BY THE HOT ROCK AS USUAL ?
BY THE "GLUE-WOIKS" AS "UN UJIL"
CANTINA TRES FLORES
JOSE CUERVO
Copr. 1943, King Features Syndicate, Inc., World rights reserved.
4-4
GLUE

April 4th, 1943.

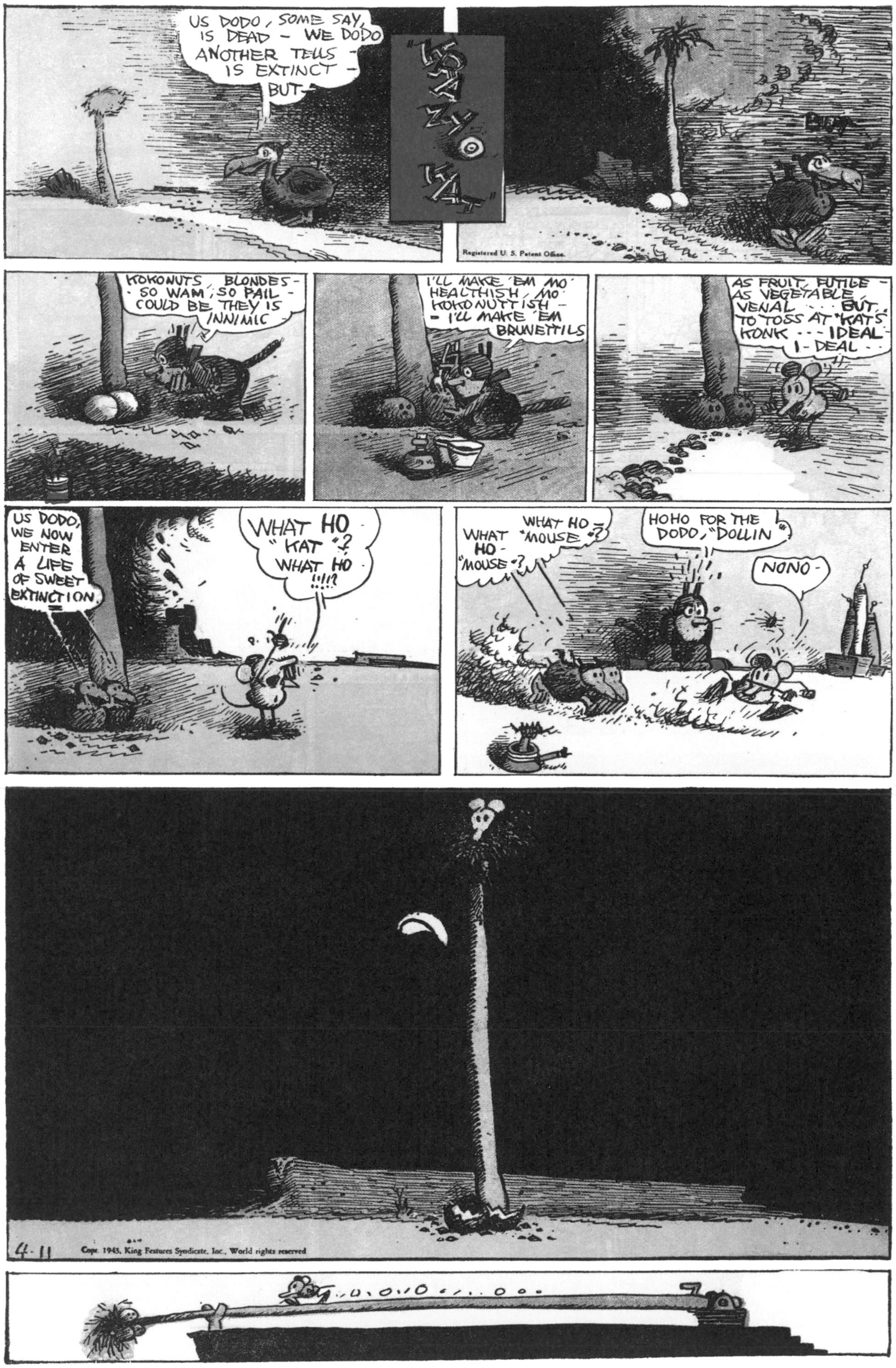
US DODO, SOME SAY, IS DEAD - WE DODO ANOTHER TELLS - IS EXTINCT - BUT-
"KRAZY KAT"
Registered U. S. Patent Office.
KOKONUTS BLONDES - SO WAM, SO PAIL - COULD BE THEY IS INNIMIC
I'LL MAKE 'EM MO' HEALTHISH, MO' KOKONUTTISH - - I'LL MAKE 'EM BRUNETTILS
AS FRUIT, FUTILE - AS VEGETABLE, VENAL - - BUT, TO TOSS AT "KATS" KONK - - - IDEAL I-DEAL - -
US DODO, WE NOW ENTER A LIFE OF SWEET EXTINCTION.
WHAT HO "KAT"? WHAT HO !!!!?
WHAT HO - "MOUSE"?
WHAT HO "MOUSE"?
HOHO FOR THE DODO, "DOLLIN".
NONO -
4-11
Copr. 1943, King Features Syndicate, Inc., World rights reserved

April 11th, 1943.

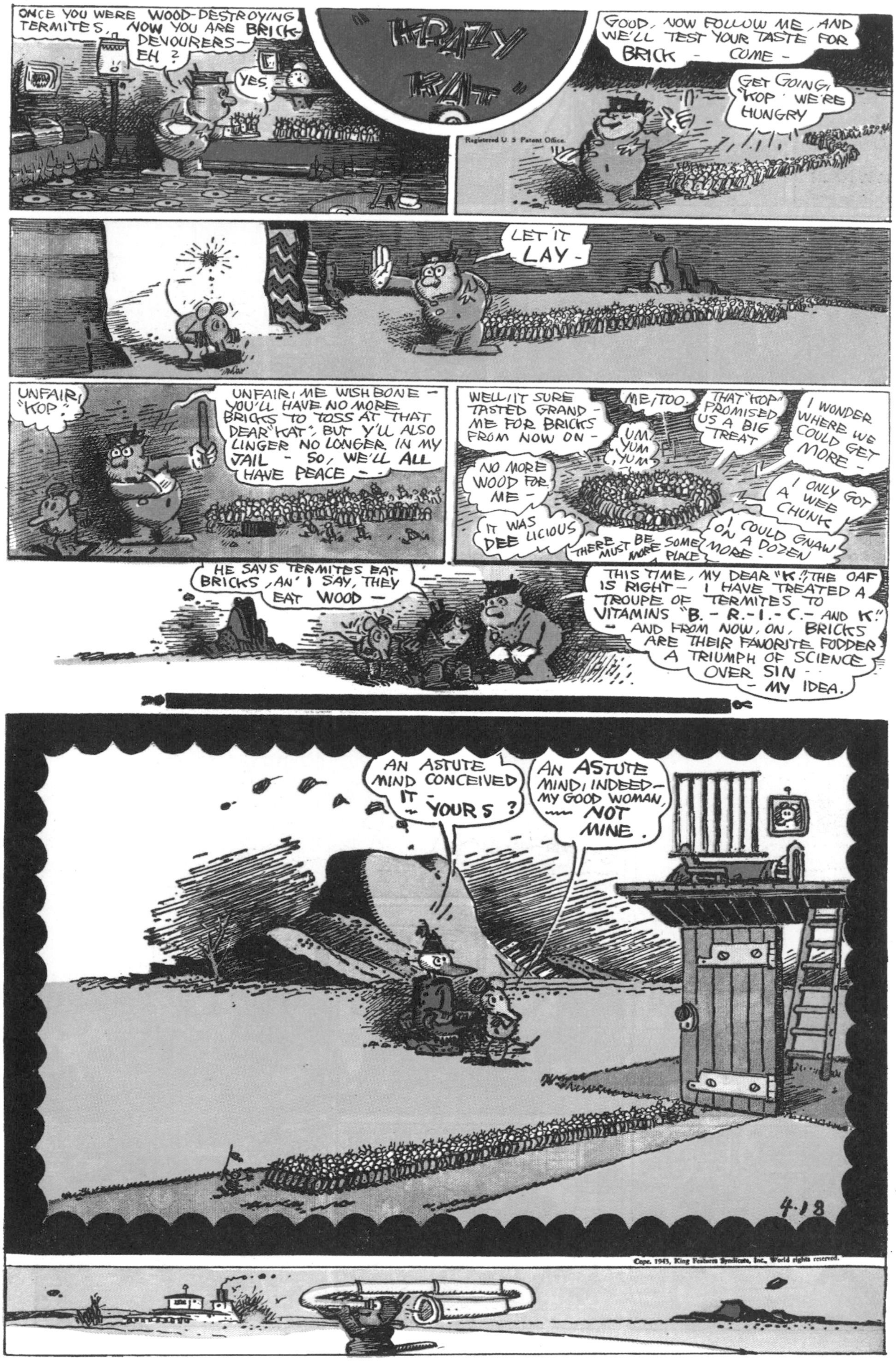
ONCE YOU WERE WOOD-DESTROYING TERMITES, NOW YOU ARE BRICK-DEVOURERS— EH?
YES.
"KRAZY KAT"
Registered U. S. Patent Office.
GOOD, NOW FOLLOW ME, AND WE'LL TEST YOUR TASTE FOR BRICK - COME -
GET GOING, "KOP" WE'RE HUNGRY
LET IT LAY -
UNFAIR, "KOP."
UNFAIR, ME WISHBONE - YOU'LL HAVE NO MORE BRICKS TO TOSS AT THAT DEAR "KAT", BUT Y'LL ALSO LINGER NO LONGER IN MY JAIL - SO, WE'LL ALL HAVE PEACE - -
WELL, IT SURE TASTED GRAND - ME FOR BRICKS FROM NOW ON -
ME, TOO.
THAT "KOP" PROMISED US A BIG TREAT
I WONDER WHERE WE COULD GET MORE -
UM, YUM, YUM
NO MORE WOOD FOR ME -
I ONLY GOT A WEE CHUNK
IT WAS DEE LICIOUS
THERE MUST BE MORE SOME PLACE
I COULD GNAW ON A DOZEN MORE -
HE SAYS TERMITES EAT BRICKS, AN' I SAY, THEY EAT WOOD -
THIS TIME, MY DEAR "K." THE OAF IS RIGHT - I HAVE TREATED A TROUPE OF TERMITES TO VITAMINS "B. - R. - I. - C. - AND K." - AND FROM NOW, ON, BRICKS ARE THEIR FAVORITE FODDER - A TRIUMPH OF SCIENCE OVER SIN - - MY IDEA.
AN ASTUTE MIND CONCEIVED IT - - YOURS?
AN ASTUTE MIND, INDEED - MY GOOD WOMAN, - NOT MINE.
4-18
Copr. 1943, King Features Syndicate, Inc., World rights reserved.

April 18th, 1943.

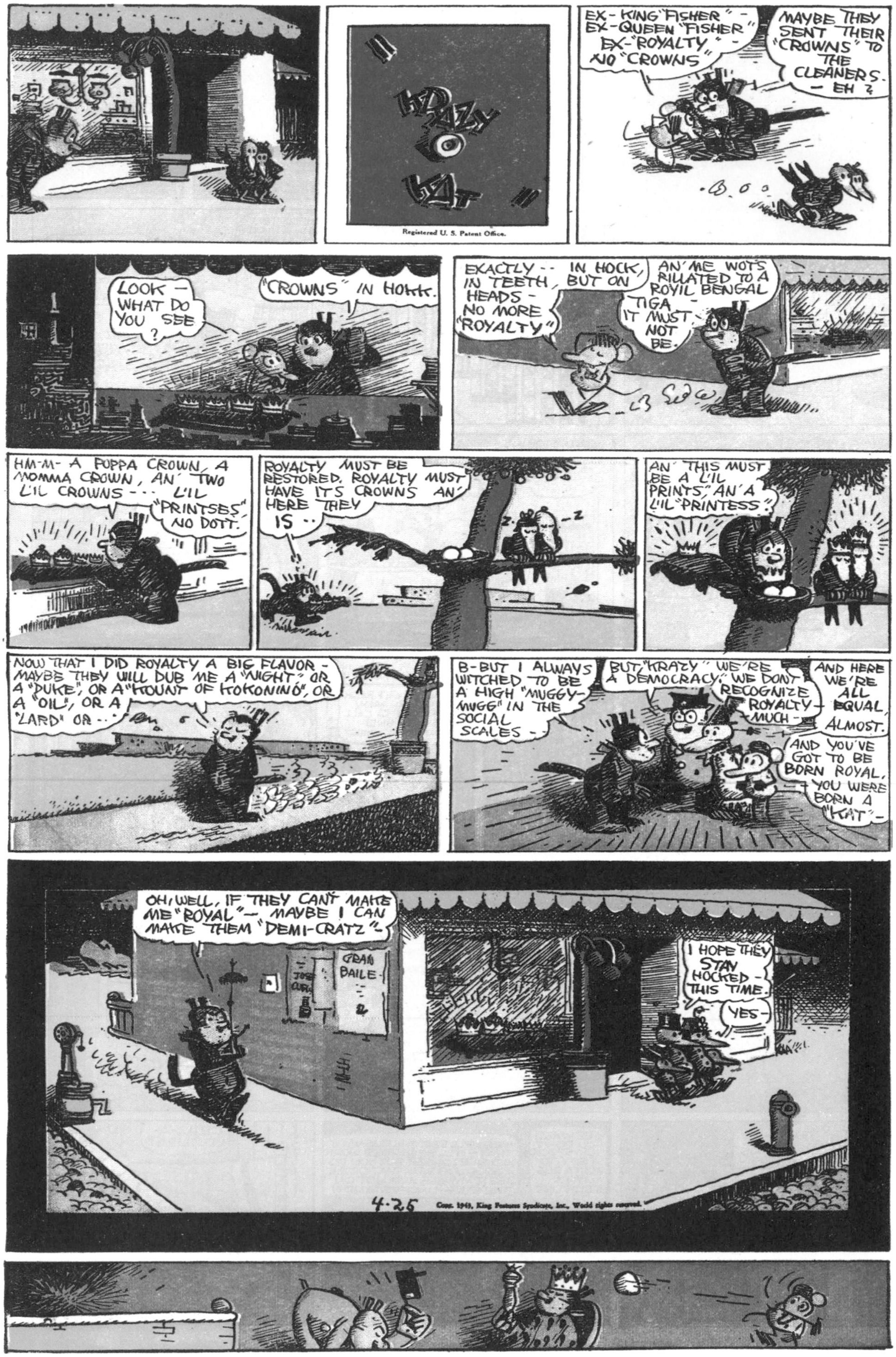
KRAZY KAT
Registered U. S. Patent Office.
EX-KING "FISHER" - EX-QUEEN "FISHER" EX-"ROYALTY" - NO "CROWNS"
MAYBE THEY SENT THEIR "CROWNS" TO THE CLEANERS - EH ?
LOOK - WHAT DO YOU SEE ?
"CROWNS" IN HOKK.
EXACTLY -- IN TEETH, HEADS - NO MORE "ROYALTY"
IN HOCK, BUT ON
AN' ME WOT'S RILLATED TO A ROYIL BENGAL TIGA - IT MUST NOT BE.
HM-M- A POPPA CROWN, A MOMMA CROWN, AN' TWO L'IL CROWNS ---
L'IL "PRINTSES" NO DOTT.
ROYALTY MUST BE RESTORED. ROYALTY MUST HAVE ITS CROWNS AN' HERE THEY IS ..
AN' THIS MUST BE A L'IL PRINTS, AN' A L'IL "PRINTESS".
NOW THAT I DID ROYALTY A BIG FLAVOR - MAYBE THEY WILL DUB ME A "NIGHT", OR A "DUKE", OR A "KOUNT OF KOKONINO", OR A "OIL", OR A "LARD" OR - -
B-BUT I ALWAYS WITCHED TO BE A HIGH "MUGGY-MUGG" IN THE SOCIAL SCALES -
BUT, "KRAZY" WE'RE A DEMOCRACY, WE DON'T RECOGNIZE ROYALTY - MUCH -
AND HERE WE'RE ALL EQUAL, ALMOST.
AND YOU'VE GOT TO BE BORN ROYAL, YOU WERE BORN A "KAT" -
OH, WELL, IF THEY CAN'T MAKE ME "ROYAL" - MAYBE I CAN MAKE THEM "DEMI-CRATZ" -
GRAN BAILE
I HOPE THEY STAY HOCKED - THIS TIME.
YES -
4-25
Copr. 1943, King Features Syndicate, Inc., World rights reserved.

April 25th, 1943.

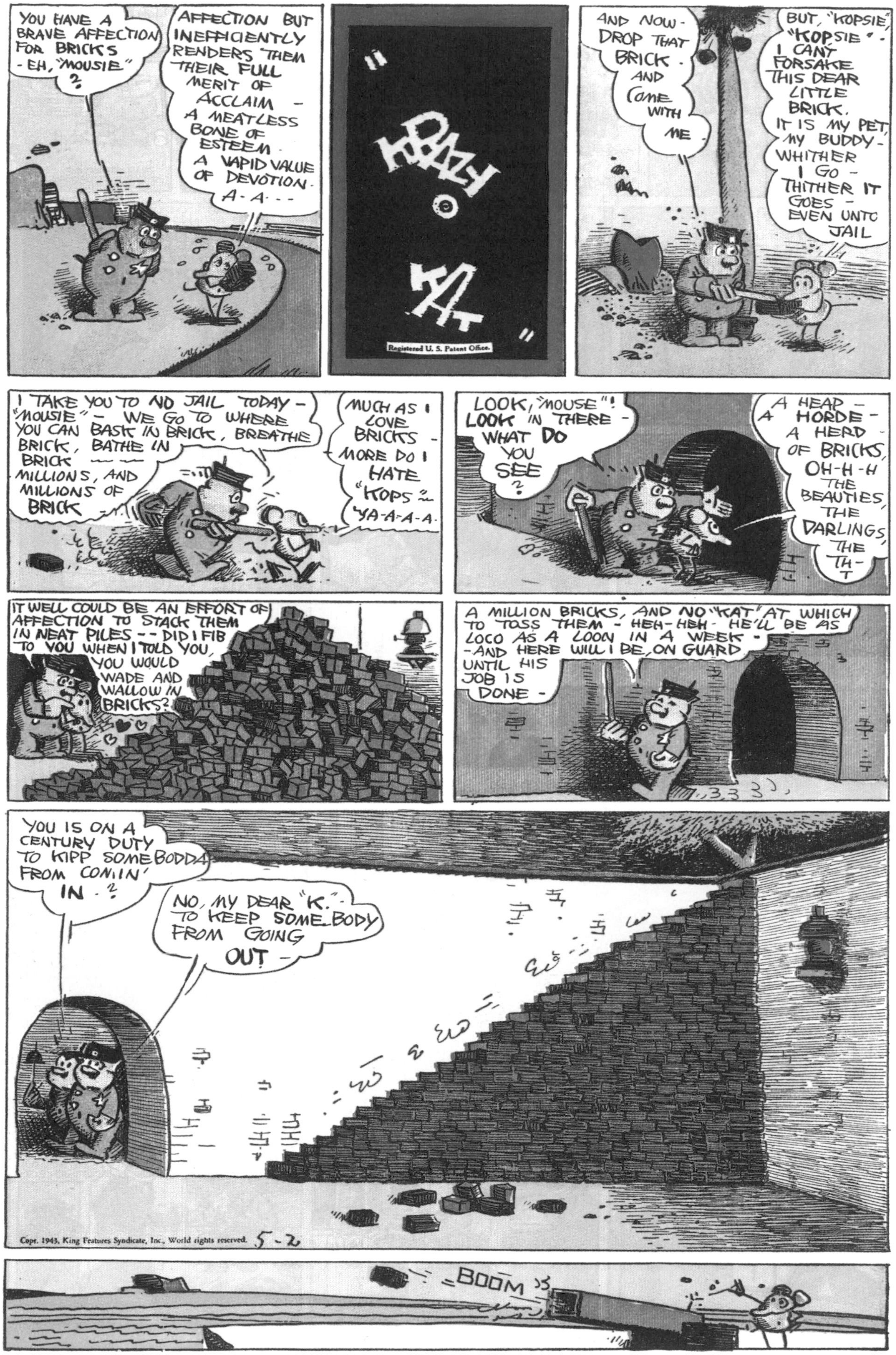
YOU HAVE A BRAVE AFFECTION FOR BRICKS - EH, "MOUSIE" ?
AFFECTION BUT INEFFICIENTLY RENDERS THEM THEIR FULL MERIT OF ACCLAIM - A MEATLESS BONE OF ESTEEM - A VAPID VALUE OF DEVOTION - A - A - - -
"KRAZY KAT"
Registered U. S. Patent Office.
AND NOW - DROP THAT BRICK - AND COME WITH ME
BUT, "KOPSIE", "KOPSIE" - I CAN'T FORSAKE THIS DEAR LITTLE BRICK. IT IS MY PET, MY BUDDY - WHITHER I GO - THITHER IT GOES - EVEN UNTO JAIL
I TAKE YOU TO NO JAIL TODAY - "MOUSIE" - WE GO TO WHERE YOU CAN BASK IN BRICK, BREATHE BRICK, BATHE IN BRICK —— MILLIONS, AND MILLIONS OF BRICK
MUCH AS I LOVE BRICKS - MORE DO I HATE "KOPS" YA-A-A-A
LOOK, "MOUSE"! LOOK IN THERE - WHAT DO YOU SEE ?
A HEAP - A HORDE - A HERD OF BRICKS, OH-H-H THE BEAUTIES, THE DARLINGS, THE TH-T
IT WELL COULD BE AN EFFORT OF AFFECTION TO STACK THEM IN NEAT PILES - - DID I FIB TO YOU WHEN I TOLD YOU, YOU WOULD WADE AND WALLOW IN BRICKS?
A MILLION BRICKS, AND NO "KAT" AT WHICH TO TOSS THEM - HEH-HEH - HE'LL BE AS LOCO AS A LOON IN A WEEK - -AND HERE WILL I BE, ON GUARD UNTIL HIS JOB IS DONE -
YOU IS ON A CENTURY DUTY TO KIPP SOME BODDA FROM COMIN' IN - ?
NO, MY DEAR "K." - TO KEEP SOME-BODY FROM GOING OUT -
Copr. 1943, King Features Syndicate, Inc., World rights reserved. 5-2
BOOM

May 2nd, 1943.

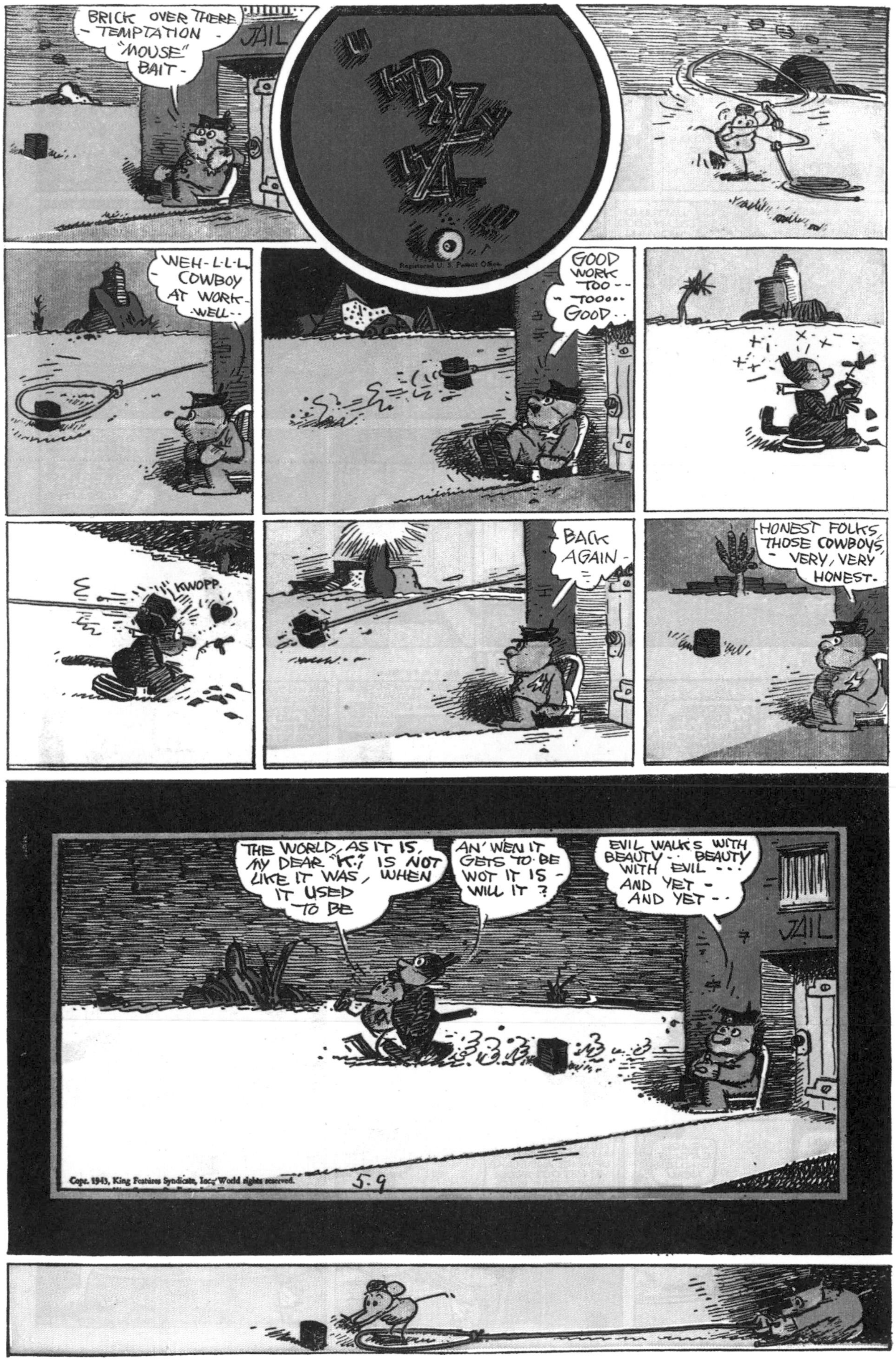

BRICK OVER THERE - TEMPTATION - "MOUSE" BAIT -
JAIL
KRAZY KAT
WEH-L-L-L COWBOY AT WORK - WELL -
GOOD WORK TOO - - TOO... GOOD -
KNOPP
BACK AGAIN -
HONEST FOLKS, THOSE COWBOYS - VERY, VERY HONEST -
THE WORLD, AS IT IS, MY DEAR "K," IS NOT LIKE IT WAS, WHEN IT USED TO BE
AN' WEN IT GETS TO BE WOT IT IS - WILL IT ?
EVIL WALKS WITH BEAUTY - - BEAUTY WITH EVIL - - - AND YET - AND YET - -
JAIL
Copr. 1943, King Features Syndicate, Inc., World rights reserved.
5.9

May 9th, 1943.

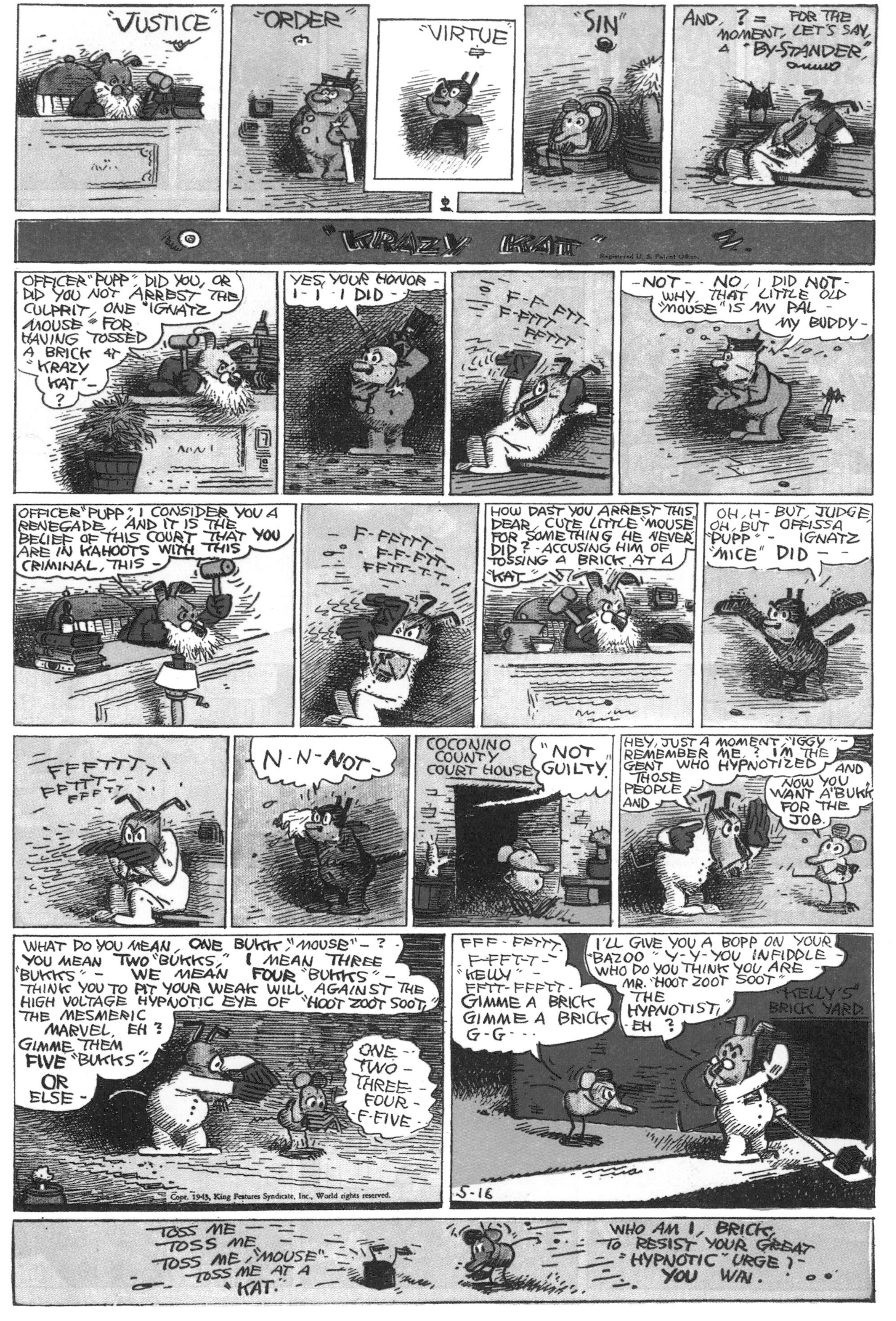

"JUSTICE"
"ORDER"
"VIRTUE"
"SIN"
AND, ? = FOR THE MOMENT, LET'S SAY, A "BY-STANDER"
"KRAZY KAT"
Registered U. S. Patent Office.
OFFICER "PUPP", DID YOU, OR DID YOU NOT ARREST THE CULPRIT, ONE "IGNATZ MOUSE" FOR HAVING TOSSED A BRICK AT "KRAZY KAT" - ?
YES, YOUR HONOR - I - I - I DID -
F-F-FTT F-FTT FFTTT
-NOT - - NO, I DID NOT - WHY, THAT LITTLE OLD "MOUSE" IS MY PAL - MY BUDDY -
OFFICER "PUPP", I CONSIDER YOU A RENEGADE, AND IT IS THE BELIEF OF THIS COURT THAT YOU ARE IN KAHOOTS WITH THIS CRIMINAL, THIS -
F-FFTTT - F-F-FTT - FFTT-T-T-
HOW DAST YOU ARREST THIS DEAR, CUTE LITTLE "MOUSE" FOR SOMETHING HE NEVER DID? - ACCUSING HIM OF TOSSING A BRICK AT A "KAT" -
OH, H - BUT, JUDGE, OH, BUT OFFISSA "PUPP" - IGNATZ "MICE" DID - -
FFFTTTT FFTTT FFFTT
N-N-NOT -
COCONINO COUNTY COURT HOUSE
"NOT GUILTY"
HEY, JUST A MOMENT, "IGGY" - REMEMBER ME? I'M THE GENT WHO HYPNOTIZED THOSE PEOPLE AND -
AND NOW YOU WANT A "BUKK" FOR THE JOB.
WHAT DO YOU MEAN, ONE "BUKK", "MOUSE" - ? YOU MEAN TWO "BUKKS", I MEAN THREE "BUKKS" - WE MEAN FOUR "BUKKS" - THINK YOU TO PIT YOUR WEAK WILL AGAINST THE HIGH VOLTAGE HYPNOTIC EYE OF "HOOT ZOOT SOOT", THE MESMERIC MARVEL, EH? GIMME THEM FIVE "BUKKS" - OR ELSE -
ONE - TWO - THREE - FOUR - F-FIVE
Copr. 1943, King Features Syndicate, Inc., World rights reserved.
FFF-FFTTT- F-FFT-T- "KELLY" - FFTT-FFFTT- GIMME A BRICK GIMME A BRICK G-G- - -
I'LL GIVE YOU A BOPP ON YOUR "BAZOO" Y-Y-YOU INFIDDLE - WHO DO YOU THINK YOU ARE - MR. "HOOT ZOOT SOOT" THE HYPNOTIST, EH ?
"KELLY'S" BRICK YARD
5-16
TOSS ME - TOSS ME - TOSS ME, "MOUSE" - TOSS ME AT A "KAT".
WHO AM I, BRICK, TO RESIST YOUR GREAT "HYPNOTIC" URGE? - YOU WAI.

May 16th, 1943.

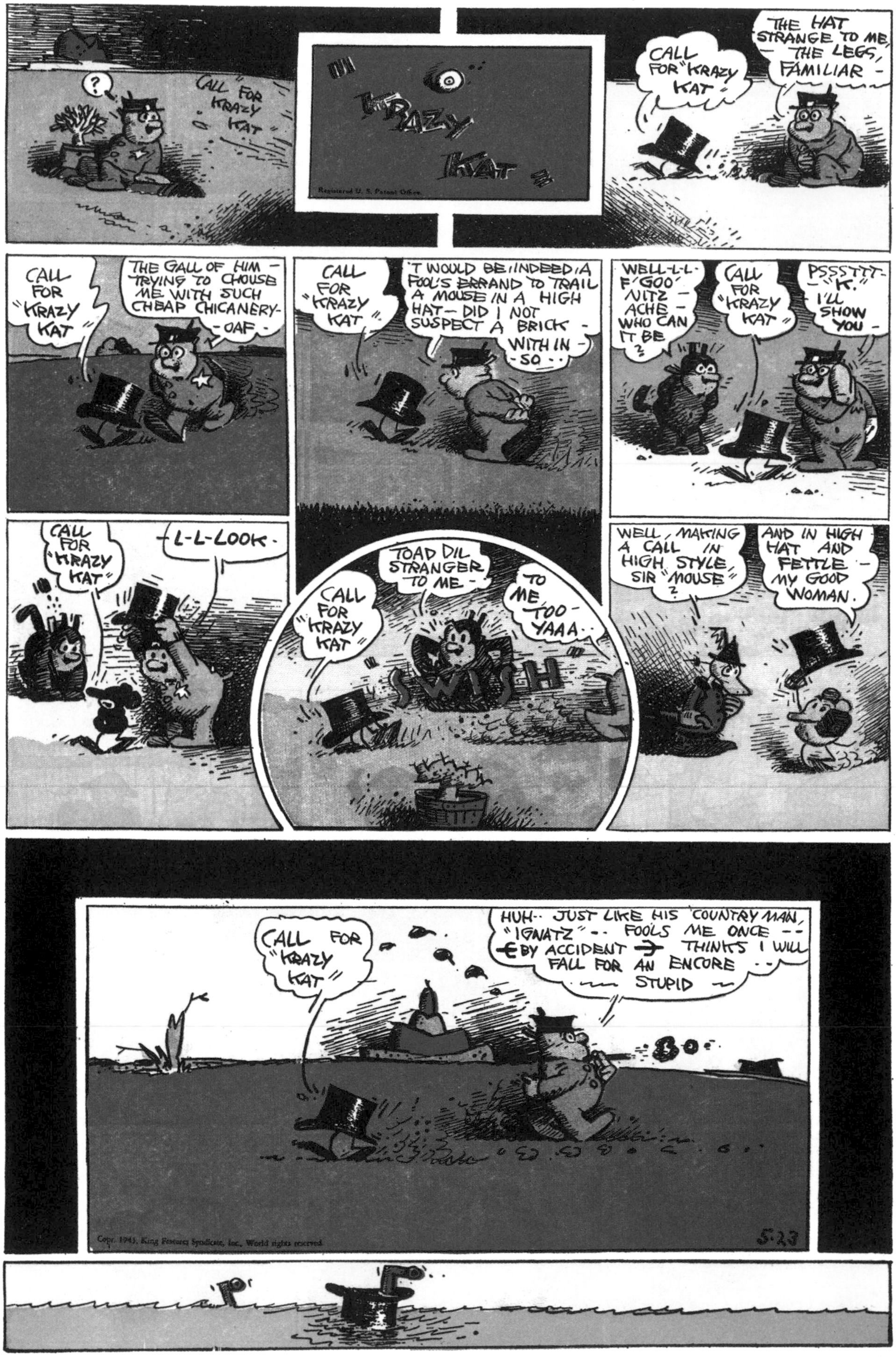
CALL FOR "KRAZY KAT"
?
KRAZY KAT
Registered U. S. Patent Office.
CALL FOR "KRAZY KAT"
THE HAT STRANGE TO ME, THE LEGS, FAMILIAR -
CALL FOR "KRAZY KAT"
THE GALL OF HIM - TRYING TO CHOUSE ME WITH SUCH CHEAP CHICANERY - OAF.
CALL FOR "KRAZY KAT"
'T WOULD BE, INDEED, A FOOL'S ERRAND TO TRAIL A MOUSE IN A HIGH HAT - DID I NOT SUSPECT A BRICK - WITH IN - SO - -
WELL-L-L F'GOO NITZ - ACHE - WHO CAN IT BE ?
CALL FOR "KRAZY KAT"
PSSSTTT "K." I'LL SHOW YOU -
CALL FOR "KRAZY KAT"
L-L-LOOK -
TOAD DIL STRANGER TO ME -
CALL FOR "KRAZY KAT"
TO ME TOO YAAA.
SWISH
WELL, MAKING A CALL IN HIGH STYLE SIR "MOUSE" ?
AND IN HIGH HAT AND FETTLE - MY GOOD WOMAN.
CALL FOR "KRAZY KAT"
HUH - JUST LIKE HIS COUNTRY MAN, "IGNATZ" - FOOLS ME ONCE - BY ACCIDENT - THINKS I WILL FALL FOR AN ENCORE - - STUPID
Copr. 1943, King Features Syndicate, Inc., World rights reserved.
5-23

May 23rd, 1943.

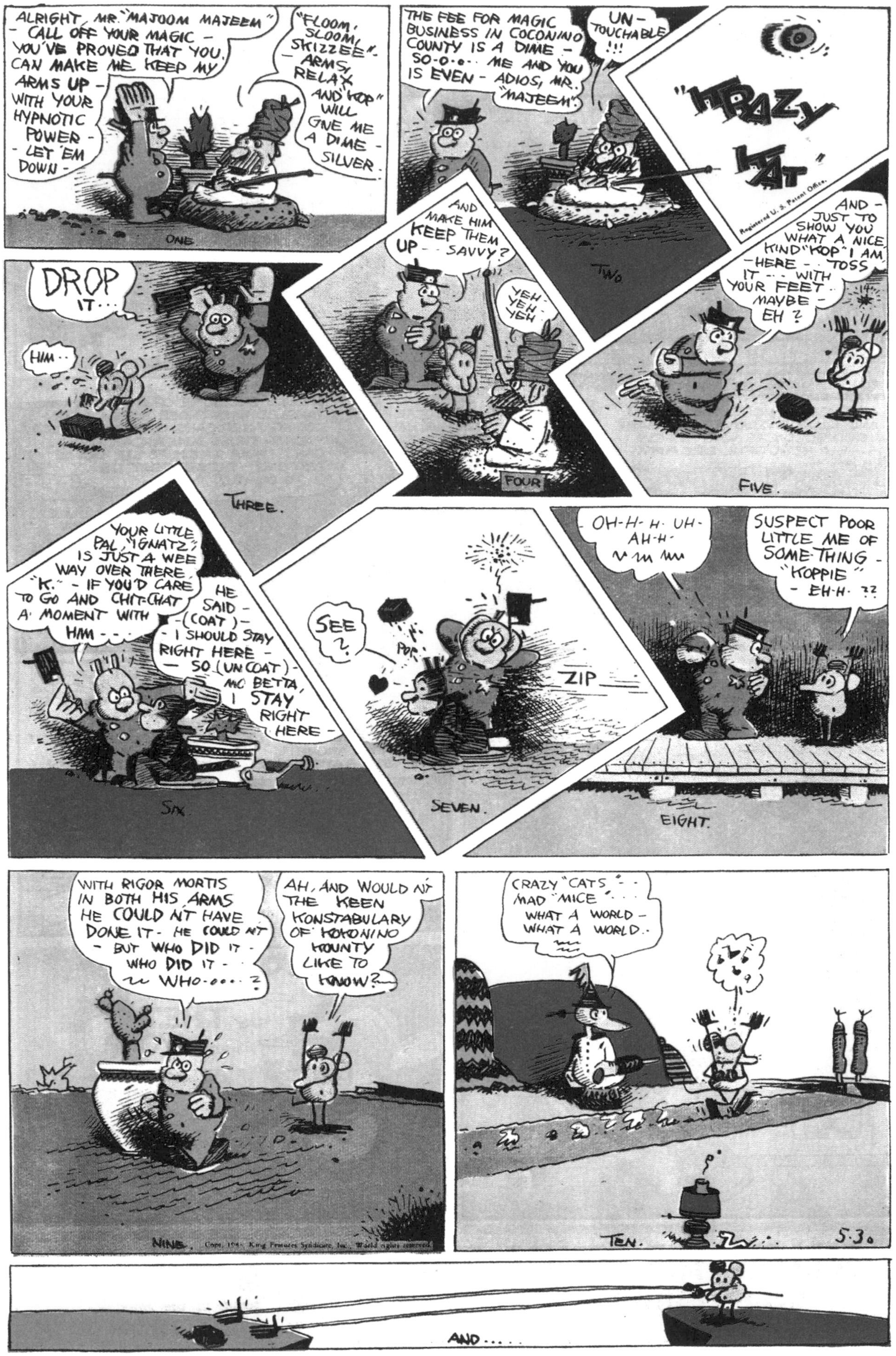
ALRIGHT, MR. "MAJOOM MAJEEM" - CALL OFF YOUR MAGIC - YOU'VE PROVED THAT YOU CAN MAKE ME KEEP MY ARMS UP - WITH YOUR HYPNOTIC POWER - LET 'EM DOWN -
"FLOOM, SLOOM, SKIZZEE" - ARMS, RELAX AND "KOP" WILL GIVE ME A DIME - SILVER
ONE
THE FEE FOR MAGIC BUSINESS IN COCONINO COUNTY IS A DIME - SO-O-o.. ME AND YOU IS EVEN - ADIOS, MR. "MAJEEM".
UN-TOUCHABLE !!!
"KRAZY KAT"
Registered U. S. Patent Office.
TWO
DROP IT...
HIM...
THREE.
AND MAKE HIM KEEP THEM UP - - SAVVY?
YEH YEH YEH
FOUR
AND - JUST TO SHOW YOU WHAT A NICE, KIND "KOP" I AM, - HERE - - TOSS IT - - WITH YOUR FEET MAYBE - EH ?
FIVE.
YOUR LITTLE PAL, "IGNATZ", IS JUST A WEE WAY OVER THERE, "K." - IF YOU'D CARE TO GO AND CHIT-CHAT A MOMENT WITH HIM - -
HE SAID - (COAT) - I SHOULD STAY RIGHT HERE - SO (UN COAT) - MO BETTA, I STAY RIGHT HERE -
SIX
SEE ?
POP
ZIP
SEVEN.
- OH-H- H. UH - AH-H -
SUSPECT POOR LITTLE ME OF SOME-THING - "KOPPIE" - EH-H- ??
EIGHT.
WITH RIGOR MORTIS IN BOTH HIS ARMS HE COULD N'T HAVE DONE IT - HE COULD N'T - BUT WHO DID IT - WHO DID IT - WHO-... ?
AH, AND WOULD N'T THE KEEN KONSTABULARY OF KOKONINO KOUNTY LIKE TO KNOW?
NINE
Copr. 194- King Features Syndicate, Inc., World rights reserved.
CRAZY "CATS" - - MAD "MICE" - - WHAT A WORLD - WHAT A WORLD..
TEN.
5.30
AND....

May 30th, 1943.

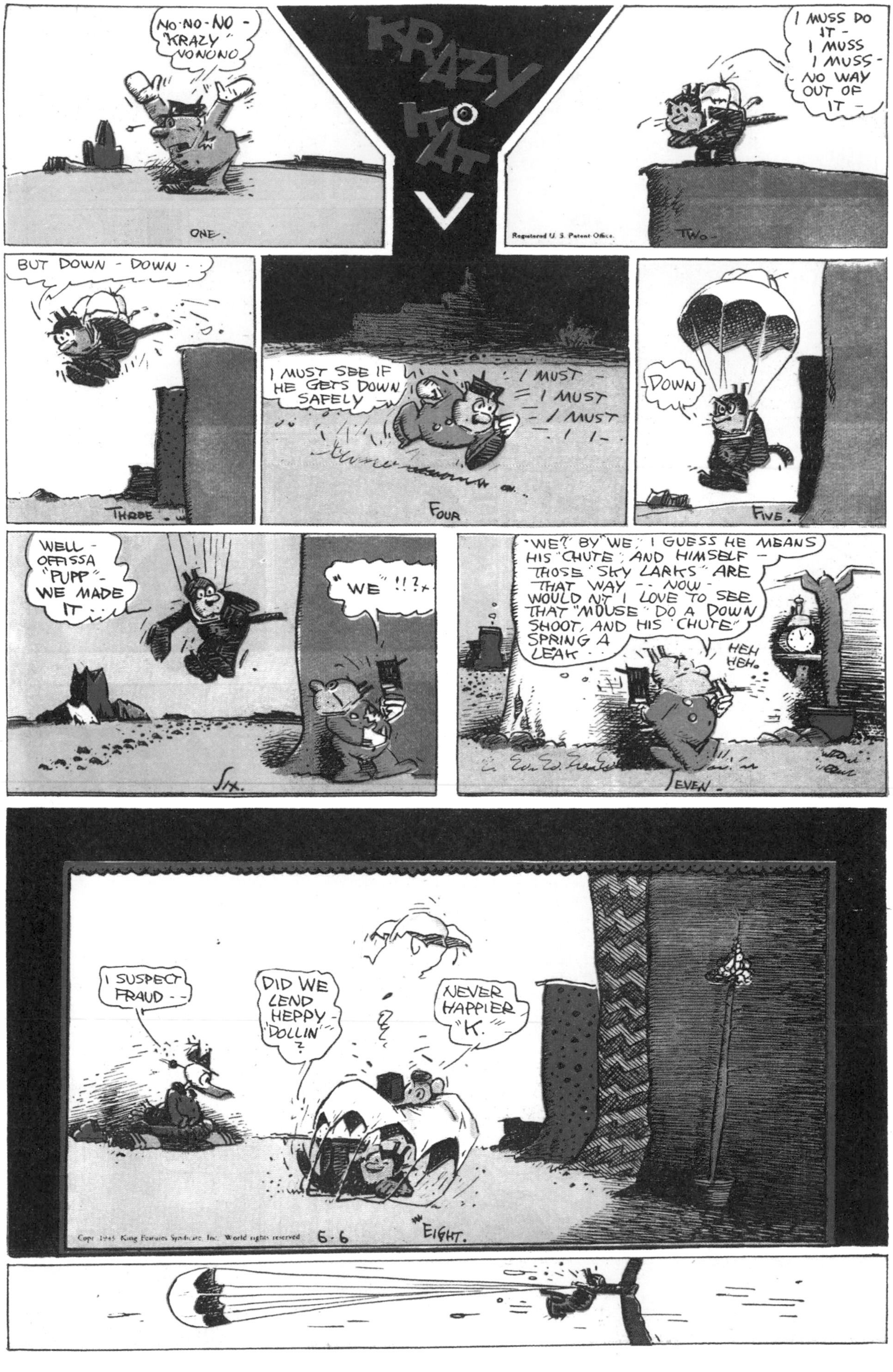

KRAZY KAT
NO-NO-NO - "KRAZY" VONONO
ONE.
I MUSS DO IT - I MUSS I MUSS - NO WAY OUT OF IT -
Registered U. S. Patent Office.
TWO-
BUT DOWN - DOWN -
THREE
I MUST SEE IF HE GETS DOWN SAFELY
I MUST - I MUST - I MUST
FOUR
DOWN
FIVE.
WELL - OFFISSA "PUPP" WE MADE IT
"WE" !!?
SIX.
"WE"? BY "WE" I GUESS HE MEANS HIS "CHUTE" AND HIMSELF - THOSE "SKY LARKS" ARE THAT WAY - - NOW - WOULD N'T I LOVE TO SEE THAT "MOUSE" DO A DOWN SHOOT, AND HIS "CHUTE" SPRING A LEAK -
HEH HEH.
SEVEN -
I SUSPECT FRAUD - -
DID WE LEND HEPPY DOLLIN ?
NEVER HAPPIER "K."
Copr 1943 King Features Syndicate, Inc. World rights reserved
6-6
EIGHT.

June 6th, 1943.

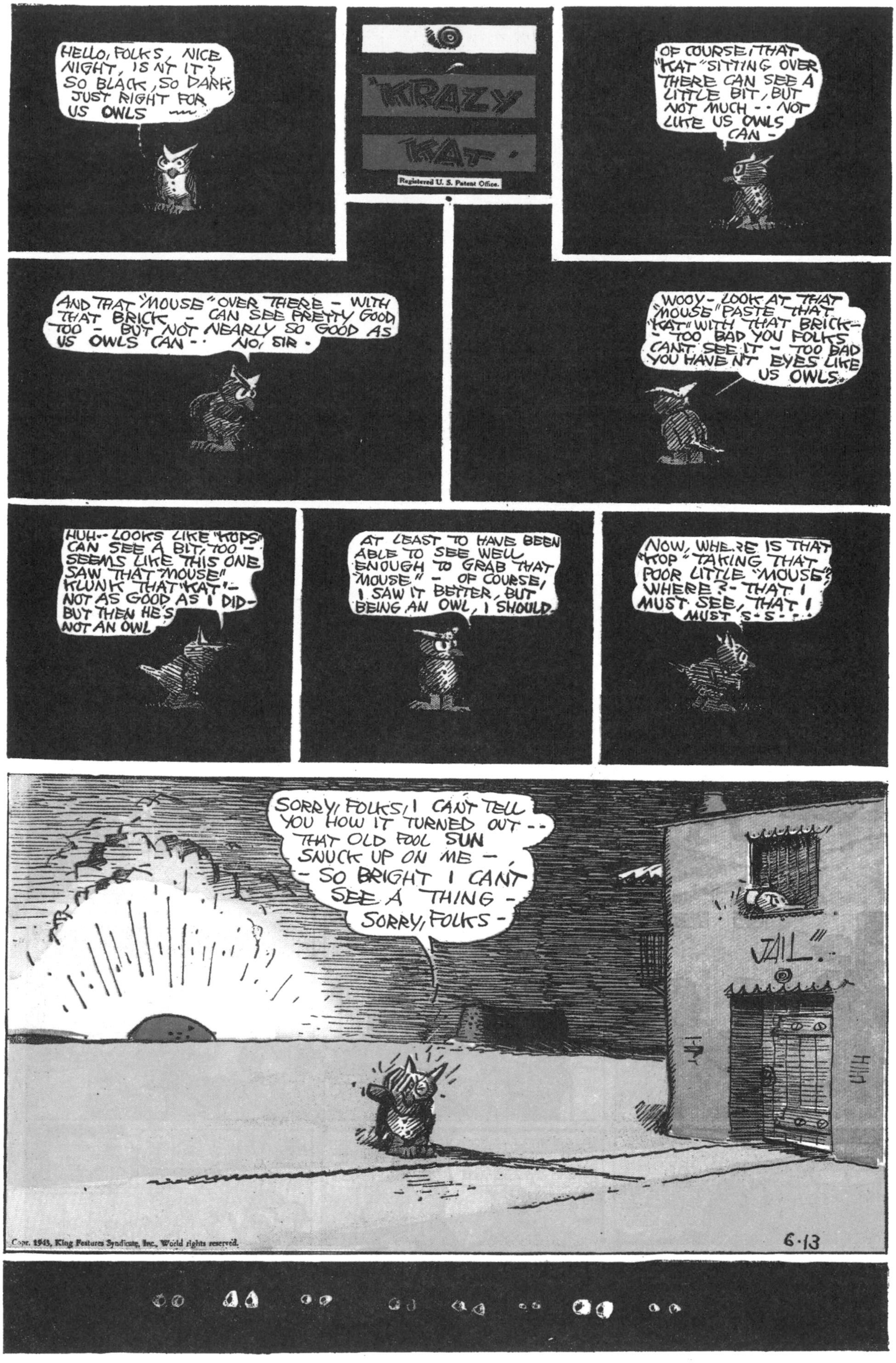
HELLO, FOLKS, NICE NIGHT, IS N'T IT? SO BLACK, SO DARK, JUST RIGHT FOR US OWLS
"KRAZY KAT"
Registered U. S. Patent Office.
OF COURSE, THAT "KAT" SITTING OVER THERE CAN SEE A LITTLE BIT, BUT NOT MUCH - - NOT LIKE US OWLS CAN -
AND THAT "MOUSE" OVER THERE - WITH THAT BRICK - CAN SEE PRETTY GOOD TOO - BUT NOT NEARLY SO GOOD AS US OWLS CAN - - NO, SIR -
WOOY - LOOK AT THAT "MOUSE" PASTE THAT "KAT" WITH THAT BRICK - - TOO BAD YOU FOLKS CAN'T SEE IT - TOO BAD YOU HAVE N'T EYES LIKE US OWLS.
HUH - - LOOKS LIKE "KOPS" CAN SEE A BIT, TOO - SEEMS LIKE THIS ONE SAW THAT "MOUSE" KLUNK THAT "KAT" - NOT AS GOOD AS I DID - BUT THEN HE'S NOT AN OWL
AT LEAST TO HAVE BEEN ABLE TO SEE WELL ENOUGH TO GRAB THAT "MOUSE" - OF COURSE, I SAW IT BETTER, BUT BEING AN OWL, I SHOULD.
NOW, WHERE IS THAT "KOP" TAKING THAT POOR LITTLE "MOUSE"? WHERE? - THAT I MUST SEE, THAT I MUST S-S-
SORRY, FOLKS, I CAN'T TELL YOU HOW IT TURNED OUT - - THAT OLD FOOL SUN SNUCK UP ON ME - - SO BRIGHT I CAN'T SEE A THING - SORRY, FOLKS -
JAIL
Copr. 1943, King Features Syndicate, Inc., World rights reserved.
6·13

June 13th, 1943.

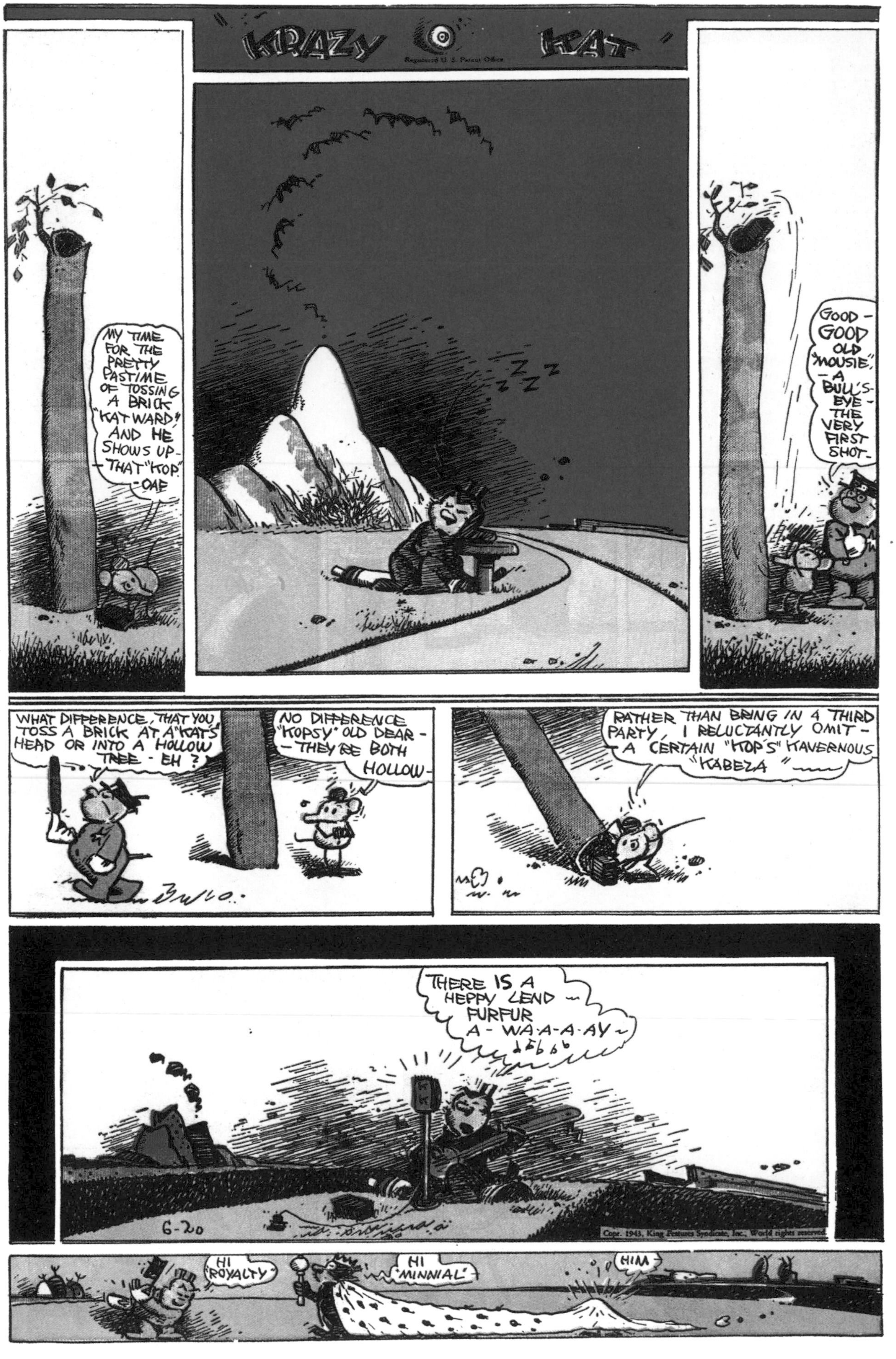
KRAZY KAT
Registered U. S. Patent Office.
MY TIME FOR THE PRETTY PASTIME OF TOSSING A BRICK "KAT WARD," AND HE SHOWS UP - THAT "KOP" - OAF
GOOD - GOOD OLD "MOUSIE," - A BULL'S-EYE THE VERY FIRST SHOT-
WHAT DIFFERENCE, THAT YOU TOSS A BRICK AT A "KAT'S" HEAD OR INTO A HOLLOW TREE - EH ?
NO DIFFERENCE "KOPSY" OLD DEAR - THEY'RE BOTH HOLLOW-
RATHER THAN BRING IN A THIRD PARTY, I RELUCTANTLY OMIT - A CERTAIN "KOP'S" KAVERNOUS "KABEZA"
THERE IS A HEPPY LEND - FURFUR A-WA-A-A-AY -
6-20
Copr. 1943, King Features Syndicate, Inc., World rights reserved.
HI "ROYALTY"
HI "MINNIAL"
HIM-

June 20th, 1943.

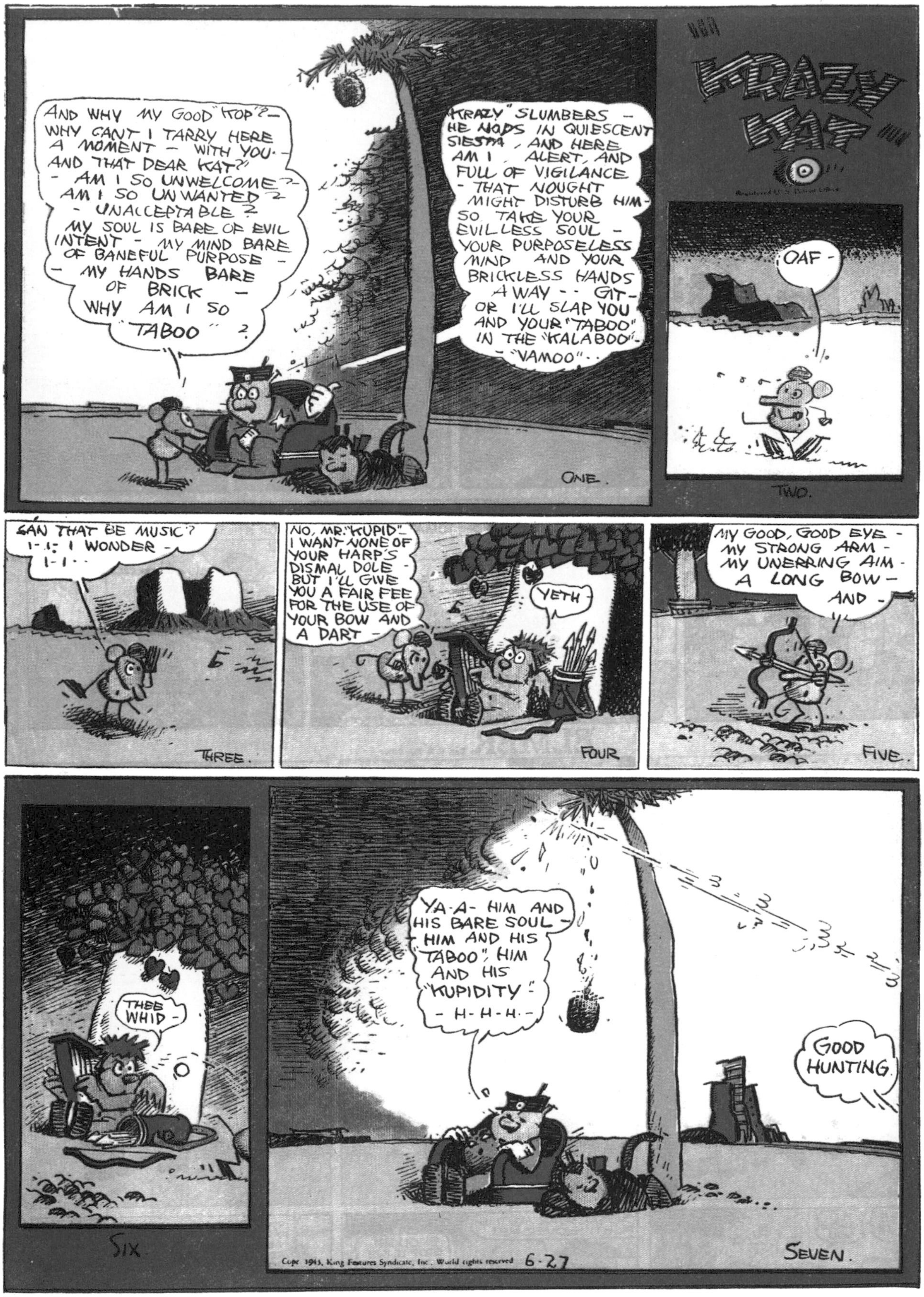
KRAZY KAT
AND WHY MY GOOD "KOP"? — WHY CANT I TARRY HERE A MOMENT — WITH YOU — AND THAT DEAR KAT? — AM I SO UNWELCOME? — AM I SO UNWANTED? — UNACCEPTABLE? MY SOUL IS BARE OF EVIL INTENT — MY MIND BARE OF BANEFUL PURPOSE — MY HANDS BARE OF BRICK — WHY AM I SO "TABOO"?
"KRAZY" SLUMBERS — HE NODS IN QUIESCENT SIESTA, AND HERE AM I, ALERT, AND FULL OF VIGILANCE — THAT NOUGHT MIGHT DISTURB HIM — SO TAKE YOUR EVILLESS SOUL — YOUR PURPOSELESS MIND AND YOUR BRICKLESS HANDS AWAY — GIT — OR I'LL SLAP YOU AND YOUR "TABOO" IN THE "KALABOO" — "VAMOO"
ONE.
OAF —
TWO.
CAN THAT BE MUSIC? I - I - I WONDER - I - I -
THREE.
NO, MR. "KUPID" I WANT NONE OF YOUR HARP'S DISMAL DOLE — BUT I'LL GIVE YOU A FAIR FEE FOR THE USE OF YOUR BOW AND A DART
YETH
FOUR
MY GOOD, GOOD EYE — MY STRONG ARM — MY UNERRING AIM — A LONG BOW — AND —
FIVE.
THEE WHID
SIX
YA-A- HIM AND HIS BARE SOUL — HIM AND HIS "TABOO", HIM AND HIS "KUPIDITY" — H-H-H —
GOOD HUNTING
Copr 1943, King Features Syndicate, Inc., World rights reserved 6-27
SEVEN.
"SPANIOLA"

June 27th, 1943.

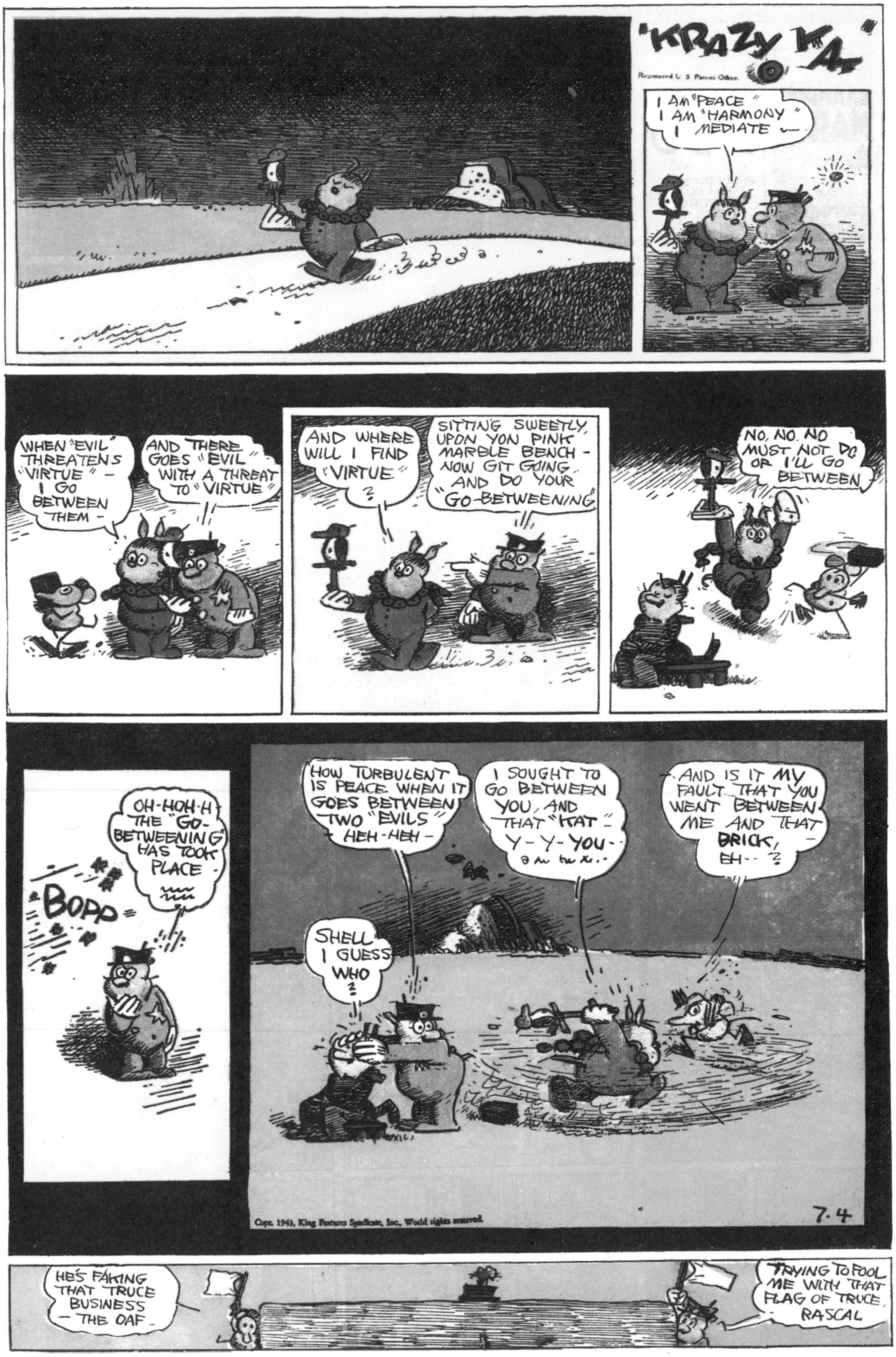
"KRAZY KAT"
Registered U. S. Patent Office.
I AM "PEACE" I AM "HARMONY" I MEDIATE ~~
WHEN "EVIL" THREATENS "VIRTUE" — I GO BETWEEN THEM —
AND THERE GOES "EVIL" WITH A THREAT TO "VIRTUE"
AND WHERE WILL I FIND "VIRTUE" ?
SITTING SWEETLY, UPON YON PINK MARBLE BENCH — NOW GIT GOING AND DO YOUR "GO-BETWEENING"
NO, NO, NO MUST NOT DO OR I'LL GO BETWEEN
OH-HOH-H THE "GO-BETWEENING" HAS TOOK PLACE
BOPP
HOW TURBULENT IS PEACE WHEN IT GOES BETWEEN TWO "EVILS" HEH-HEH —
I SOUGHT TO GO BETWEEN YOU, AND THAT "KAT" — Y-Y-YOU —
AND IS IT MY FAULT THAT YOU WENT BETWEEN ME AND THAT BRICK, — EH — ?
SHELL I GUESS WHO ?
Copr. 1943, King Features Syndicate, Inc., World rights reserved.
7.4
HE'S FAKING THAT TRUCE BUSINESS — THE OAF —
TRYING TO FOOL ME WITH THAT FLAG OF TRUCE, RASCAL

July 4th, 1943.

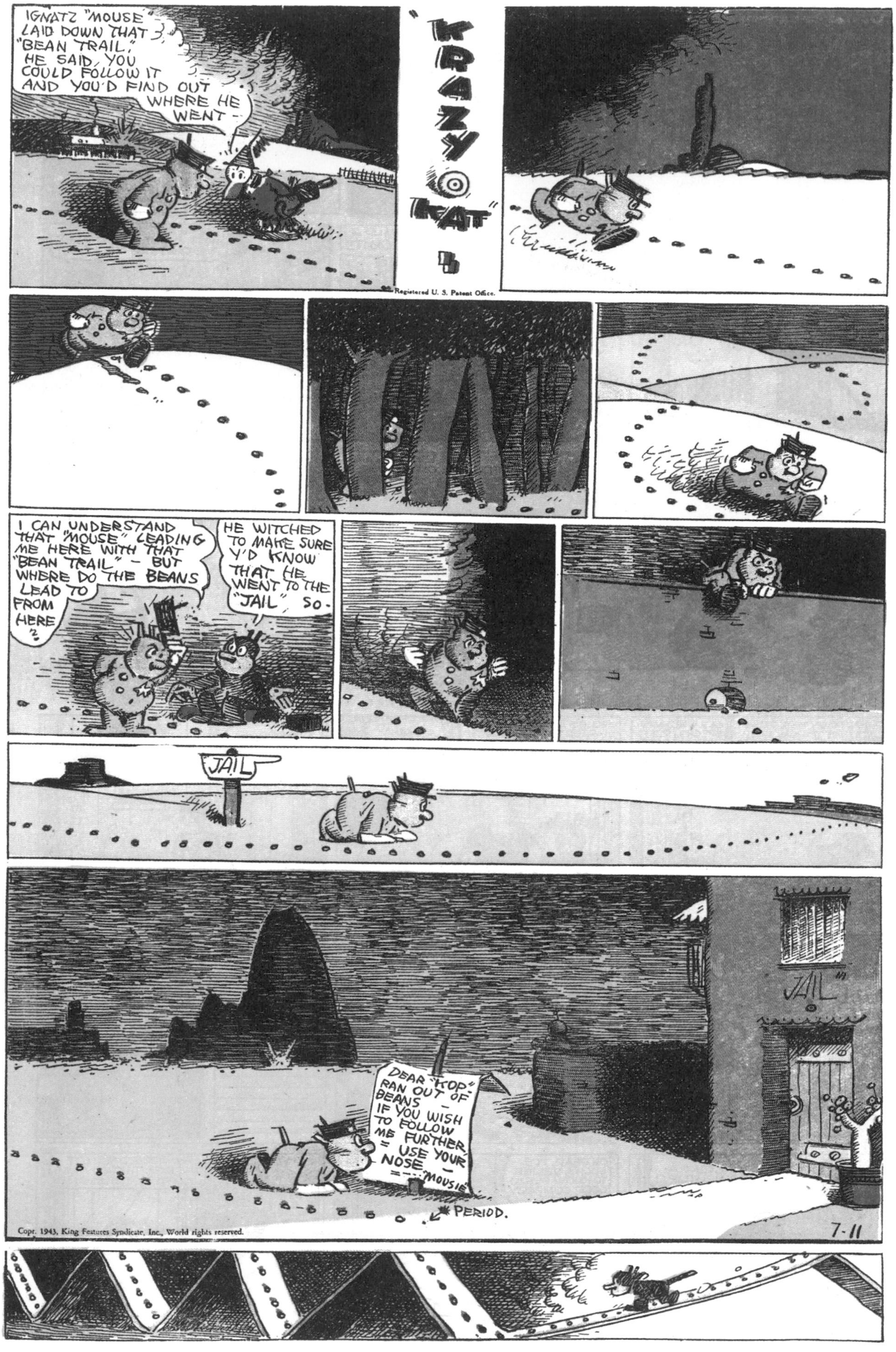

IGNATZ "MOUSE" LAID DOWN THAT "BEAN TRAIL," HE SAID, YOU COULD FOLLOW IT AND YOU'D FIND OUT WHERE HE WENT –
"KRAZY KAT"
Registered U. S. Patent Office.
I CAN UNDERSTAND THAT "MOUSE" LEADING ME HERE WITH THAT "BEAN TRAIL" – BUT WHERE DO THE BEANS LEAD TO FROM HERE ?
HE WITCHED TO MAKE SURE Y'D KNOW THAT HE WENT TO THE "JAIL", SO.
JAIL
"JAIL"
DEAR "KOP" RAN OUT OF BEANS – IF YOU WISH TO FOLLOW ME FURTHER, = USE YOUR NOSE. = "MOUSIE"
PERIOD.
Copr. 1943, King Features Syndicate, Inc., World rights reserved.
7-11

July 11th, 1943.

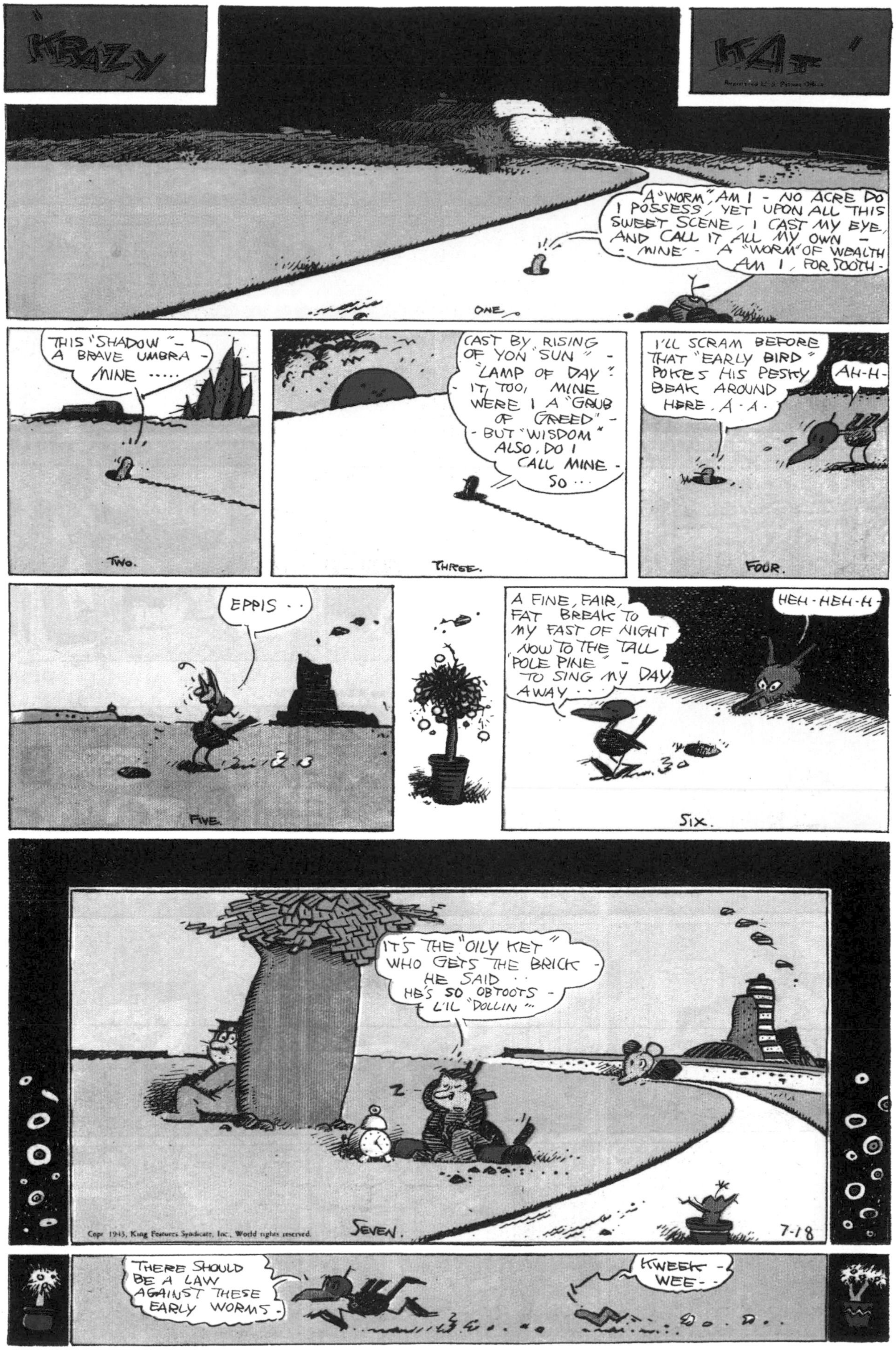
KRAZY KAT
A "WORM" AM I - NO ACRE DO I POSSESS, YET UPON ALL THIS SWEET SCENE, I CAST MY EYE, AND CALL IT ALL MY OWN - - MINE - - A "WORM" OF WEALTH AM I, FORSOOTH -
ONE
THIS "SHADOW" - A BRAVE UMBRA - MINE .....
TWO.
CAST BY RISING OF YON "SUN" - "LAMP OF DAY" - IT, TOO, MINE. WERE I A "GRUB OF GREED" - - BUT "WISDOM" ALSO, DO I CALL MINE - SO ...
THREE.
I'LL SCRAM BEFORE THAT "EARLY BIRD" POKES HIS PESKY BEAK AROUND HERE. A - A -
AH-H-
FOUR.
EPPIS - -
FIVE.
A FINE, FAIR, FAT BREAK TO MY FAST OF NIGHT NOW TO THE TALL "POLE PINE" - TO SING MY DAY AWAY - - -
HEH - HEH - H -
SIX.
IT'S THE "OILY KET" WHO GETS THE BRICK - HE SAID - - HE'S SO OBTOOTS - L'IL "DOLLIN" "
Z
Copr 1943, King Features Syndicate, Inc., World rights reserved.
SEVEN.
7-18
THERE SHOULD BE A LAW AGAINST THESE EARLY WORMS.
KWEEK - WEE - -

July 18th, 1943.

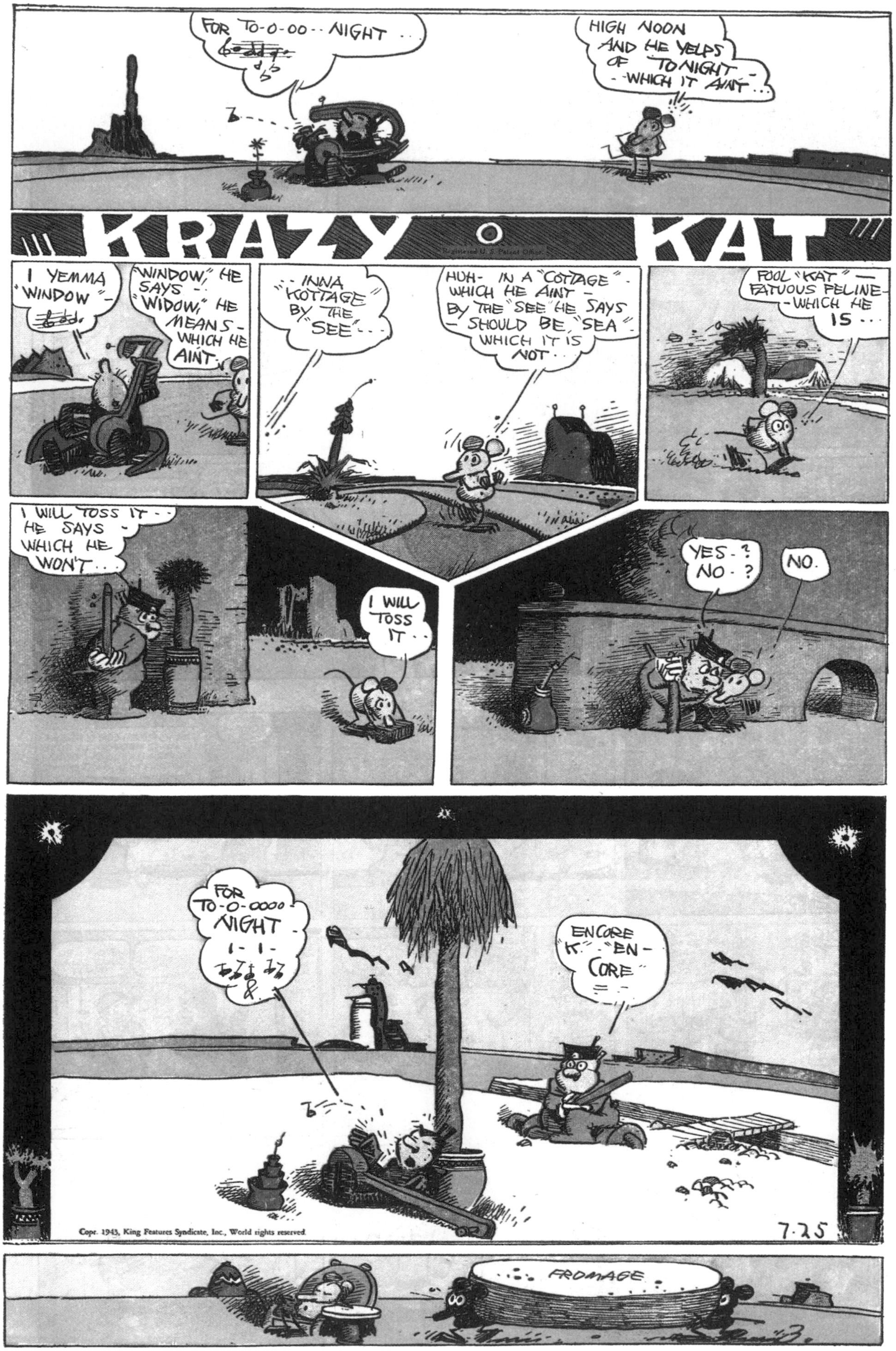
FOR TO-O-OO.. NIGHT...
HIGH NOON AND HE YELPS OF "TONIGHT" - - WHICH IT AINT...
KRAZY KAT
Registered U. S. Patent Office
I YEMMA "WINDOW" -
"WINDOW," HE SAYS - "WIDOW," HE MEANS - WHICH HE AINT.
- INNA "KOTTAGE" BY THE "SEE" - - -
HUH - IN A "COTTAGE" - WHICH HE AINT - BY THE "SEE" HE SAYS - SHOULD BE "SEA" - WHICH IT IS NOT - -
FOOL "KAT" - FATUOUS FELINE - - WHICH HE IS...
I WILL TOSS IT - - HE SAYS - WHICH HE WON'T - -
I WILL TOSS IT
YES - ? NO - ?
NO.
FOR TO-O-OOOO NIGHT - I - I -
ENCORE K. "EN-CORE"
Copr. 1943, King Features Syndicate, Inc., World rights reserved.
7-25
FROMAGE

July 25th, 1943.

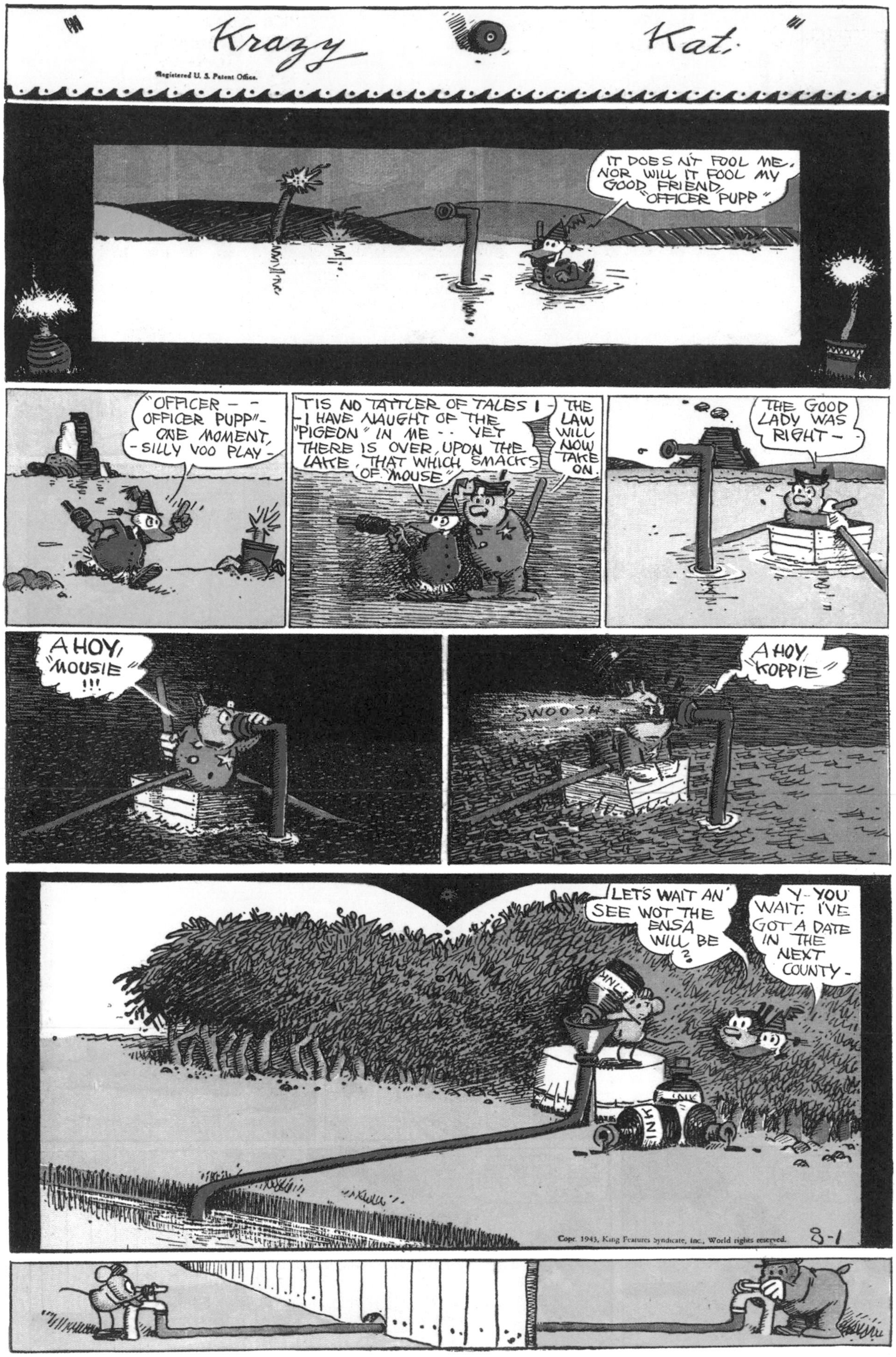
Krazy Kat
Registered U. S. Patent Office.
IT DOES N'T FOOL ME, NOR WILL IT FOOL MY GOOD FRIEND, "OFFICER PUPP"
"OFFICER - - OFFICER PUPP" - ONE MOMENT, - SILLY VOO PLAY -
TIS NO TATTLER OF TALES I - I HAVE NAUGHT OF THE "PIGEON" IN ME - - YET THERE IS OVER, UPON THE LAKE, THAT WHICH SMACKS OF "MOUSE"
THE LAW WILL NOW TAKE ON.
THE GOOD LADY WAS RIGHT -
A HOY, "MOUSIE" !!!
SWOOSH
A HOY, "KOPPIE"
LET'S WAIT AN' SEE WOT THE ENSA WILL BE ?
Y- YOU WAIT. I'VE GOT A DATE IN THE NEXT COUNTY -
INK
Copr. 1943, King Features Syndicate, Inc., World rights reserved.
8-1

August 1st, 1943.

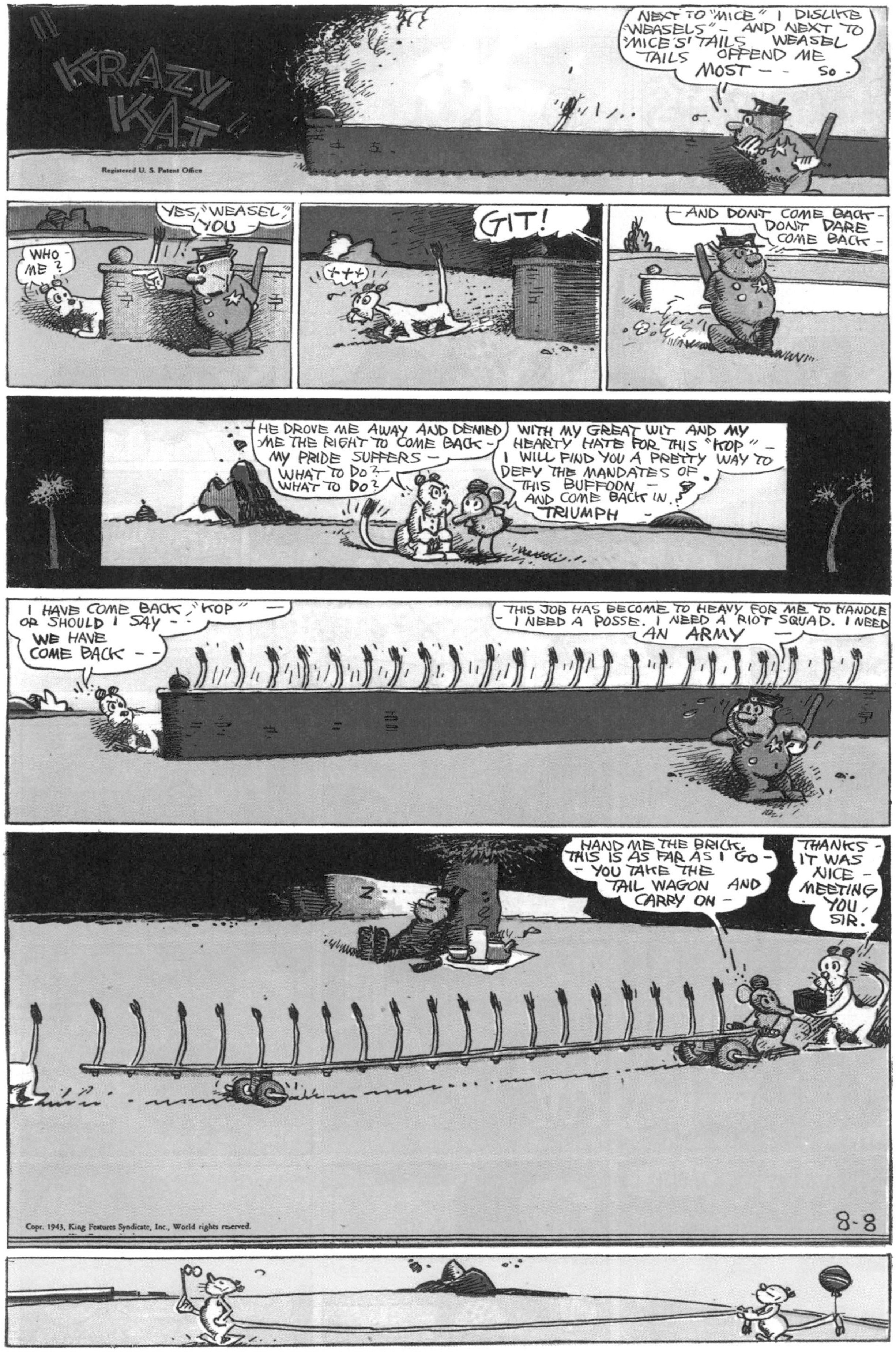
KRAZY KAT
Registered U. S. Patent Office
NEXT TO "MICE" I DISLIKE "WEASELS" – AND NEXT TO "MICE'S" TAILS WEASEL TAILS OFFEND ME MOST – – SO –
YES, "WEASEL" YOU
WHO ME ?
GIT!
– AND DON'T COME BACK – DON'T DARE COME BACK –
HE DROVE ME AWAY AND DENIED ME THE RIGHT TO COME BACK – MY PRIDE SUFFERS – WHAT TO DO? WHAT TO DO?
WITH MY GREAT WIT AND MY HEARTY HATE FOR THIS "KOP" – I WILL FIND YOU A PRETTY WAY TO DEFY THE MANDATES OF THIS BUFFOON – AND COME BACK IN TRIUMPH
I HAVE COME BACK, "KOP" – OR SHOULD I SAY – WE HAVE COME BACK – –
– THIS JOB HAS BECOME TO HEAVY FOR ME TO HANDLE – I NEED A POSSE. I NEED A RIOT SQUAD. I NEED AN ARMY –
HAND ME THE BRICK. THIS IS AS FAR AS I GO – YOU TAKE THE TAIL WAGON AND CARRY ON –
THANKS – IT WAS NICE – MEETING YOU, SIR.
Copr. 1943, King Features Syndicate, Inc., World rights reserved.
8-8

August 8th, 1943.

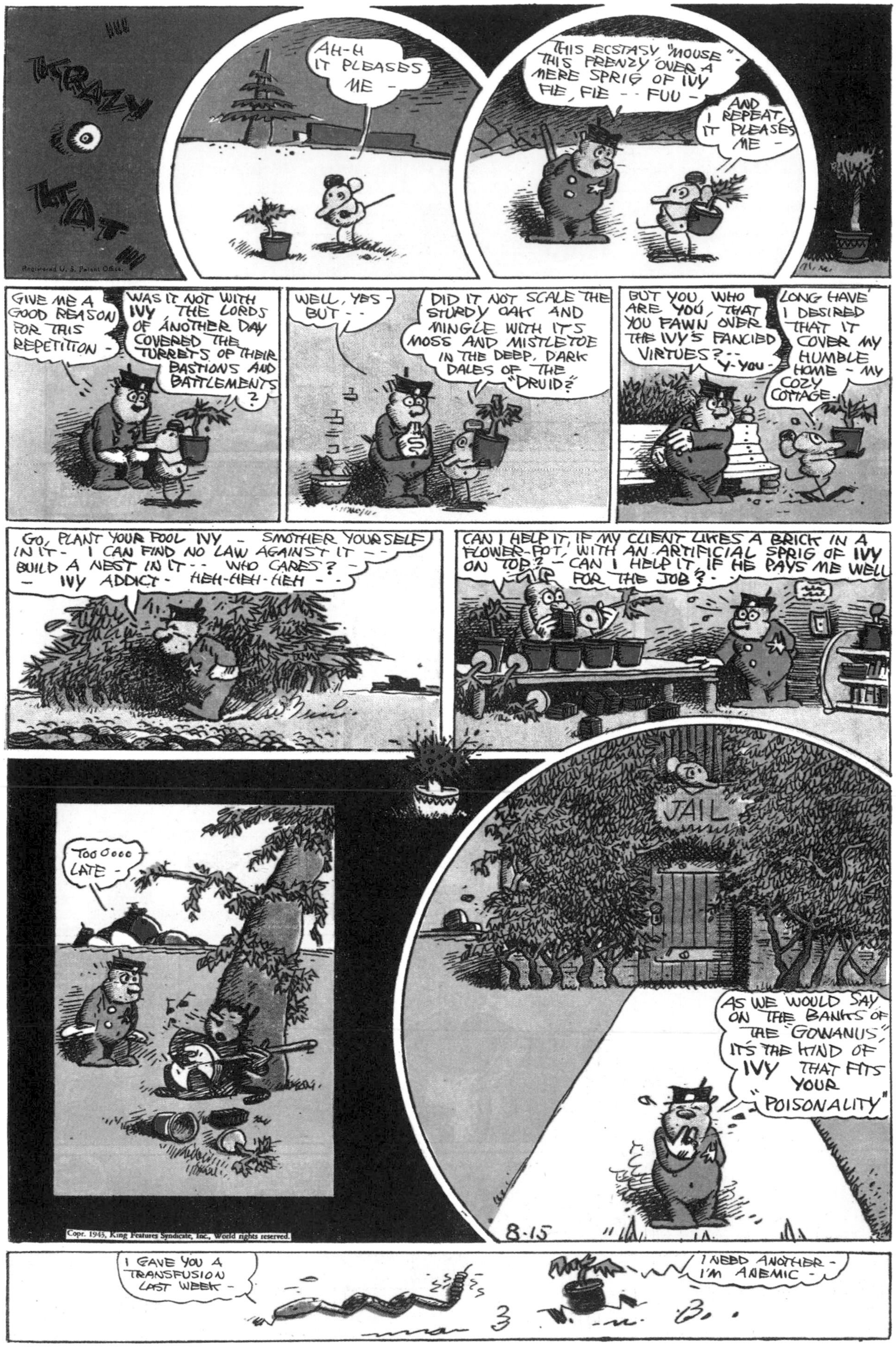

Krazy Kat
Registered U. S. Patent Office.
AH-H IT PLEASES ME -
THIS ECSTASY "MOUSE" - THIS FRENZY OVER A MERE SPRIG OF IVY FIE, FIE - - FUU -
AND I REPEAT, IT PLEASES ME -
GIVE ME A GOOD REASON FOR THIS REPETITION -
WAS IT NOT WITH IVY THE LORDS OF ANOTHER DAY COVERED THE TURRETS OF THEIR BASTIONS AND BATTLEMENTS ?
WELL, YES - BUT - -
DID IT NOT SCALE THE STURDY OAK AND MINGLE WITH IT'S MOSS AND MISTLETOE IN THE DEEP, DARK DALES OF THE "DRUID"?
BUT YOU, WHO ARE YOU, THAT YOU FAWN OVER THE IVY'S FANCIED VIRTUES? - -
Y-YOU -
LONG HAVE I DESIRED THAT IT COVER MY HUMBLE HOME - MY COZY COTTAGE -
GO, PLANT YOUR FOOL IVY - SMOTHER YOURSELF IN IT - I CAN FIND NO LAW AGAINST IT - - BUILD A NEST IN IT - - WHO CARES? - - IVY ADDICT - HEH-HEH-HEH - -
CAN I HELP IT, IF MY CLIENT LIKES A BRICK IN A FLOWER-POT, WITH AN ARTIFICIAL SPRIG OF IVY ON TOP? - CAN I HELP IT, IF HE PAYS ME WELL FOR THE JOB? -
TOO OOOO LATE -
JAIL
AS WE WOULD SAY ON THE BANKS OF THE "GOWANUS" IT'S THE KIND OF IVY THAT FITS YOUR "POISONALITY"
8-15
Copr. 1943, King Features Syndicate, Inc., World rights reserved.
I GAVE YOU A TRANSFUSION LAST WEEK -
I NEED ANOTHER - I'M ANEMIC -

August 15th, 1943.

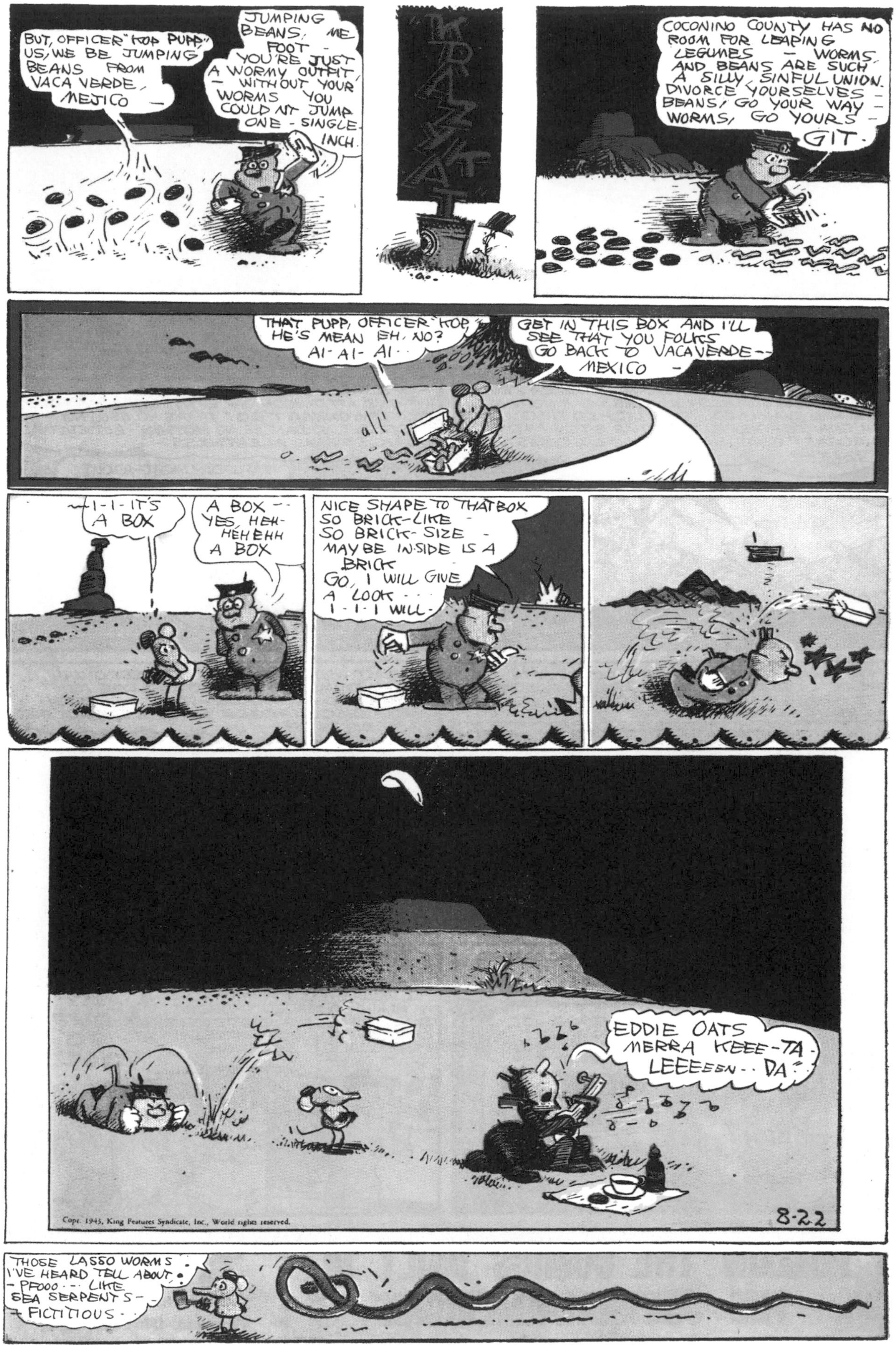
BUT, OFFICER "KOP PUPP" US, WE BE JUMPING BEANS FROM VACA VERDE, MEJICO —
JUMPING BEANS, ME FOOT — YOU'RE JUST A WORMY OUTFIT, — WITHOUT YOUR WORMS YOU COULD NT JUMP ONE - SINGLE - INCH.
KRAZY KAT
COCONINO COUNTY HAS NO ROOM FOR LEAPING LEGUMES — WORMS, AND BEANS ARE SUCH A SILLY, SINFUL UNION. DIVORCE YOURSELVES — BEANS, GO YOUR WAY — WORMS, GO YOURS — GIT.
THAT PUPP, OFFICER "KOP" HE'S MEAN EH, NO? AI - AI - AI.
GET IN THIS BOX AND I'LL SEE THAT YOU FOLKS GO BACK TO VACAVERDE — MEXICO —
I - I - IT'S A BOX
A BOX — YES, HEH-HEH EHH A BOX
NICE SHAPE TO THAT BOX SO BRICK-LIKE — SO BRICK-SIZE — MAYBE IN-SIDE IS A BRICK. GO, I WILL GIVE A LOOK — I - I - I WILL.
EDDIE OATS MERRA KEEE-TA LEEEEEN - - DA
Copr. 1943, King Features Syndicate, Inc., World rights reserved.
8-22
THOSE LASSO WORMS I'VE HEARD TELL ABOUT — PFOOO — LIKE SEA SERPENTS — FICTITIOUS —

August 22nd, 1943.

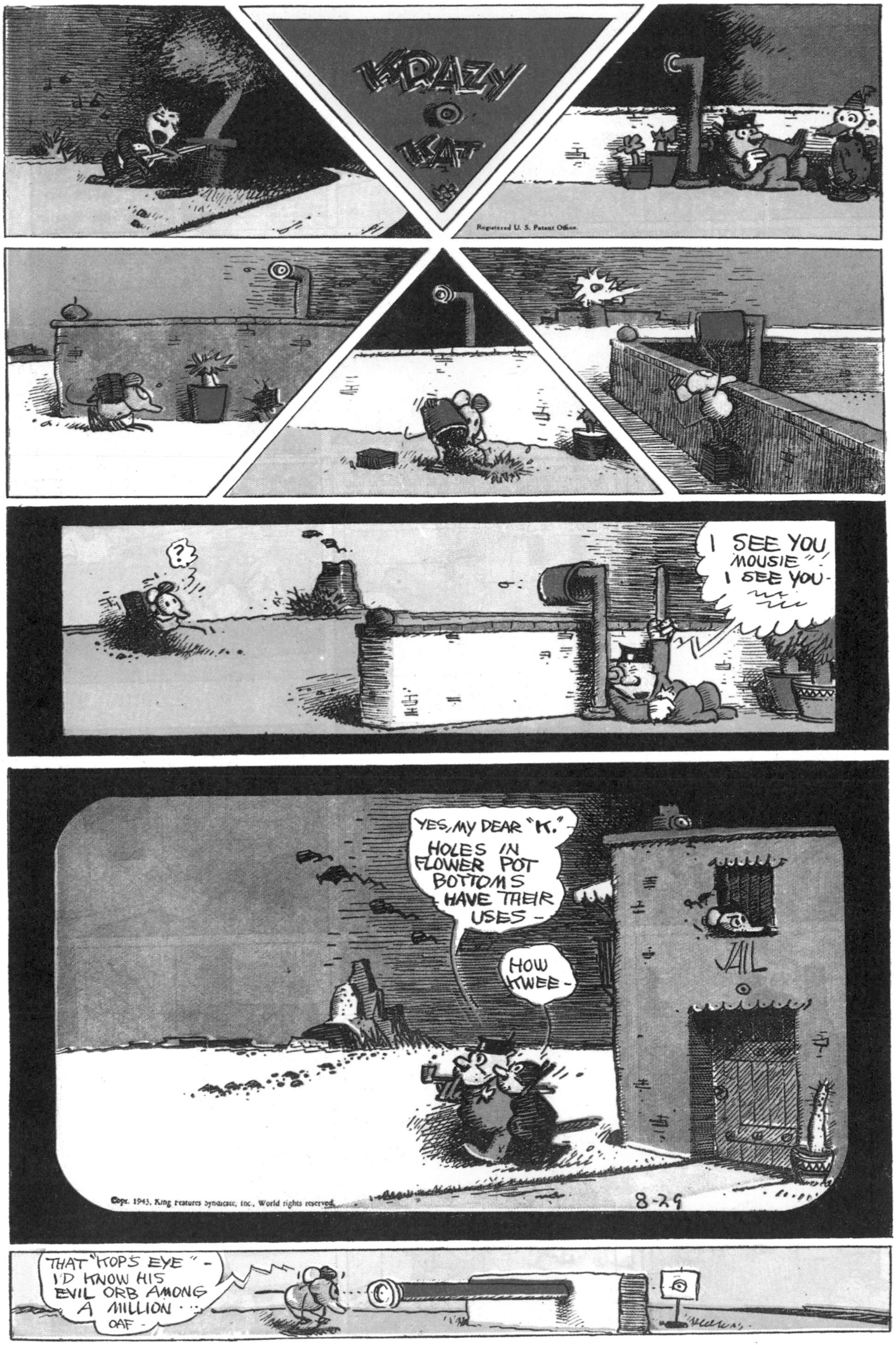
KRAZY KAT
Registered U. S. Patent Office.
I SEE YOU "MOUSIE" ! I SEE YOU -
YES, MY DEAR "K." HOLES IN FLOWER POT BOTTOMS HAVE THEIR USES -
HOW KWEE -
JAIL
Copr. 1943, King Features Syndicate, Inc., World rights reserved.
8-29
THAT "KOP'S EYE" - I'D KNOW HIS EVIL ORB AMONG A MILLION · · OAF

August 29th, 1943.

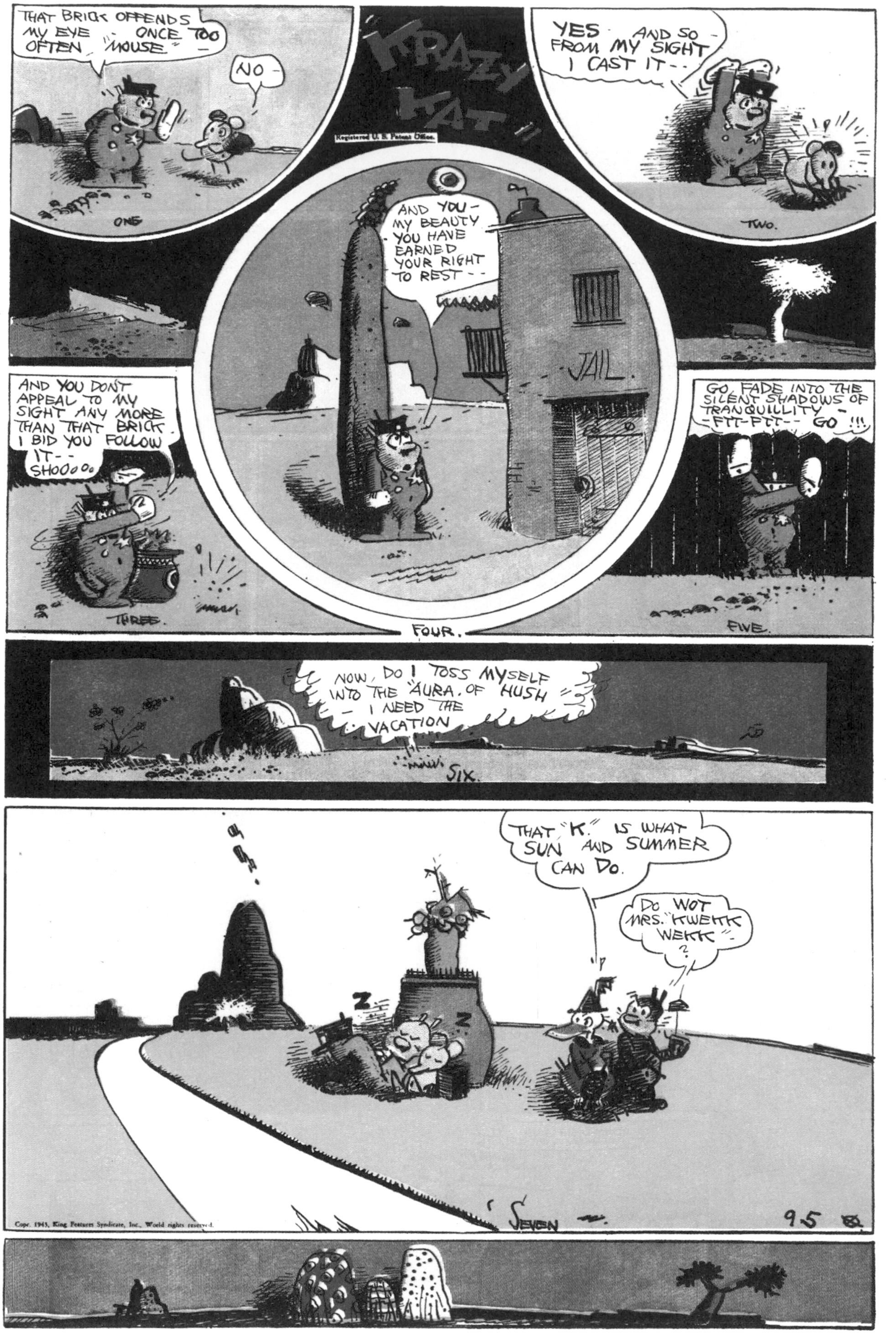
KRAZY KAT
Registered U. S. Patent Office.
THAT BRICK OFFENDS MY EYE - ONCE TOO OFTEN "MOUSE" -
NO -
ONE
YES - AND SO FROM MY SIGHT I CAST IT - -
TWO.
AND YOU DONT APPEAL TO MY SIGHT ANY MORE THAN THAT BRICK I BID YOU FOLLOW IT - - SHOOooo
THREE.
AND YOU - MY BEAUTY YOU HAVE EARNED YOUR RIGHT TO REST - -
JAIL
FOUR.
GO FADE INTO THE SILENT SHADOWS OF TRANQUILLITY - FTT-FTT - - GO !!!
FIVE.
NOW, DO I TOSS MYSELF INTO THE "AURA" OF "HUSH" - I NEED THE VACATION
SIX.
THAT "K." IS WHAT SUN AND SUMMER CAN DO.
DO WOT MRS. KWEKK WEKK ?
Copr. 1943, King Features Syndicate, Inc., World rights reserved.
SEVEN
9-5

September 5th, 1943.

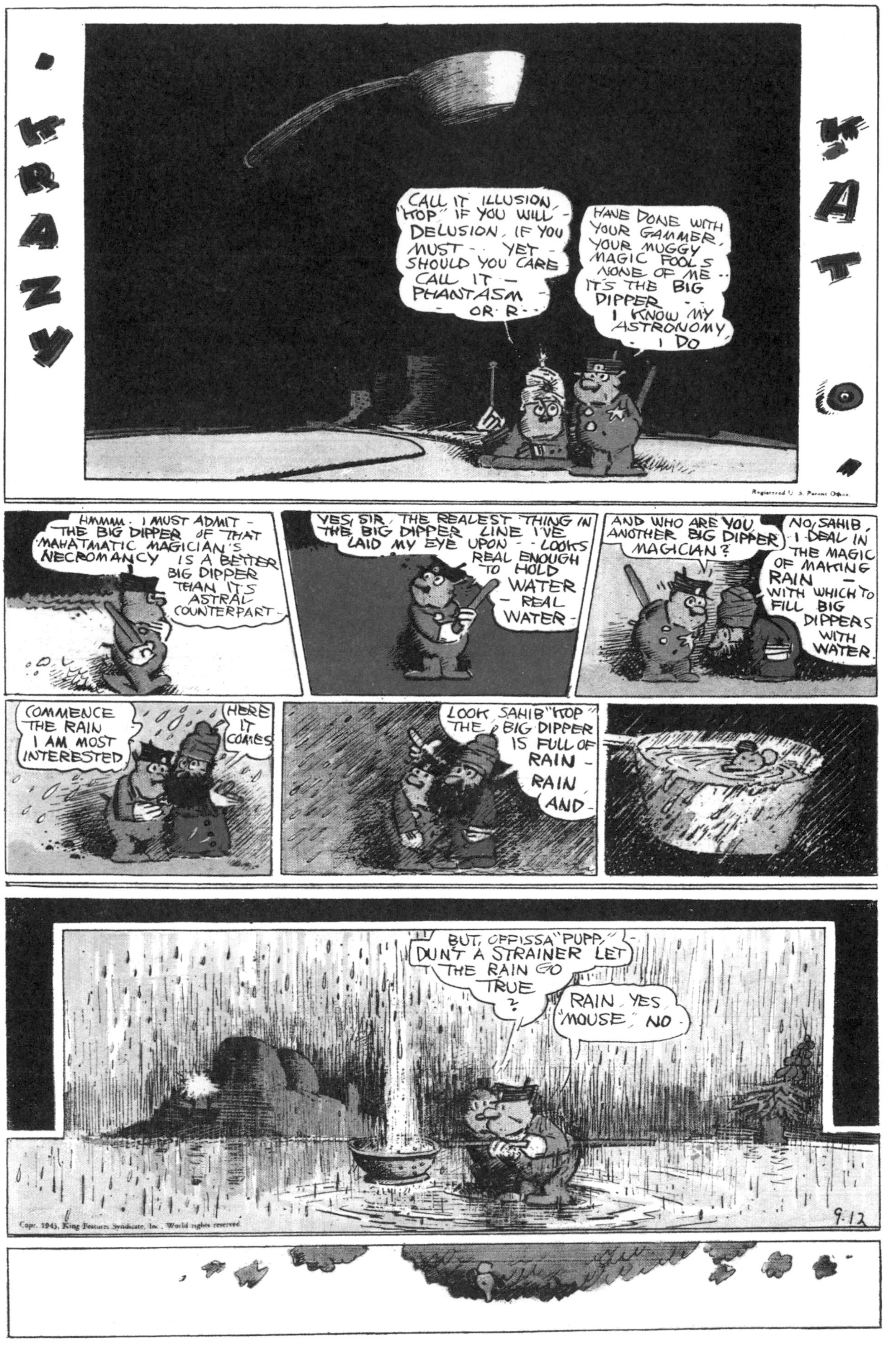
KRAZY KAT
CALL IT ILLUSION, "KOP" IF YOU WILL - DELUSION, IF YOU MUST - YET - SHOULD YOU CARE CALL IT - PHANTASM - OR R -
HAVE DONE WITH YOUR GAMMER, YOUR MUGGY MAGIC FOOLS NONE OF ME - IT'S THE BIG DIPPER - I KNOW MY ASTRONOMY, I DO
Registered U. S. Patent Office.
HMMM - I MUST ADMIT - THE BIG DIPPER OF THAT MAHATMATIC MAGICIAN'S NECROMANCY IS A BETTER BIG DIPPER THAN IT'S ASTRAL COUNTERPART -
YES, SIR, THE REALEST THING IN THE BIG DIPPER LINE I'VE LAID MY EYE UPON - LOOKS REAL ENOUGH TO HOLD WATER - REAL WATER -
AND WHO ARE YOU, ANOTHER BIG DIPPER MAGICIAN?
NO, SAHIB, I DEAL IN THE MAGIC OF MAKING RAIN - WITH WHICH TO FILL BIG DIPPERS WITH WATER.
COMMENCE THE RAIN I AM MOST INTERESTED
HERE IT COMES
LOOK SAHIB "KOP" THE BIG DIPPER IS FULL OF RAIN - RAIN AND -
BUT, OFFISSA "PUPP," DUN'T A STRAINER LET THE RAIN GO TRUE ?
RAIN, YES "MOUSE," NO
Copr. 1943, King Features Syndicate, Inc., World rights reserved.
9-12

September 12th, 1943.

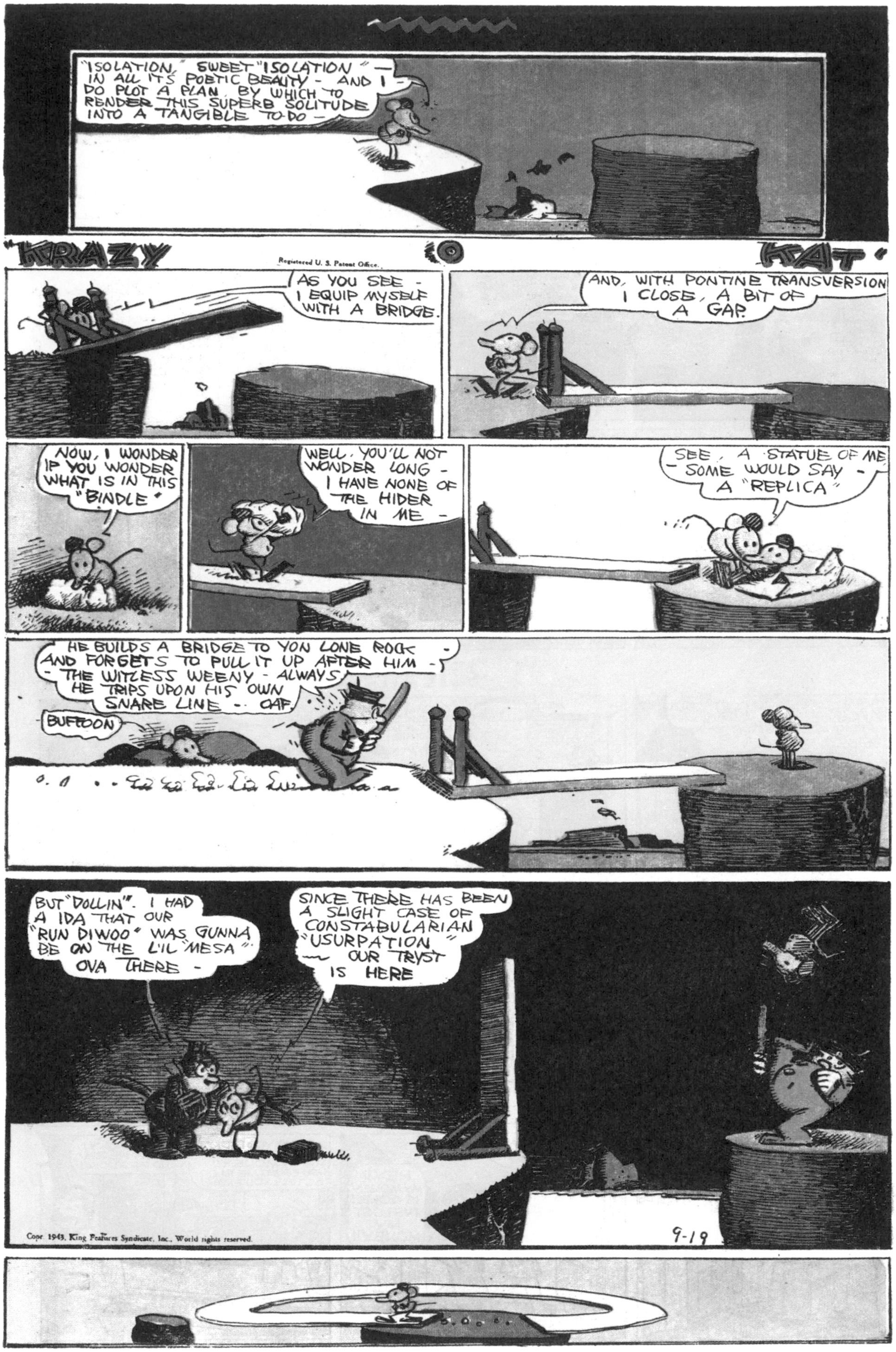
"ISOLATION," SWEET "ISOLATION" — IN ALL ITS POETIC BEAUTY - AND I DO PLOT A PLAN, BY WHICH TO RENDER THIS SUPERB SOLITUDE INTO A TANGIBLE TO-DO -
"KRAZY
KAT"
Registered U. S. Patent Office.
AS YOU SEE - I EQUIP MYSELF WITH A BRIDGE.
AND, WITH PONTINE TRANSVERSION I CLOSE, A BIT OF A GAP.
NOW, I WONDER IF YOU WONDER WHAT IS IN THIS "BINDLE"
WELL, YOU'LL NOT WONDER LONG - I HAVE NONE OF THE HIDER IN ME -
SEE, A STATUE OF ME - SOME WOULD SAY - A "REPLICA"
HE BUILDS A BRIDGE TO YON LONE ROCK - AND FORGETS TO PULL IT UP AFTER HIM - THE WITLESS WEENY - ALWAYS HE TRIPS UPON HIS OWN SNARE LINE - - OAF
BUFFOON
BUT "DOLLIN". I HAD A IDA THAT OUR "RUN DIWOO" WAS GUNNA BE ON THE "L'IL MESA" OVA THERE -
SINCE THERE HAS BEEN A SLIGHT CASE OF CONSTABULARIAN "USURPATION" — OUR TRYST IS HERE
Copr. 1943, King Features Syndicate, Inc., World rights reserved.
9-19

September 19th, 1943.

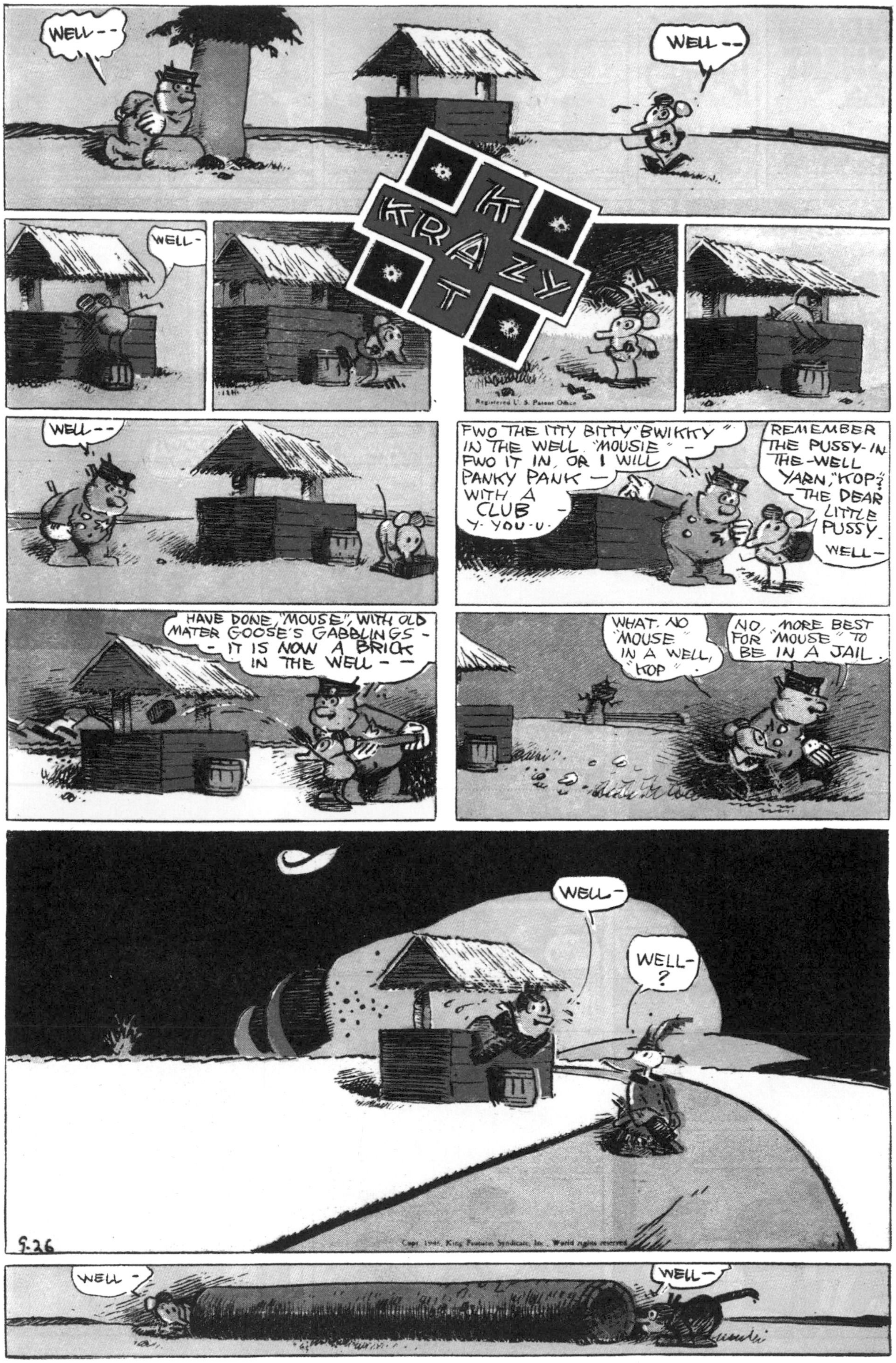
WELL--
WELL--
KRAZY KAT
WELL-
Registered U. S. Patent Office
WELL--
FWO THE ITTY BITTY "BWIKKY" IN THE WELL, "MOUSIE" – FWO IT IN, OR I WILL PANKY PANK – WITH A CLUB – Y-YOU-U-
REMEMBER THE PUSSY-IN-THE-WELL YARN, "KOP"? THE DEAR LITTLE PUSSY-
WELL-
HAVE DONE, "MOUSE", WITH OLD MATER GOOSE'S GABBLINGS – IT IS NOW A BRICK IN THE WELL--
WHAT, NO "MOUSE" IN A WELL, "KOP"
NO, MORE BEST FOR "MOUSE" TO BE IN A JAIL.
WELL-
WELL- ?
9-26
WELL-
WELL-

September 26th, 1943.

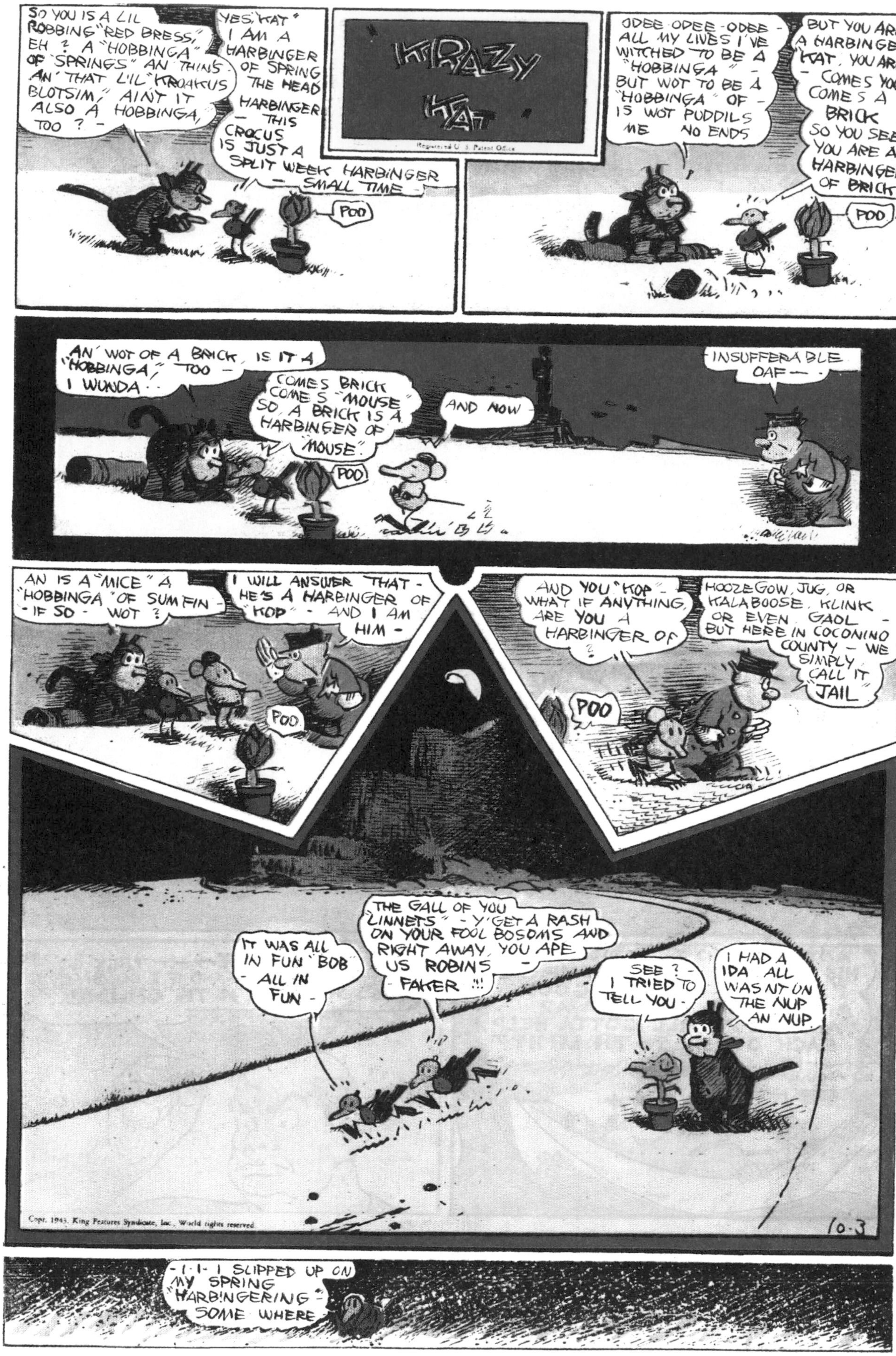
SO YOU IS A LIL ROBBING "RED BRESS," EH ? A "HOBBINGA" OF "SPRINGS" AN' THINS - AN' THAT L'IL "KROAKUS BLOTSIM," AIN'T IT ALSO A HOBBINGA, TOO ? -
"YES, KAT" I AM A HARBINGER OF SPRING THE HEAD HARBINGER - THIS CROCUS IS JUST A SPLIT WEEK HARBINGER - SMALL TIME -
POO
KRAZY KAT
Registered U. S. Patent Office
ODEE ODEE ODEE - ALL MY LIVES I'VE WITCHED TO BE A "HOBBINGA" - BUT WOT TO BE A "HOBBINGA" OF - IS WOT PUDDILS ME NO ENDS
BUT YOU ARE A HARBINGER "KAT," YOU ARE - COMES YOU, COMES A BRICK - SO YOU SEE YOU ARE A HARBINGER OF BRICK.
POO
AN' WOT OF A BRICK, IS IT A "HOBBINGA," TOO - I WUNDA -
COMES BRICK COMES "MOUSE" SO, A BRICK IS A HARBINGER OF "MOUSE".
AND NOW
POO
INSUFFERABLE OAF - -
AN IS A "MICE" A "HOBBINGA" OF SUM FIN - IF SO - WOT ?
I WILL ANSWER THAT - HE'S A HARBINGER OF "KOP" - AND I AM HIM -
POO
AND YOU "KOP" - WHAT IF ANYTHING, ARE YOU A HARBINGER OF ?
HOOZE GOW, JUG, OR KALABOOSE, KLINK OR EVEN GAOL - BUT HERE IN COCONINO COUNTY - WE SIMPLY CALL IT "JAIL"
POO
IT WAS ALL IN FUN "BOB" - ALL IN FUN -
THE GALL OF YOU "LINNETS" - Y' GET A RASH ON YOUR FOOL BOSOMS AND RIGHT AWAY YOU APE US ROBINS - FAKER !!!
SEE ? - I TRIED TO TELL YOU -
I HAD A IDA ALL WAS N'T ON THE NUP AN NUP
Copr. 1943, King Features Syndicate, Inc., World rights reserved
10-3
- I - I - I SLIPPED UP ON MY SPRING "HARBINGERING" - SOME WHERE

October 3rd, 1943.

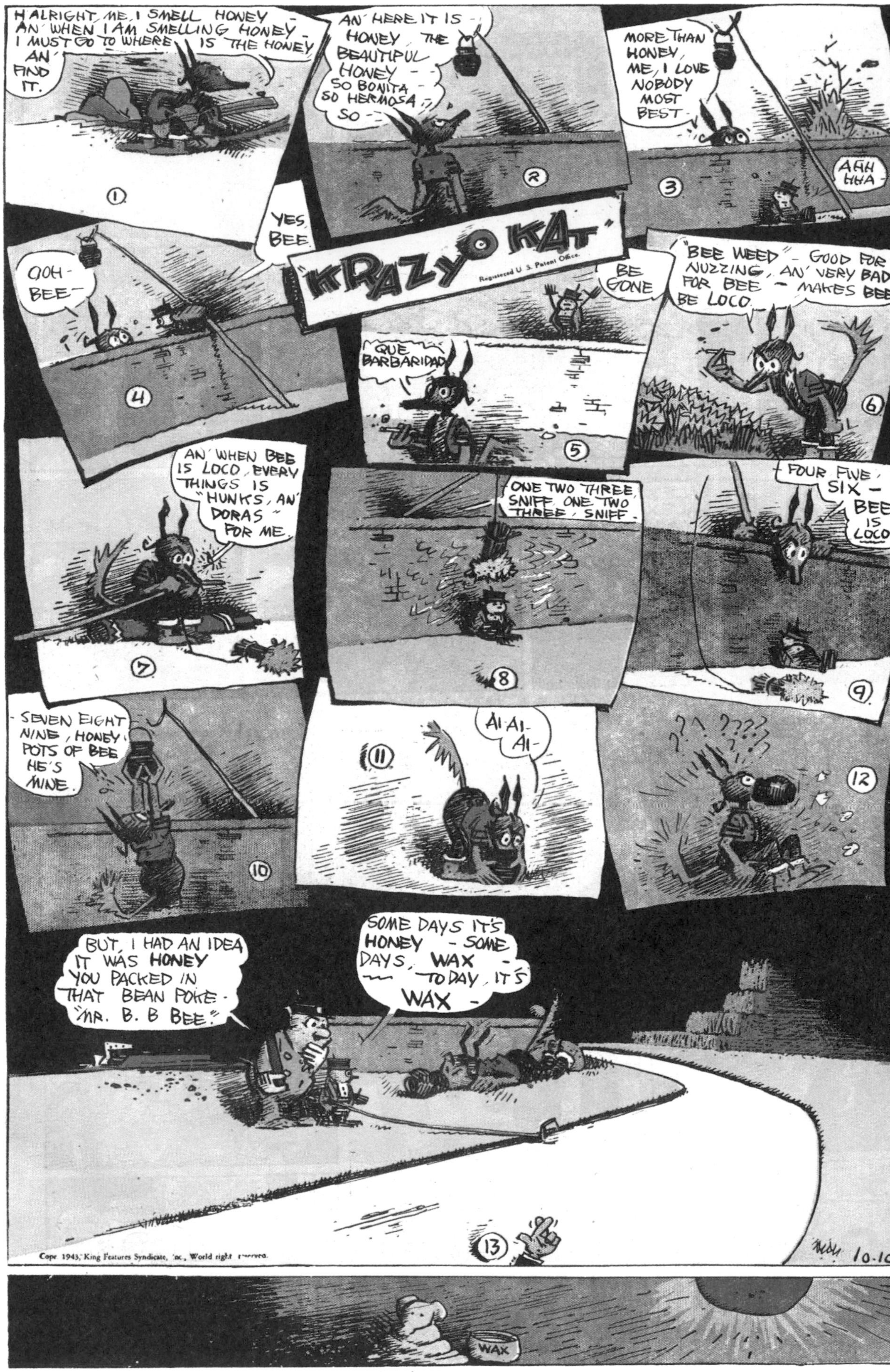
HALRIGHT, ME, I SMELL HONEY - AN' WHEN I AM SMELLING HONEY - I MUST GO TO WHERE IS THE HONEY AN' FIND IT.
AN' HERE IT IS - HONEY THE BEAUTIFUL HONEY - - SO BONITA SO HERMOSA - SO - -
MORE THAN HONEY, ME, I LOVE NOBODY MOST BEST.
AHH HHA
YES. BEE
KRAZY KAT
Registered U. S. Patent Office.
OOH - BEE -
BE GONE
"BEE WEED" - GOOD FOR NUZZING, AN' VERY BAD FOR BEE - MAKES BEE BE LOCO.
QUE BARBARIDAD
AN' WHEN BEE IS LOCO, EVERY THINGS IS "HUNKS, AN' DORAS" FOR ME.
ONE TWO THREE SNIFF ONE TWO THREE SNIFF.
FOUR FIVE SIX - BEE IS LOCO.
SEVEN EIGHT NINE, HONEY POTS OF BEE HE'S MINE.
AI AI AI -
BUT, I HAD AN IDEA IT WAS HONEY YOU PACKED IN THAT BEAN POKE - "MR. B. B BEE."
SOME DAYS IT'S HONEY - SOME DAYS, WAX - - TO DAY, IT'S WAX -
Copr 1943, King Features Syndicate, Inc., World rights reserved.
10-10
WAX

October 10th, 1943.

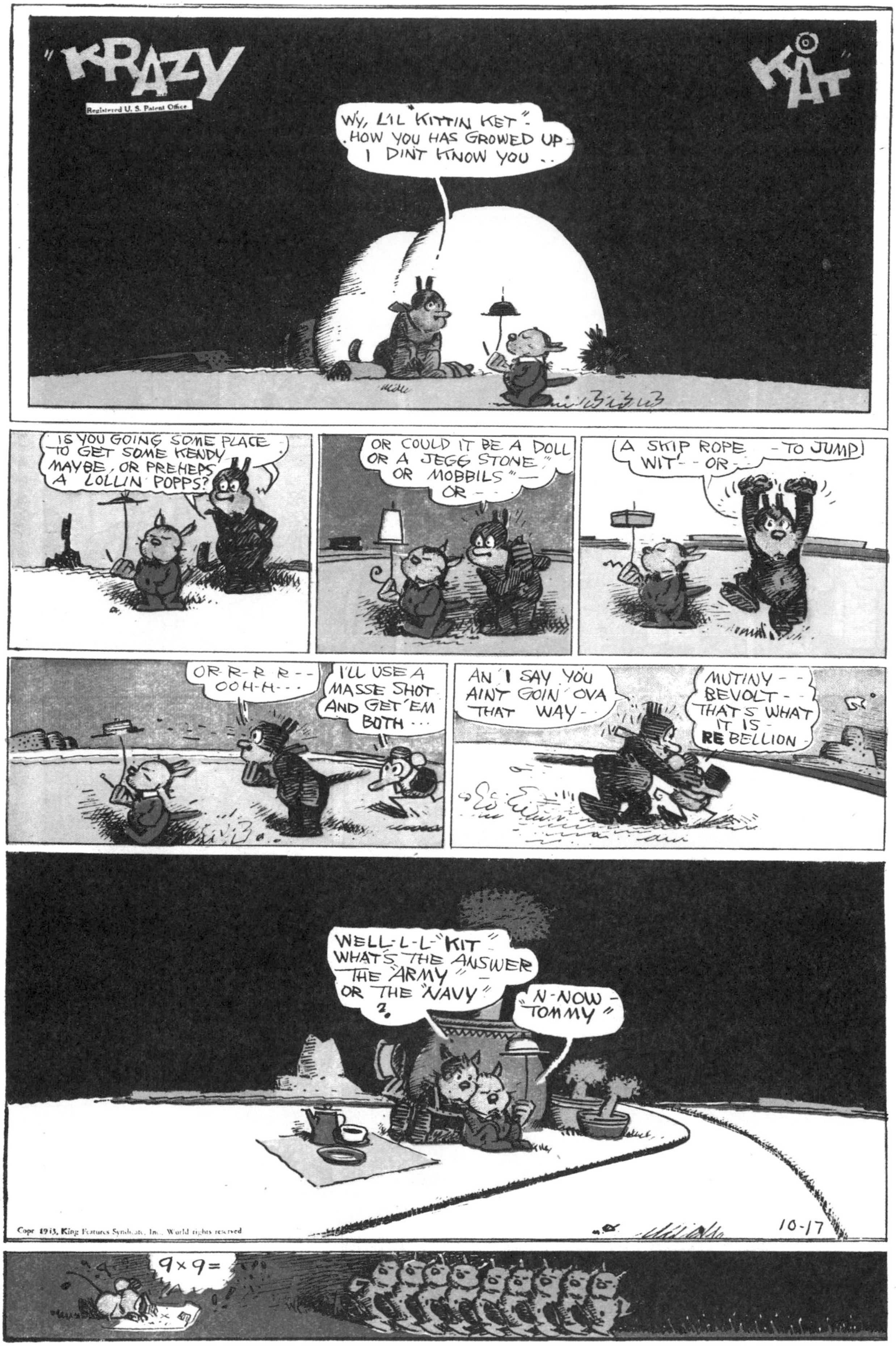
"KRAZY KAT"
Registered U. S. Patent Office
WY, L'IL "KITTIN KET" - HOW YOU HAS GROWED UP - I DINT KNOW YOU . .
IS YOU GOING SOME PLACE TO GET SOME KENDY MAYBE, OR PREHEPS A LOLLIN POPPS?
OR COULD IT BE A DOLL OR A JEGG STONE" OR MOBBILS" — OR - -
(A SKIP ROPE WIT' - - OR - - TO JUMP)
OR-R-R-R - - OOH-H - - -
I'LL USE A MASSE SHOT AND GET 'EM BOTH . . .
AN' I SAY YOU AINT GOIN' OVA THAT WAY -
MUTINY - - BEVOLT - - THAT'S WHAT IT IS - REBELLION -
WELL-L-L "KIT" WHAT'S THE ANSWER "THE ARMY" - OR THE "NAVY" ?
"N-NOW - TOMMY"
Copr. 1943, King Features Syndicate, Inc., World rights reserved
10-17
9×9=

October 17th, 1943.

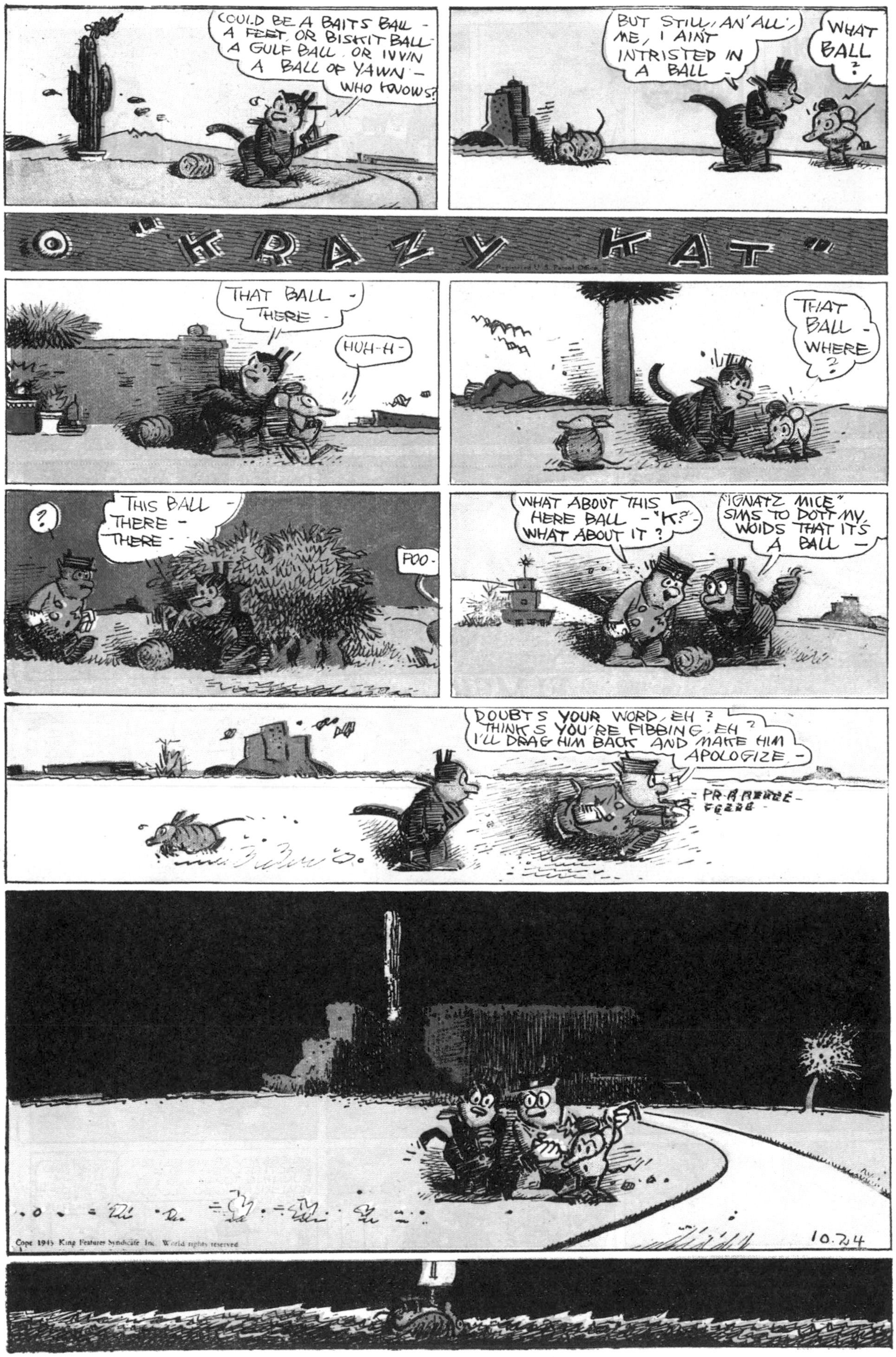
COULD BE A BAITS BALL - A FEET, OR BISKIT BALL - A GULF BALL, OR IVVIN A BALL OF YAWN - WHO KNOWS?
BUT STILL, AN' ALL, ME, I AIN'T INTRISTED IN A BALL -
WHAT BALL ?
"KRAZY KAT"
THAT BALL - THERE -
HUH-H -
THAT BALL - WHERE ?
THIS BALL - THERE - THERE -
FOO -
WHAT ABOUT THIS HERE BALL - "K?" - WHAT ABOUT IT ?
"IGNATZ MICE" SIMS TO DOTT MY WOIDS THAT IT'S A BALL -
DOUBTS YOUR WORD, EH ? THINKS YOU'RE FIBBING, EH ? I'LL DRAG HIM BACK AND MAKE HIM APOLOGIZE -
PR-R-RRRR-EEEE
Copr 1943 King Features Syndicate, Inc. World rights reserved
10.24

October 24th, 1943.

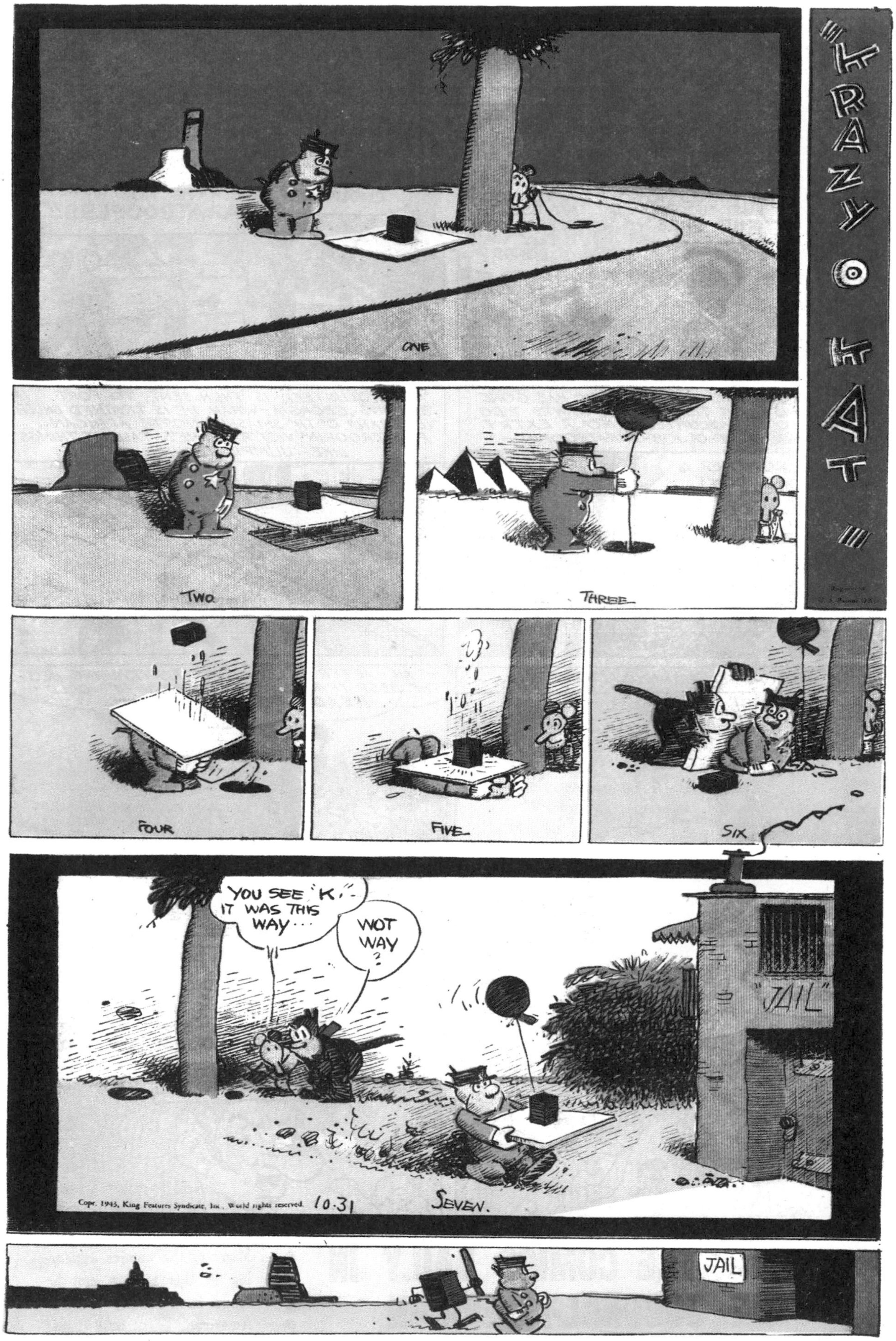
"KRAZY KAT"
ONE
TWO
THREE
FOUR
FIVE
SIX
YOU SEE "K" IT WAS THIS WAY...
WOT WAY?
"JAIL"
Copr. 1943, King Features Syndicate, Inc., World rights reserved.
10·31
SEVEN.
JAIL

October 31st, 1943.

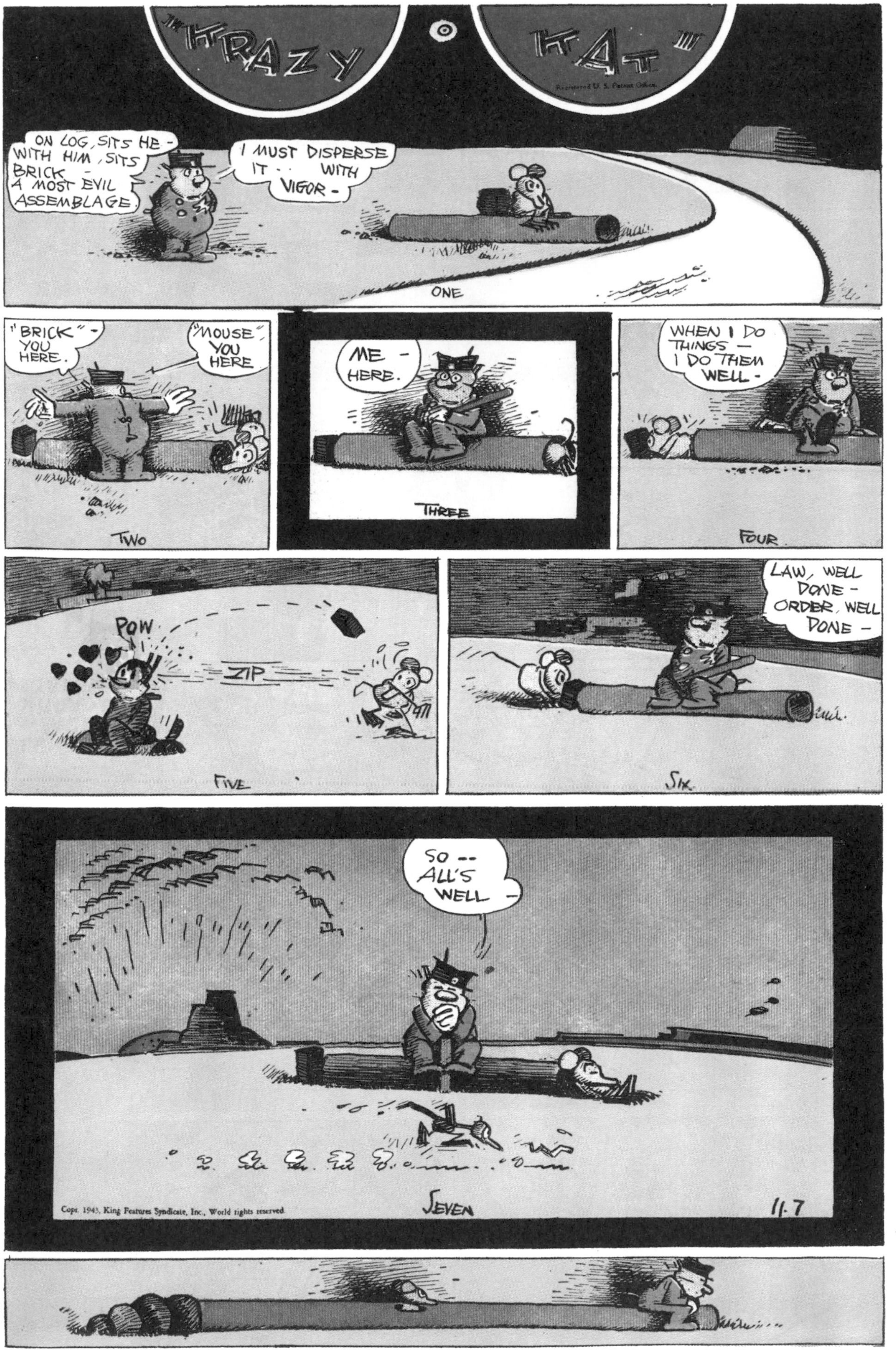
Krazy Kat
Registered U. S. Patent Office.
ON LOG, SITS HE - WITH HIM, SITS BRICK - A MOST EVIL ASSEMBLAGE.
I MUST DISPERSE IT · · WITH VIGOR -
ONE
"BRICK" - YOU HERE.
"MOUSE" YOU HERE
TWO
ME - HERE.
THREE
WHEN I DO THINGS — I DO THEM WELL -
FOUR
POW
ZIP
FIVE
LAW, WELL DONE - ORDER, WELL DONE -
SIX
SO -- ALL'S WELL -
Copr. 1943, King Features Syndicate, Inc., World rights reserved.
SEVEN
11.7

November 7th, 1943.

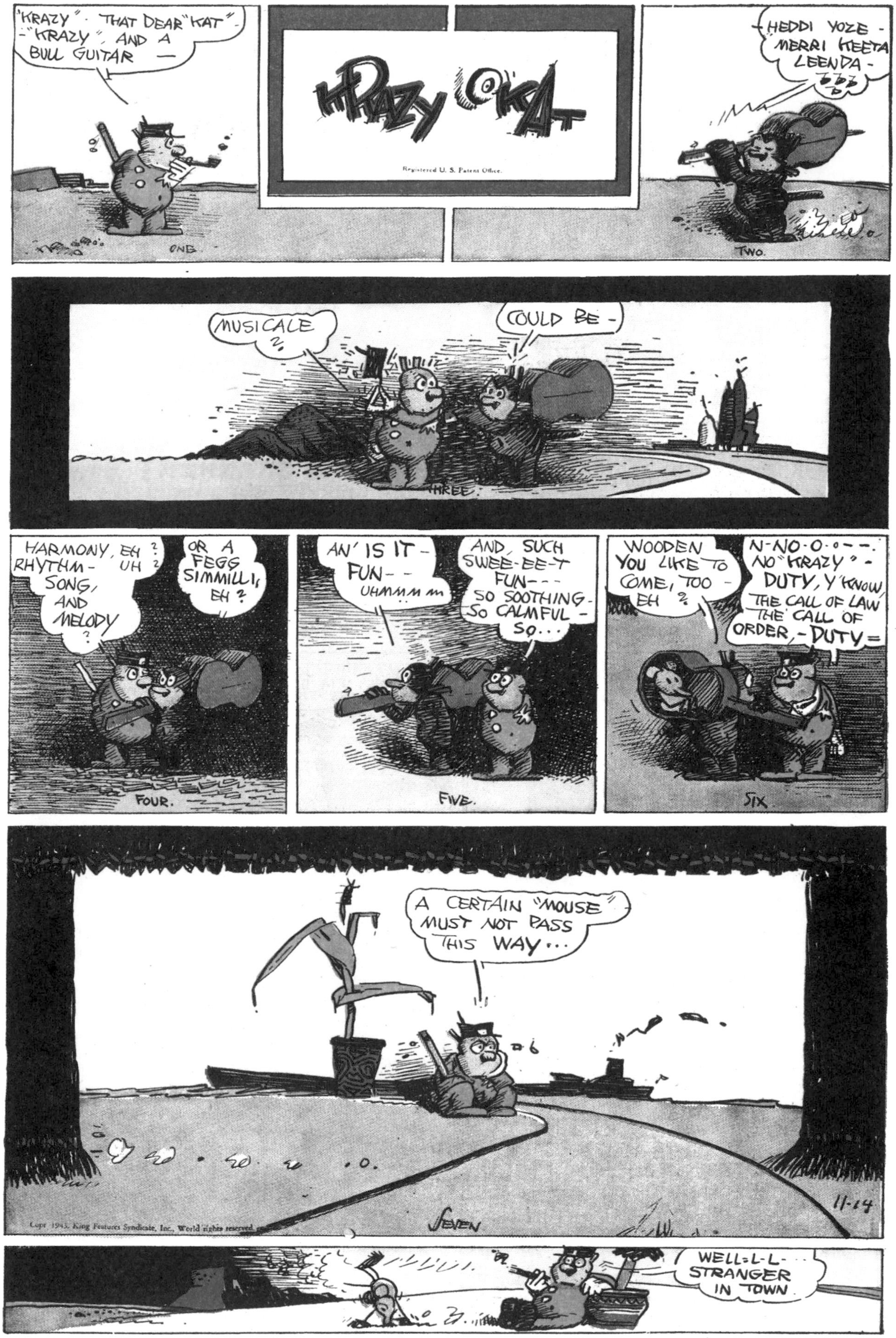
"KRAZY" - THAT DEAR "KAT" - "KRAZY" - AND A BULL GUITAR —
KRAZY KAT
Registered U. S. Patent Office.
HEDDI YOZE - MERRI KEETA LEENDA -
ONE.
TWO.
MUSICALE ?
COULD BE -
THREE
HARMONY, EH ? RHYTHM - UH SONG, AND MELODY ?
OR A FEGG SIMMILLI, EH ?
FOUR.
AN' IS IT - FUN - - UHMMMM
AND, SUCH SWEE-EE-T FUN - - - SO SOOTHING - SO CALMFUL - SO...
FIVE.
WOODEN YOU LIKE TO COME, TOO - EH ?
N-NO-O - - - NO "KRAZY" - DUTY, Y'KNOW, THE CALL OF LAW THE CALL OF ORDER, - DUTY =
SIX.
A CERTAIN "MOUSE" MUST NOT PASS THIS WAY...
Copr 1943, King Features Syndicate, Inc., World rights reserved.
SEVEN
11-14
WELL-L-L - STRANGER IN TOWN

November 14th, 1943.

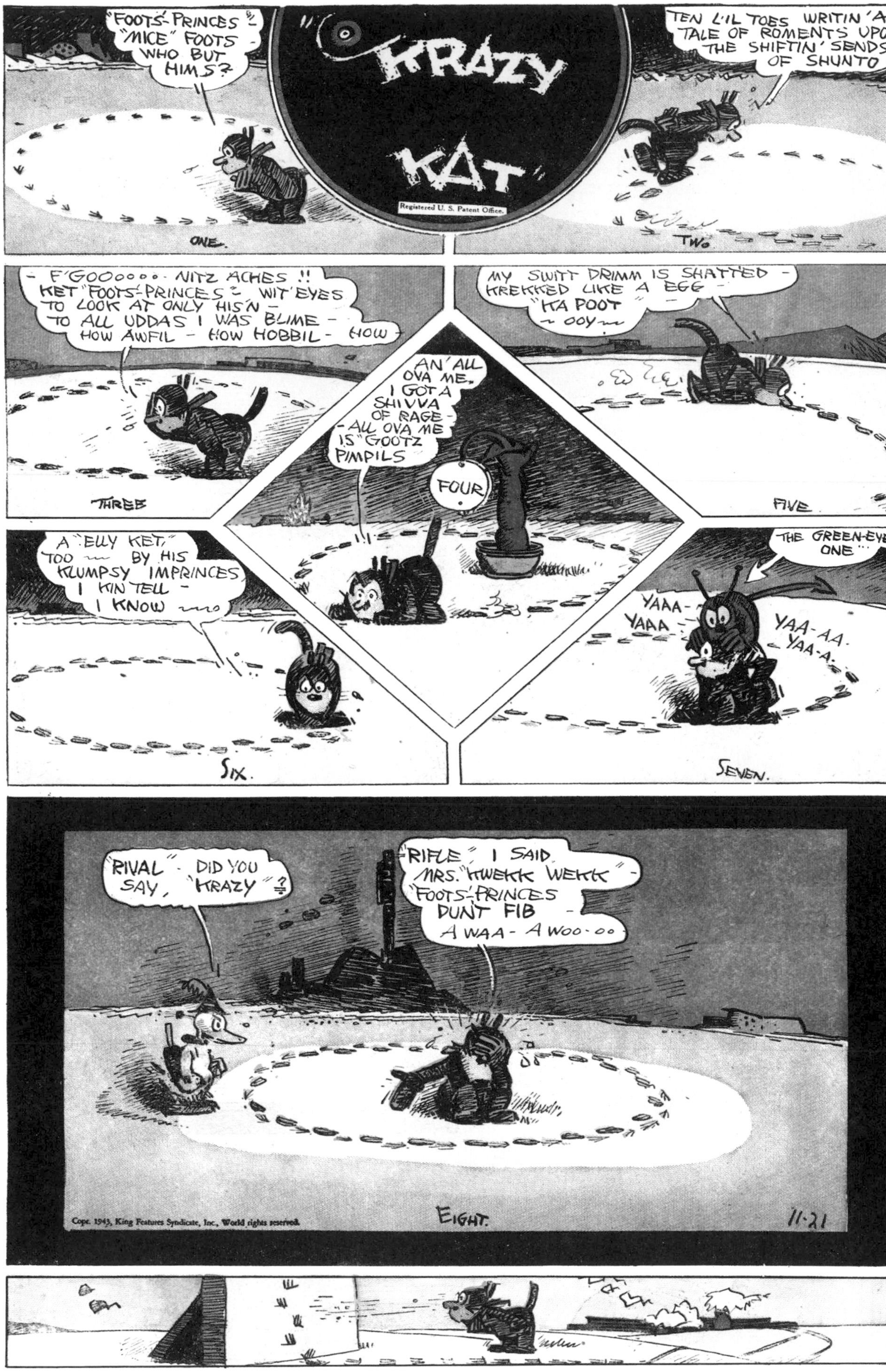
KRAZY KAT
Registered U. S. Patent Office.
"FOOTS-PRINCES" - "MICE" FOOTS - WHO BUT HIMS?
ONE.
TEN L'IL TOES WRITIN' A TALE OF ROMENTS UPON THE SHIFTIN' SENDS OF SHUNTO -
TWO
- F'GOOoooo - NITZ ACHES !! KET "FOOTS-PRINCES" - WIT EYES TO LOOK AT ONLY HIS'N - TO ALL UDDAS I WAS BLIME - HOW AWFIL - HOW HOBBIL - HOW
THREE
AN' ALL OVA ME, I GOT A SHIVVA OF RAGE - ALL OVA ME IS "GOOTZ PIMPILS
FOUR
MY SWITT DRIMM IS SHATTED - HREKKED LIKE A EGG - "KA POOT" - ooy
FIVE
A "ELLY KET," TOO - BY HIS KLUMPSY IMPRINCES, I KIN TELL - I KNOW
SIX.
THE GREEN-EYED ONE"
YAAA - YAAA -
YAA-AA - YAA-A -
SEVEN.
"RIVAL" - DID YOU SAY, "KRAZY"?
"RIFLE," I SAID, MRS. "KWEKK WEKK" - "FOOTS-PRINCES" DUNT FIB - A WAA - A WOO-OO
Copr. 1943, King Features Syndicate, Inc., World rights reserved.
EIGHT.
11-21

November 21st, 1943.

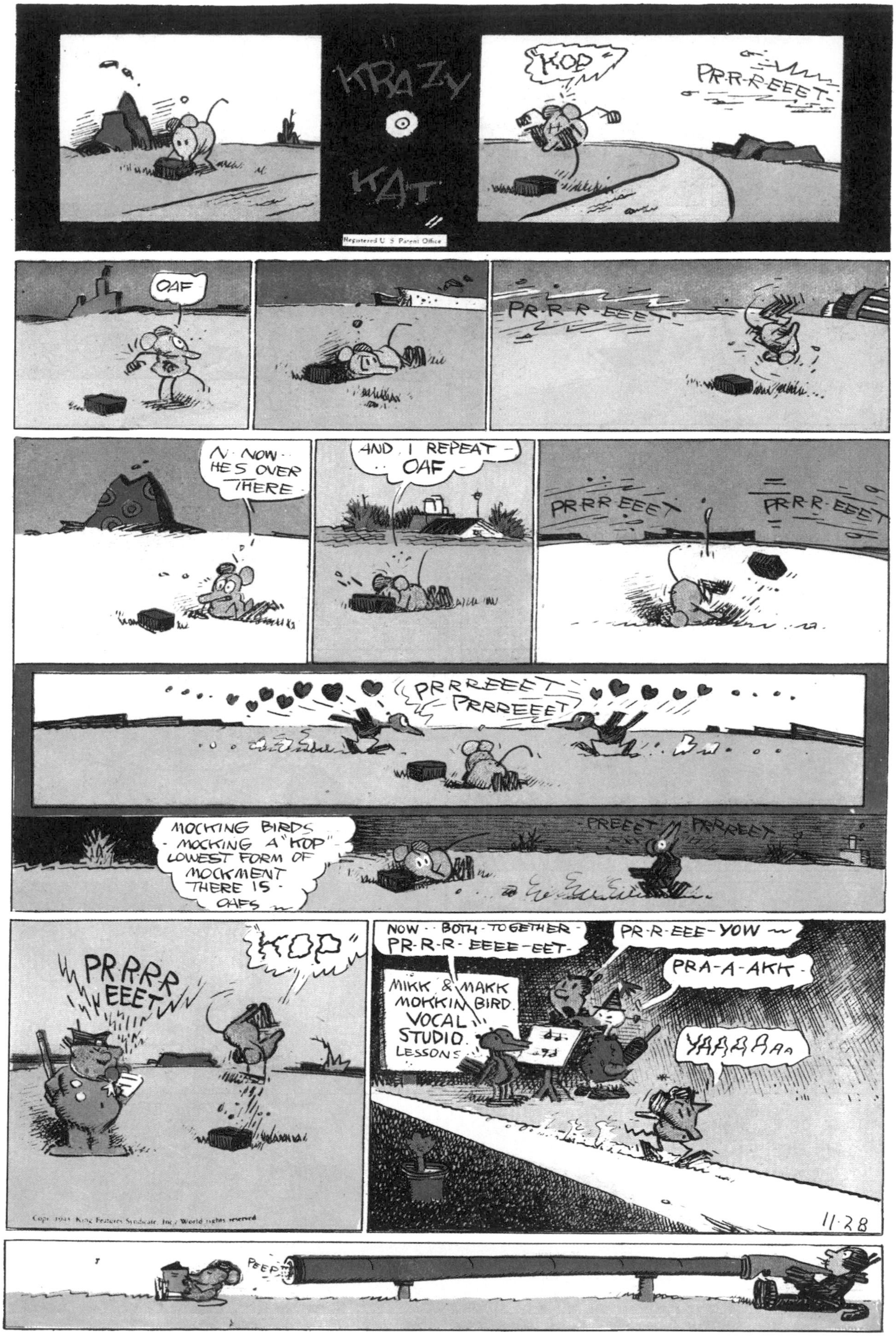
"KRAZY KAT"
Registered U S Patent Office
KOP
PR-R-R-EEET
OAF
PR-R-R-EEET
N NOW HES OVER THERE
AND I REPEAT OAF
PR-R-R-EEET
PR-R-R-EEET
PRRREEEET
PRRREEEET
MOCKING BIRDS MOCKING A "KOP" LOWEST FORM OF MOCKMENT THERE IS OAFS
PREEET
PRRREET
PR-R-R-R EEET
"KOP"
NOW BOTH TOGETHER PR-R-R-EEEE-EET
PR-R-EEE-YOW
PRA-A-AKK
MIKK & MAKK MOKKIN BIRD VOCAL STUDIO LESSONS
YAAAAAA
Copr 1943 King Features Syndicate, Inc.; World rights reserved
11-28
PEEP

November 28th, 1943.

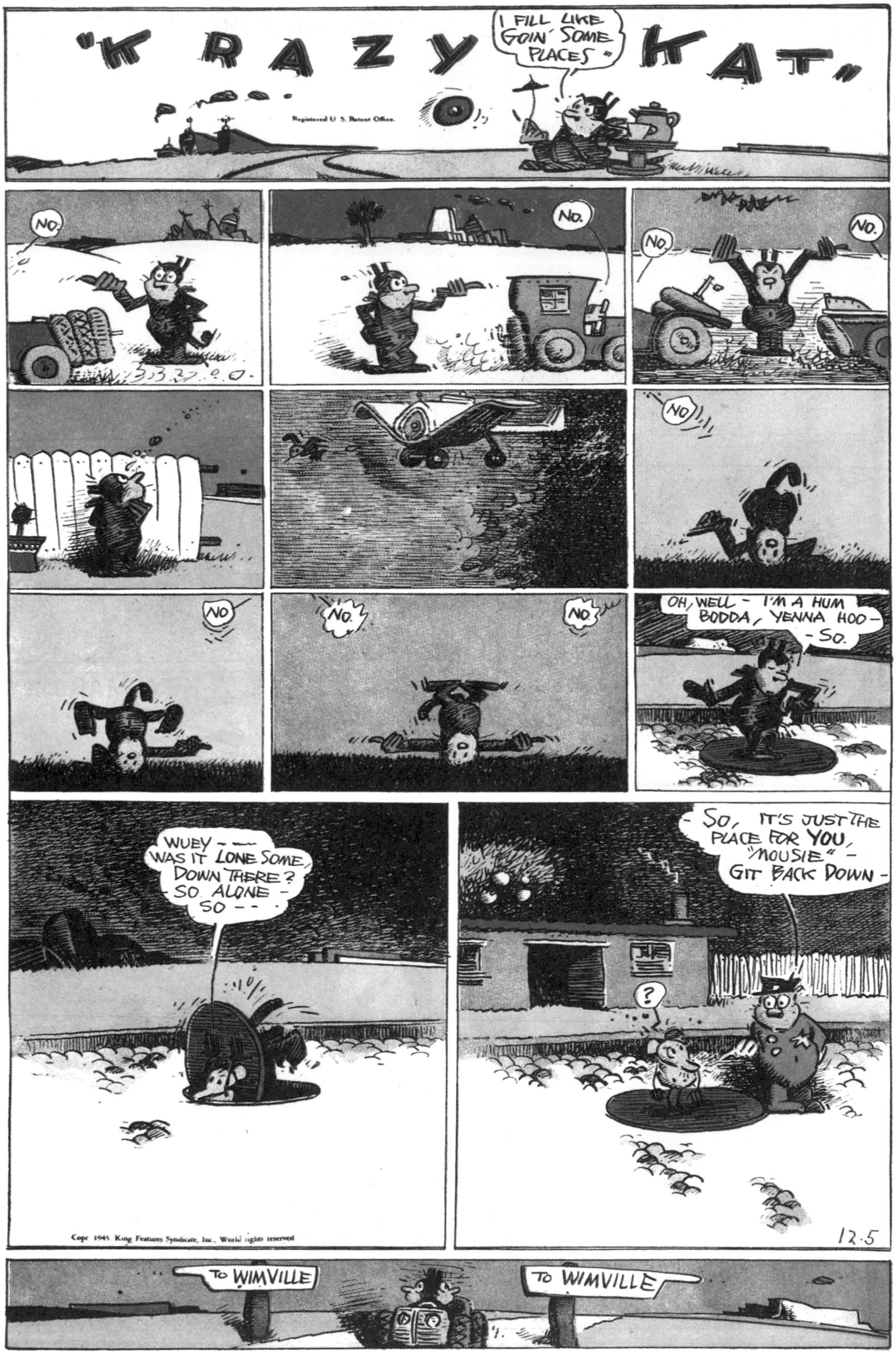
"KRAZY KAT"
I FILL LIKE GOIN' SOME PLACES -
Registered U. S. Patent Office.
NO.
NO.
NO.
NO.
NO
NO
NO.
NO
OH, WELL - I'M A HUM BODDA, YENNA HOO - SO.
WUEY - - WAS IT LONE SOME DOWN THERE? - SO ALONE - SO - -
- SO, IT'S JUST THE PLACE FOR YOU, "MOUSIE" - GIT BACK DOWN -
?
Copr 1943, King Features Syndicate, Inc., World rights reserved
12-5
TO WIMVILLE
TO WIMVILLE

December 5th, 1943.

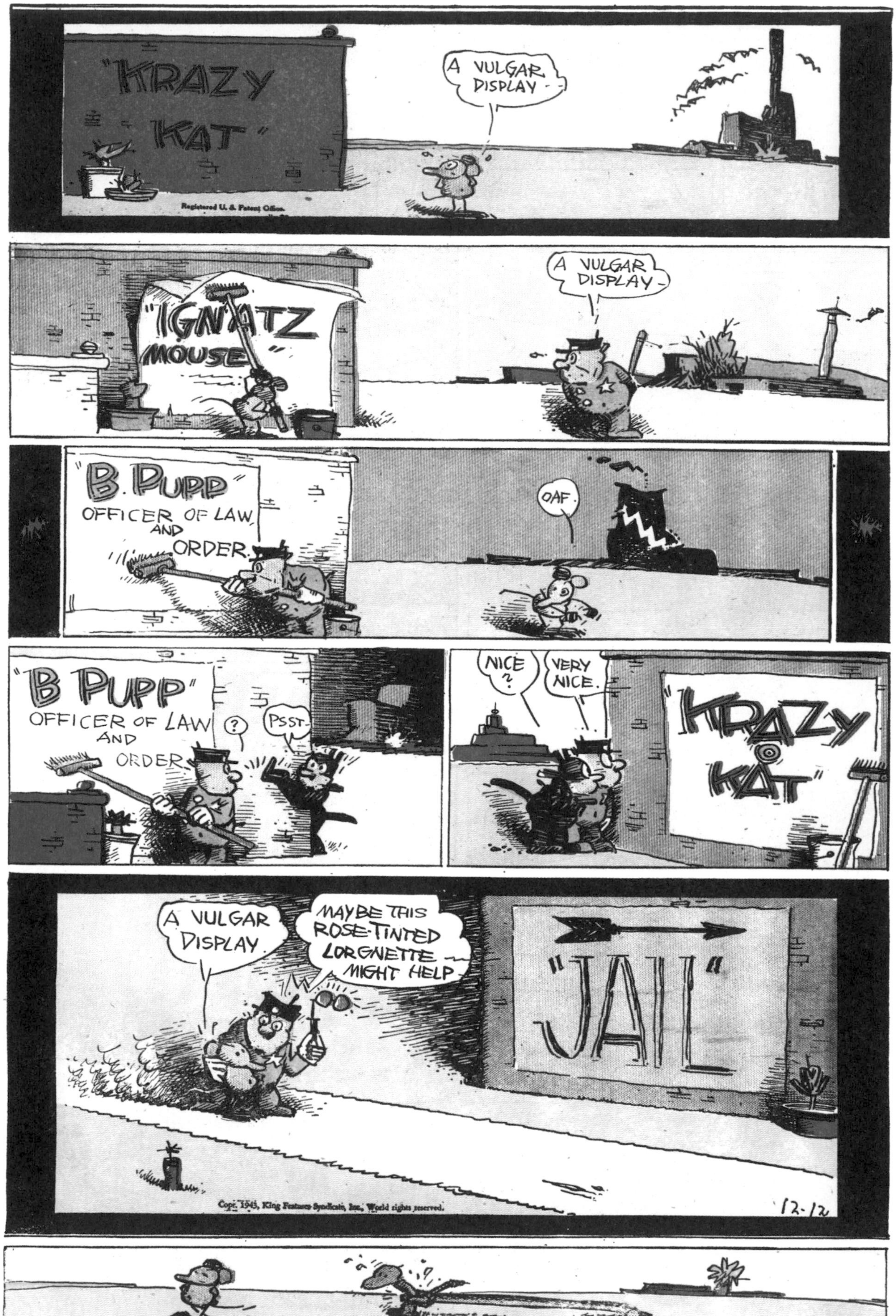
"KRAZY KAT"
Registered U.S. Patent Office.
A VULGAR DISPLAY -
"IGNATZ MOUSE"
A VULGAR DISPLAY -
"B. PUPP" OFFICER OF LAW AND ORDER.
OAF.
"B PUPP" OFFICER OF LAW AND ORDER.
?
PSST-
NICE ?
VERY NICE.
"KRAZY KAT"
A VULGAR DISPLAY.
MAYBE THIS ROSE-TINTED LORGNETTE MIGHT HELP
"JAIL"
Copr. 1943, King Features Syndicate, Inc., World rights reserved.
12-12

December 12th, 1943.

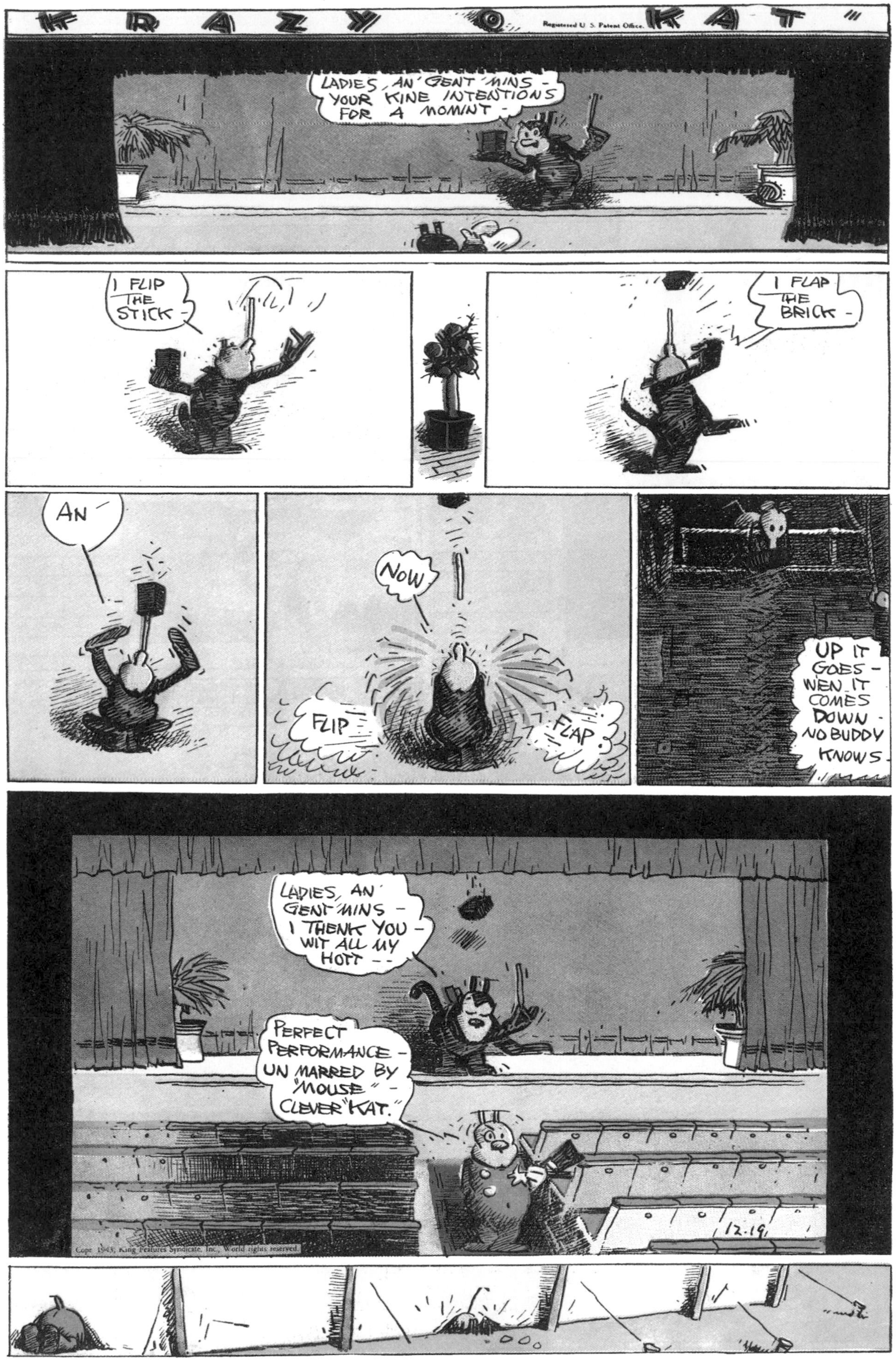
"KRAZY KAT"
Registered U. S. Patent Office.
LADIES, AN' GENT MINS - YOUR KINE INTENTIONS FOR A MOMINT -
I FLIP THE STICK -
I FLAP THE BRICK -
AN -
NOW
FLIP
FLAP
UP IT GOES - WEN IT COMES DOWN NO BUDDY KNOWS.
LADIES, AN GENT MINS - I THENK YOU - WIT ALL MY HOTT --
PERFECT PERFORMANCE - UN MARRED BY "MOUSE" - CLEVER "KAT."
12.19
Copr. 1943, King Features Syndicate, Inc., World rights reserved.

December 19th, 1943.

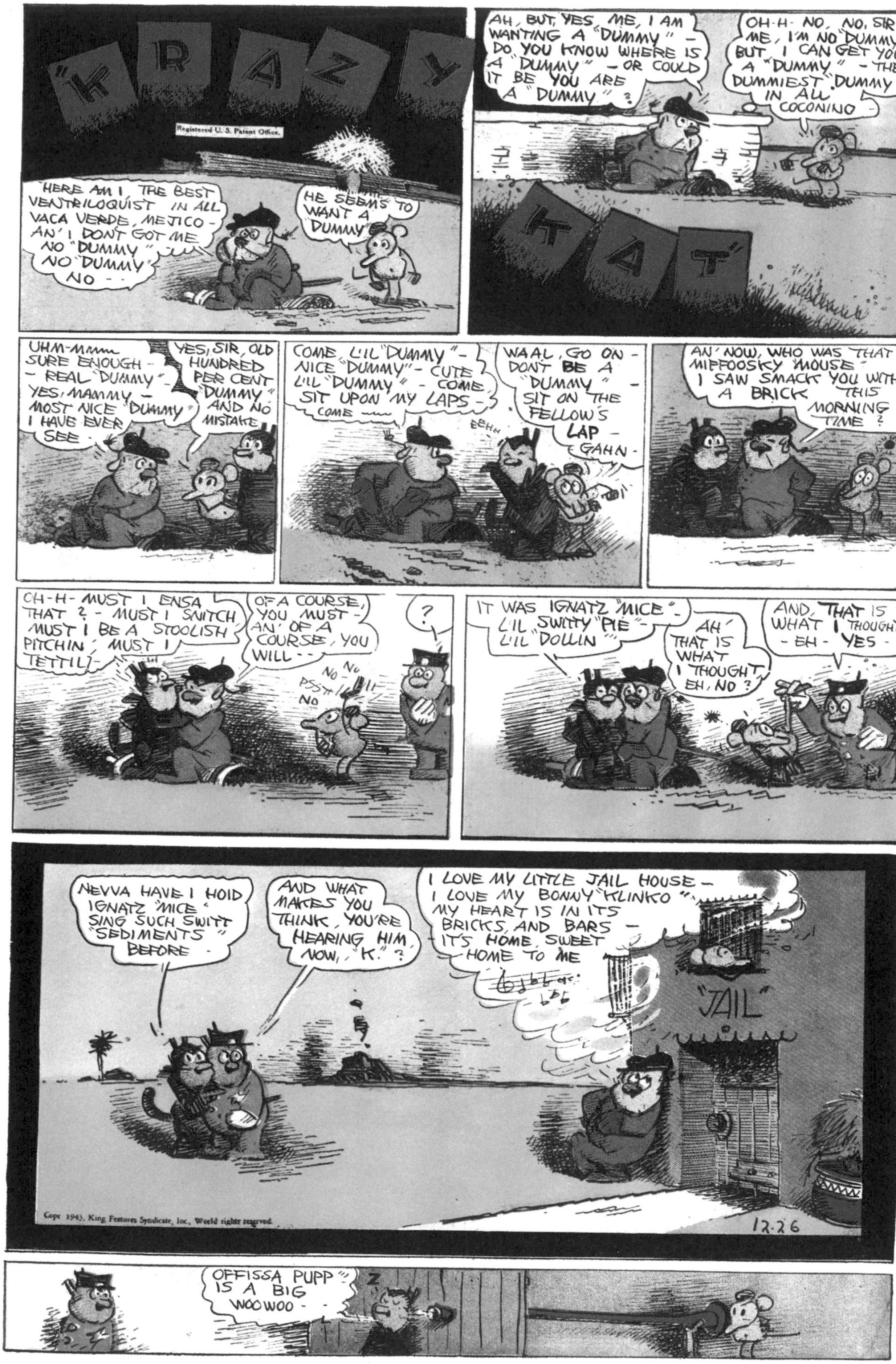
"KRAZY
Registered U. S. Patent Office.
HERE AM I, THE BEST VENTRILOQUIST IN ALL VACA VERDE, MEJICO - AN' I DON'T GOT ME NO "DUMMY" NO "DUMMY" NO - -
HE SEEMS TO WANT A "DUMMY"
AH, BUT, YES ME, I AM WANTING A "DUMMY" - DO YOU KNOW WHERE IS A "DUMMY" - OR COULD IT BE YOU ARE A "DUMMY" ?
OH-H- NO, NO, SIR - ME, I'M NO "DUMMY" BUT, I CAN GET YOU A "DUMMY" - THE DUMMIEST "DUMMY" IN ALL COCONINO -
KAT"
UHM-MMMM SURE ENOUGH - - REAL "DUMMY" - YES, MAMMY - MOST NICE "DUMMY" I HAVE EVER SEE -
YES, SIR, OLD HUNDRED PER CENT "DUMMY" AND NO MISTAKE
COME L'IL "DUMMY" - NICE "DUMMY" - CUTE L'IL "DUMMY" - COME SIT UPON MY LAPS -
COME ----
WAAL, GO ON - DON'T BE A "DUMMY" - SIT ON THE FELLOW'S LAP - GAHN -
EEHH
AN' NOW, WHO WAS THAT MIFFOOSKY MOUSE I SAW SMACK YOU WITH A BRICK THIS MORNING TIME ?
OH-H- MUST I ENSA THAT ? - MUST I SNITCH MUST I BE A STOOLISH PITCHIN', MUST I TETTIL ? -
OF A COURSE, YOU MUST - AN' OF A COURSE, YOU WILL - -
NO - NO
PSST
NO
?
IT WAS IGNATZ "MICE" - L'IL SWITTY "PIE" - L'IL DOLLIN
AH' THAT IS WHAT I THOUGHT, EH, NO ?
AND, THAT IS WHAT I THOUGHT - EH - YES -
NEVVA HAVE I HOID IGNATZ "MICE" SING SUCH SWITT "SEDIMENTS" BEFORE
AND WHAT MAKES YOU THINK, YOU'RE HEARING HIM NOW, "K." ?
I LOVE MY LITTLE JAIL HOUSE - I LOVE MY BONNY "KLINKO" - MY HEART IS IN ITS BRICKS, AND BARS - IT'S HOME, SWEET HOME TO ME
"JAIL"
Copr. 1943, King Features Syndicate, Inc., World rights reserved.
12-26
OFFISSA PUPP IS A BIG WOOWOO -
Z

December 26th, 1943.

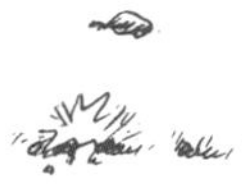

1944.

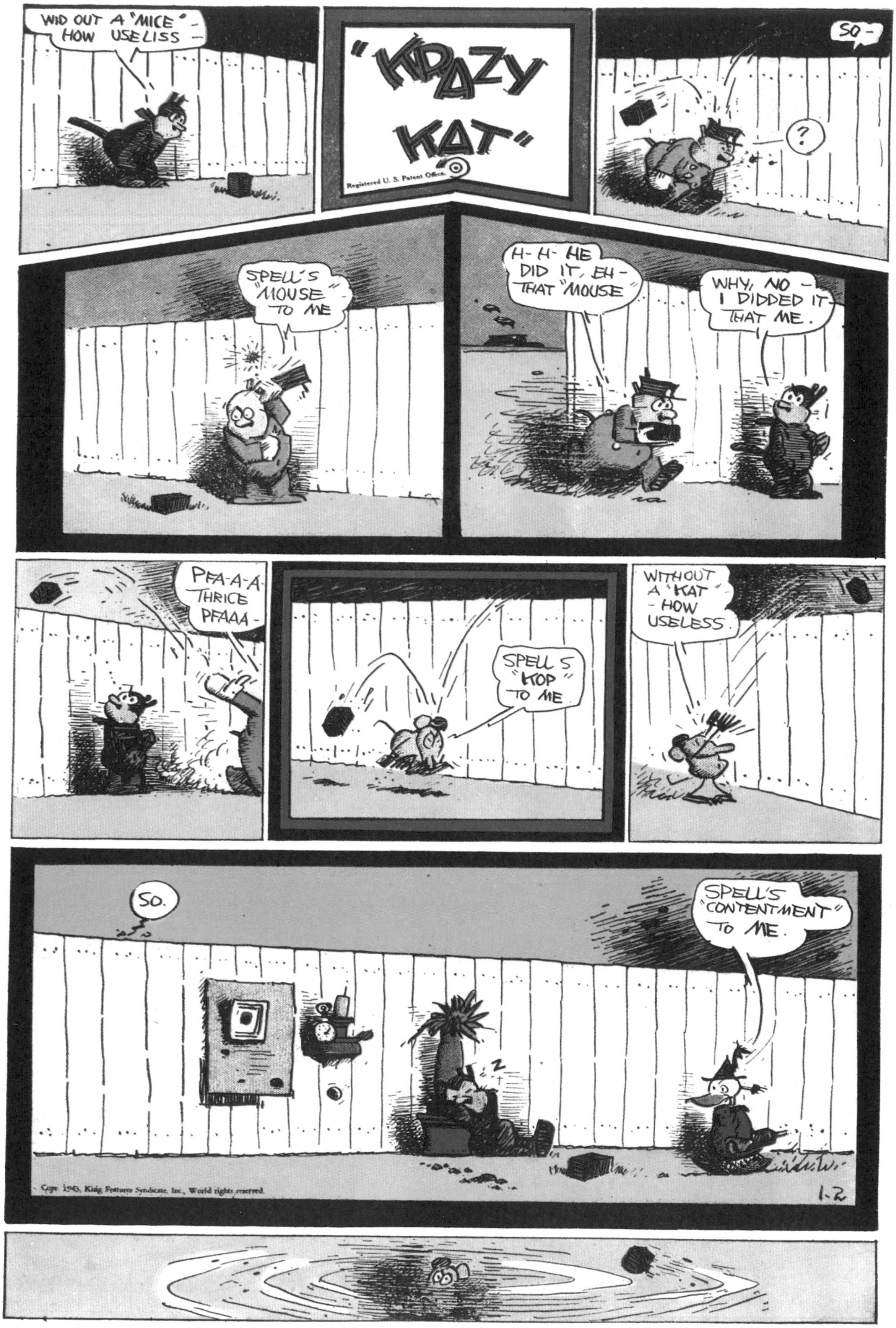
WID OUT A "MICE" - HOW USELISS -
"KRAZY KAT"
Registered U. S. Patent Office.
SO -
?
SPELL'S "MOUSE" TO ME
H- H- HE DID IT, EH - THAT "MOUSE"
WHY, NO - I DIDDED IT - THAT ME.
PFA-A-A - THRICE PFAAA -
SPELL'S "KOP" TO ME
WITHOUT A "KAT" - HOW USELESS.
SO.
SPELL'S "CONTENTMENT" TO ME.
Z
Copr. 1943, King Features Syndicate, Inc., World rights reserved.
1-2

January 2nd, 1944.

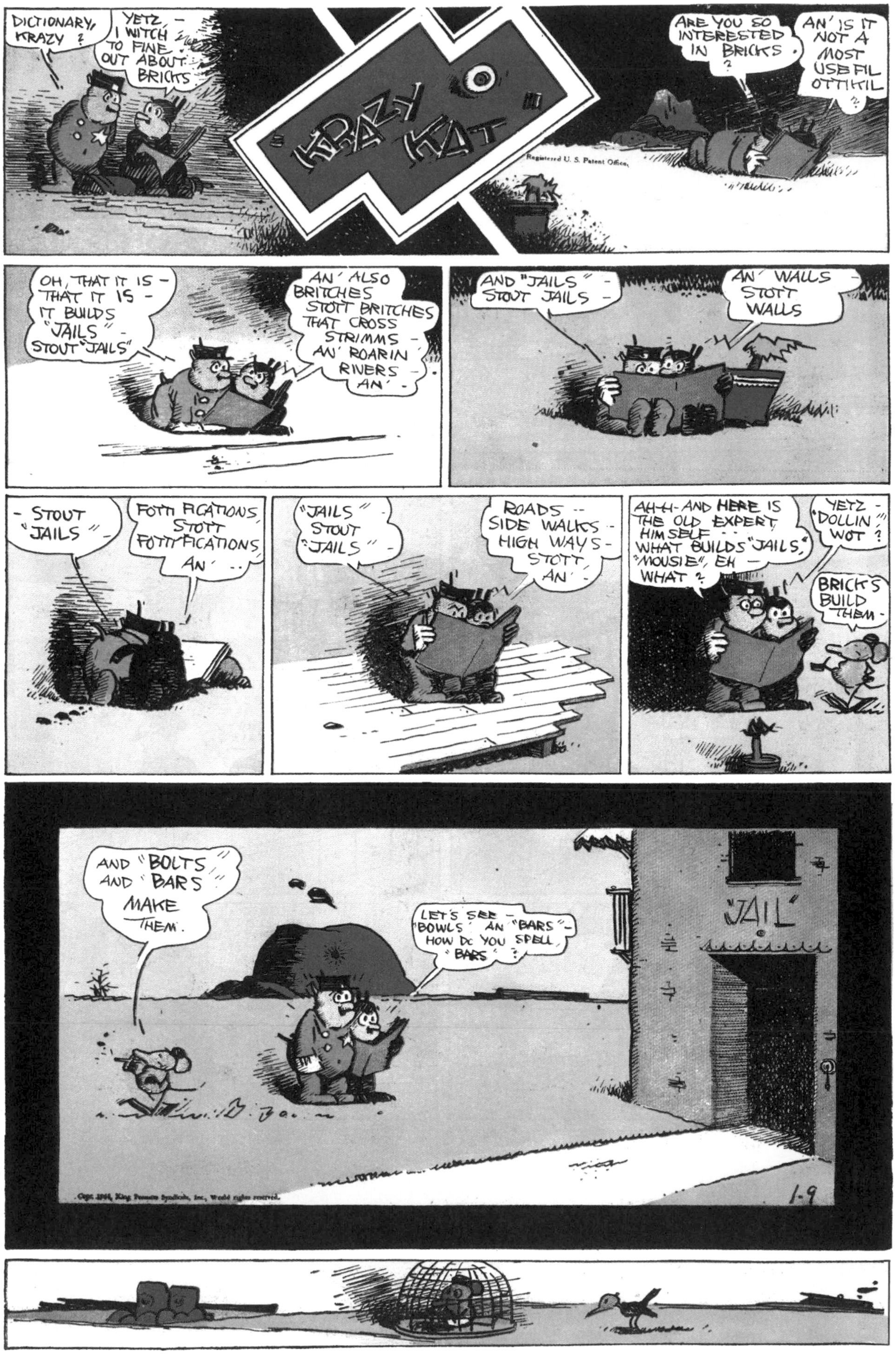

KRAZY KAT
Registered U. S. Patent Office.
DICTIONARY, KRAZY ?
YETZ, – I WITCH TO FINE OUT ABOUT BRICKS
ARE YOU SO INTERESTED IN BRICKS ?
AN' IS IT NOT A MOST USEFIL OTTIKIL ?
OH, THAT IT IS – THAT IT IS – IT BUILDS "JAILS" – STOUT "JAILS"
AN' ALSO BRITCHES STOTT BRITCHES THAT CROSS STRIMMS – AN' ROARIN RIVERS – AN' –
AND "JAILS" – STOUT JAILS –
AN' WALLS – STOTT WALLS
– STOUT "JAILS" –
FOTTI FICATIONS STOTT FOTTIFICATIONS AN' ..
"JAILS" – STOUT "JAILS" –
ROADS -- SIDE WALKS – HIGH WAYS – STOTT AN' –
AH-H- AND HERE IS THE OLD EXPERT, HIMSELF -- WHAT BUILDS "JAILS," "MOUSIE", EH – WHAT ?
YETZ – "DOLLIN" WOT ?
BRICK'S BUILD THEM –
AND "BOLTS" AND "BARS" MAKE THEM.
LET'S SEE – "BOWLS" AN "BARS" – HOW DC YOU SPELL "BARS" ?
"JAIL"
Copr. 1944, King Features Syndicate, Inc., World rights reserved.
1-9

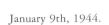

January 9th, 1944.

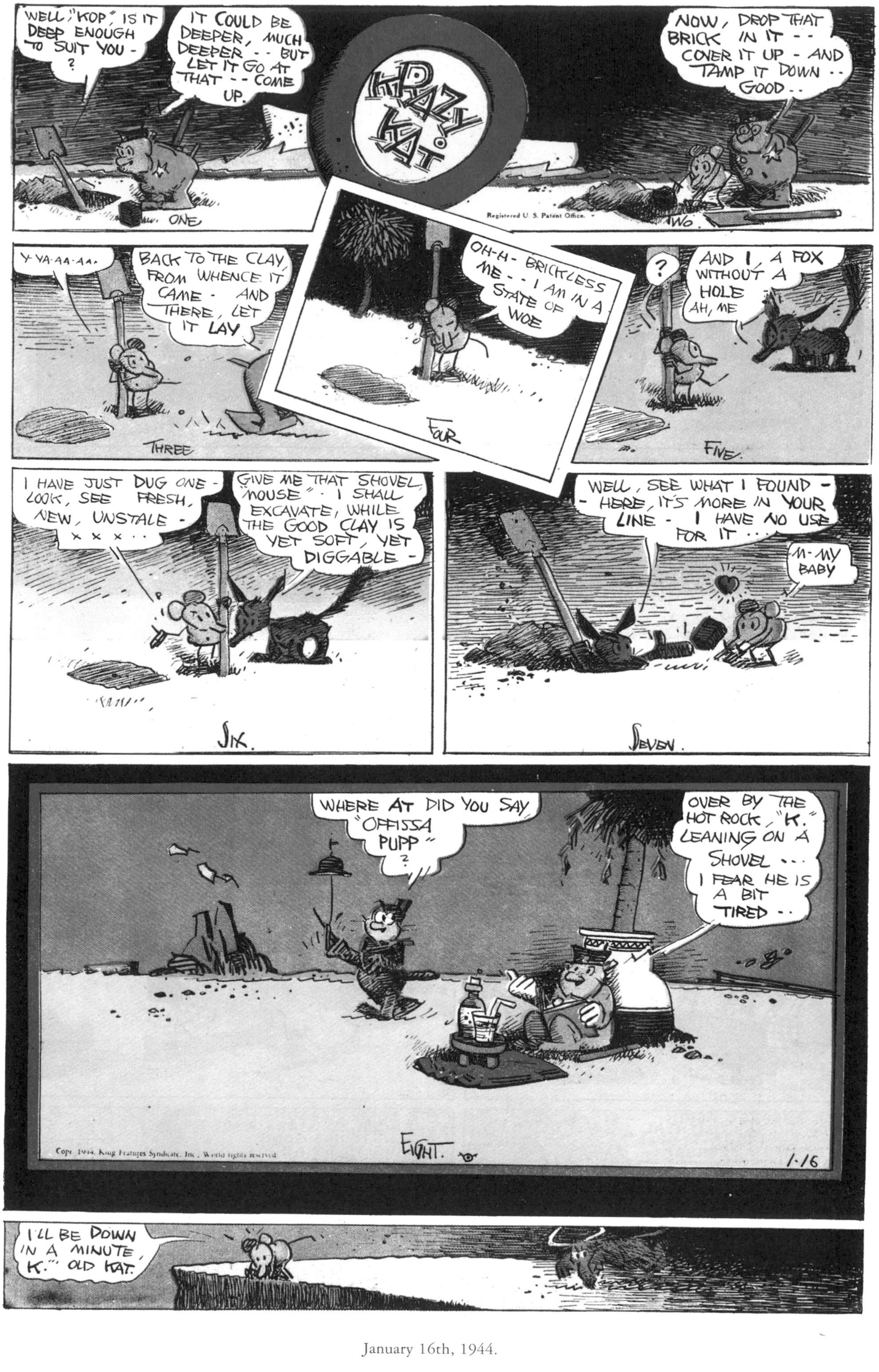
WELL, "KOP," IS IT DEEP ENOUGH TO SUIT YOU - ?
IT COULD BE DEEPER, MUCH DEEPER - - BUT LET IT GO AT THAT - - COME UP.
KRAZY KAT
ONE
NOW, DROP THAT BRICK IN IT - - COVER IT UP - AND TAMP IT DOWN - - GOOD - -
Registered U. S. Patent Office.
TWO
Y-YA-AA-AA-
BACK TO THE CLAY, FROM WHENCE IT CAME - AND THERE, LET IT LAY
THREE
OH-H - BRICKLESS ME - - I AM IN A STATE OF WOE
FOUR
?
AND I, A FOX WITHOUT A HOLE AH, ME
FIVE
I HAVE JUST DUG ONE - LOOK, SEE FRESH, NEW, UNSTALE - x x x - -
GIVE ME THAT SHOVEL, "MOUSE" - I SHALL EXCAVATE, WHILE THE GOOD CLAY IS YET SOFT, YET DIGGABLE -
SIX.
WELL, SEE WHAT I FOUND - - HERE, IT'S MORE IN YOUR LINE - I HAVE NO USE FOR IT - - -
M-MY BABY
SEVEN.
WHERE AT DID YOU SAY "OFFISSA PUPP" ?
OVER BY THE HOT ROCK, "K." LEANING ON A SHOVEL - - - I FEAR HE IS A BIT TIRED - -
Copr. 1944, King Features Syndicate, Inc., World rights reserved
EIGHT.
1-16
I'LL BE DOWN IN A MINUTE, "K." OLD KAT.

January 16th, 1944.

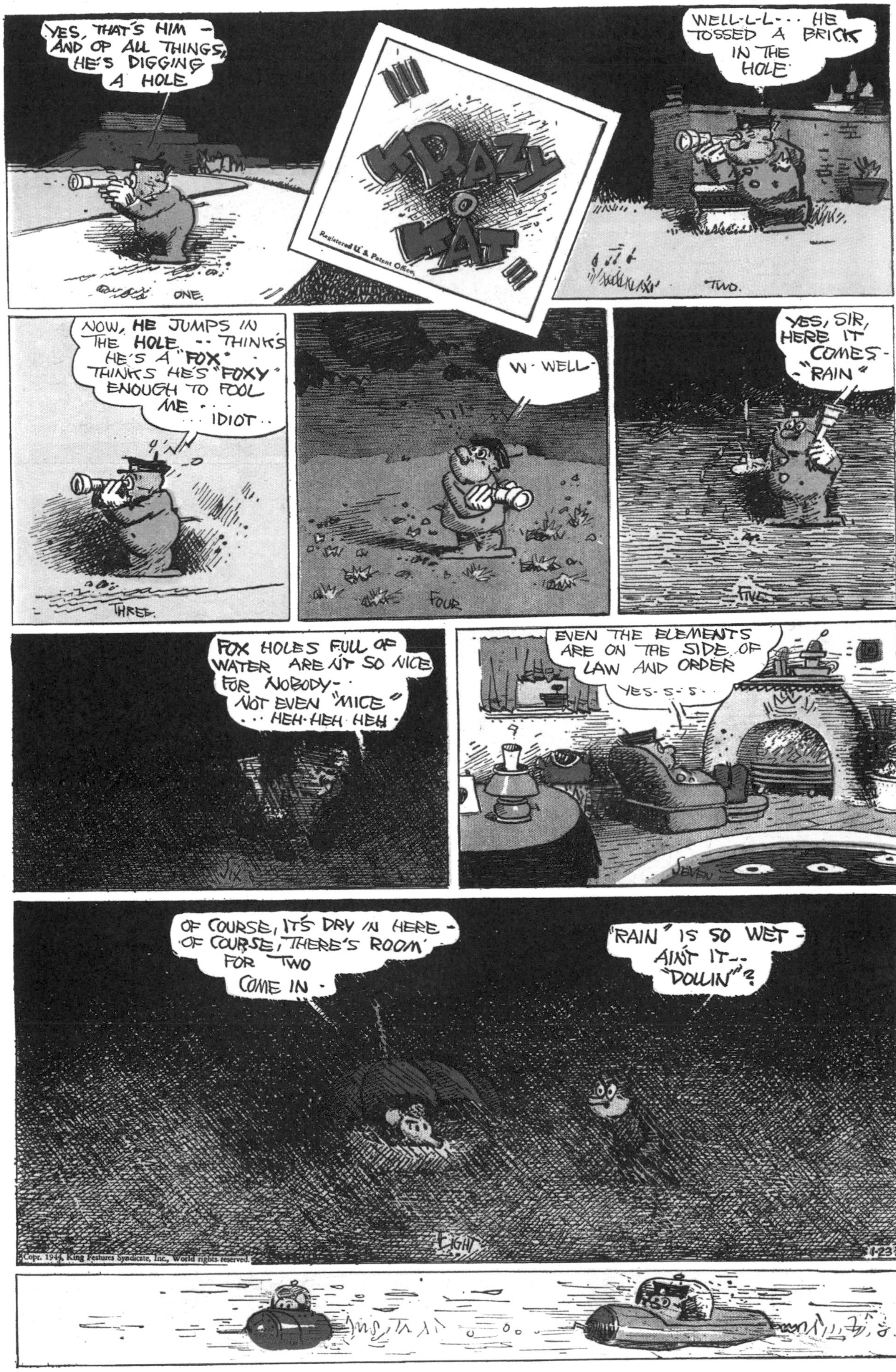
YES, THAT'S HIM - AND OF ALL THINGS, HE'S DIGGING A HOLE
KRAZY KAT
Registered U. S. Patent Office.
ONE.
WELL-L-L... HE TOSSED A BRICK IN THE HOLE
TWO.
NOW, HE JUMPS IN THE HOLE -- THINKS HE'S A "FOX" - THINKS HE'S "FOXY" ENOUGH TO FOOL ME... ...IDIOT..
THREE.
W- WELL-
FOUR
YES, SIR, HERE IT COMES - "RAIN"
FIVE
FOX HOLES FULL OF WATER ARE NOT SO NICE FOR NOBODY - NOT EVEN "MICE" ... HEH-HEH HEH
EVEN THE ELEMENTS ARE ON THE SIDE OF LAW AND ORDER
YES-S-S..
SEVEN
OF COURSE, IT'S DRY IN HERE - OF COURSE, THERE'S ROOM FOR TWO COME IN -
"RAIN" IS SO WET - AIN'T IT-.. "DOLLIN"?
EIGHT
Copr. 1944, King Features Syndicate, Inc., World rights reserved.

January 23rd, 1944.

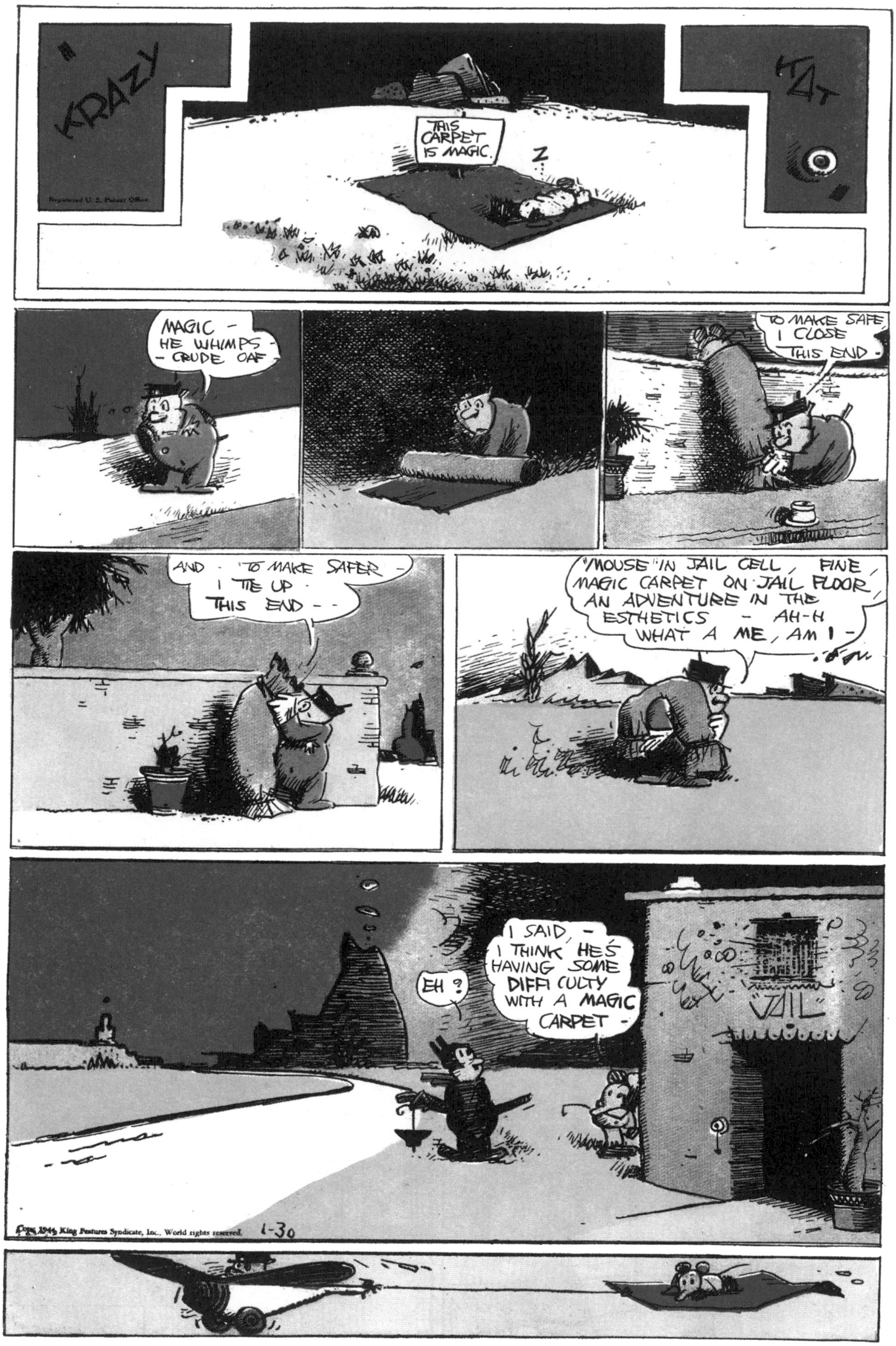
KRAZY KAT
Registered U. S. Patent Office.
THIS CARPET IS MAGIC.
Z
MAGIC - HE WHIMPS - CRUDE OAF -
TO MAKE SAFE I CLOSE THIS END -
AND - TO MAKE SAFER - I TIE UP THIS END - -
"MOUSE" IN JAIL CELL, FINE MAGIC CARPET ON JAIL FLOOR, AN ADVENTURE IN THE ESTHETICS - AH-H WHAT A ME, AM I -
EH ?
I SAID, - I THINK HE'S HAVING SOME DIFFI CULTY WITH A MAGIC CARPET -
JAIL
Copr. 1944, King Features Syndicate, Inc., World rights reserved.
1-30

January 30th, 1944.

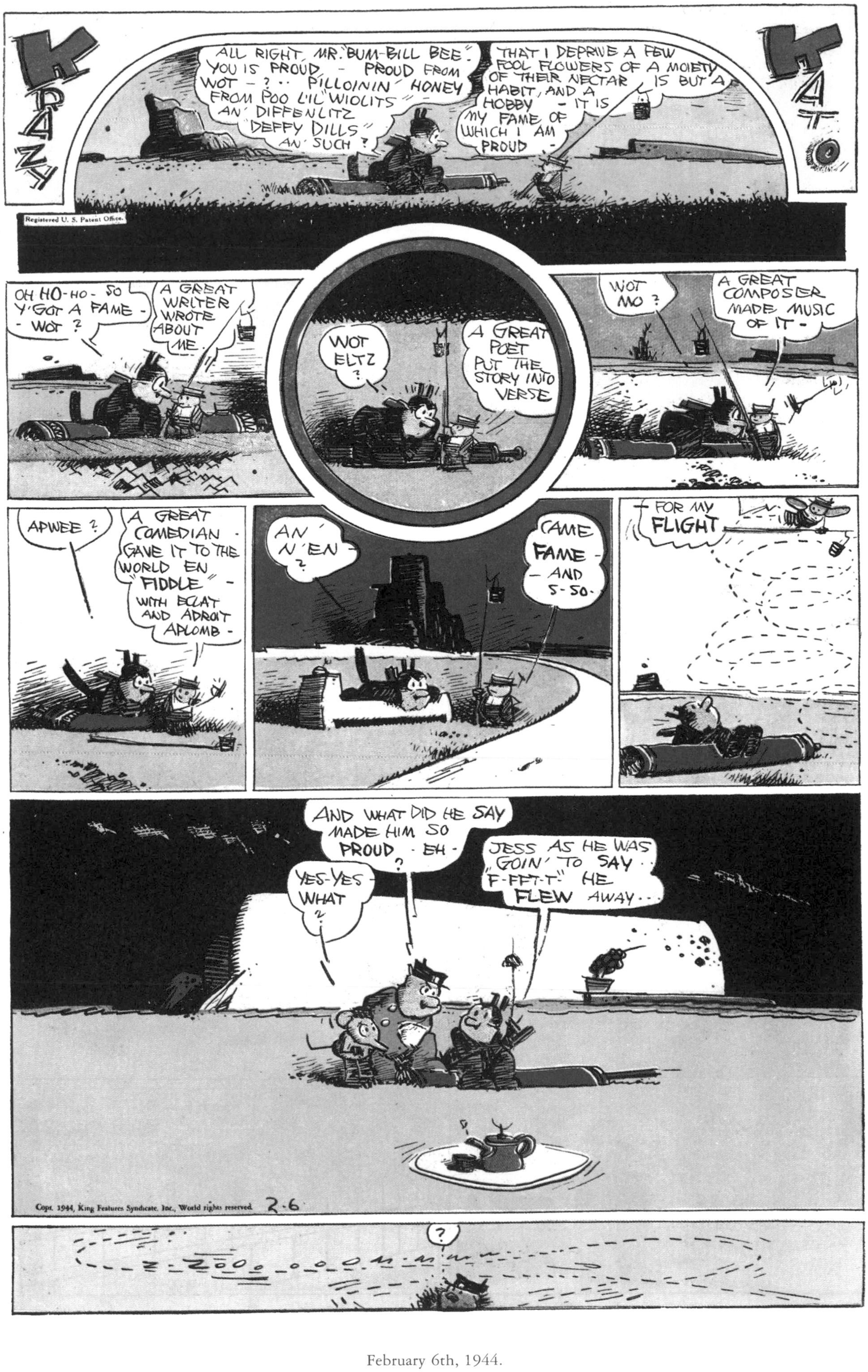

KRAZY KAT
ALL RIGHT, MR. BUM-BILL BEE. YOU IS PROUD - PROUD FROM WOT - ?.. PILLOININ' HONEY FROM POO L'IL WIOLITS AN' DIFFENLITZ "DEFFY DILLS" AN' SUCH ?
THAT I DEPRIVE A FEW FOOL FLOWERS OF A MOIETY OF THEIR NECTAR, IS BUT A HABIT, AND A HOBBY - IT IS MY FAME OF WHICH I AM PROUD -
Registered U. S. Patent Office.
OH HO-HO - SO Y'GOT A FAME - WOT ?
A GREAT WRITER WROTE ABOUT ME.
WOT ELTZ ?
A GREAT POET PUT THE STORY INTO VERSE
WOT MO ?
A GREAT COMPOSER MADE MUSIC OF IT -
APWEE ?
A GREAT COMEDIAN GAVE IT TO THE WORLD EN "FIDDLE" - WITH ECLAT AND ADROIT APLOMB -
AN' N' EN ?
CAME FAME - AND S-SO.
- FOR MY FLIGHT
AND WHAT DID HE SAY MADE HIM SO PROUD, EH ?
YES-YES WHAT ?
JESS AS HE WAS GOIN' TO SAY "F-FFT-T" HE FLEW AWAY...
Copr. 1944, King Features Syndicate, Inc., World rights reserved. 2-6
?
Z-ZOOo-o-o-O-M-M-M

February 6th, 1944.

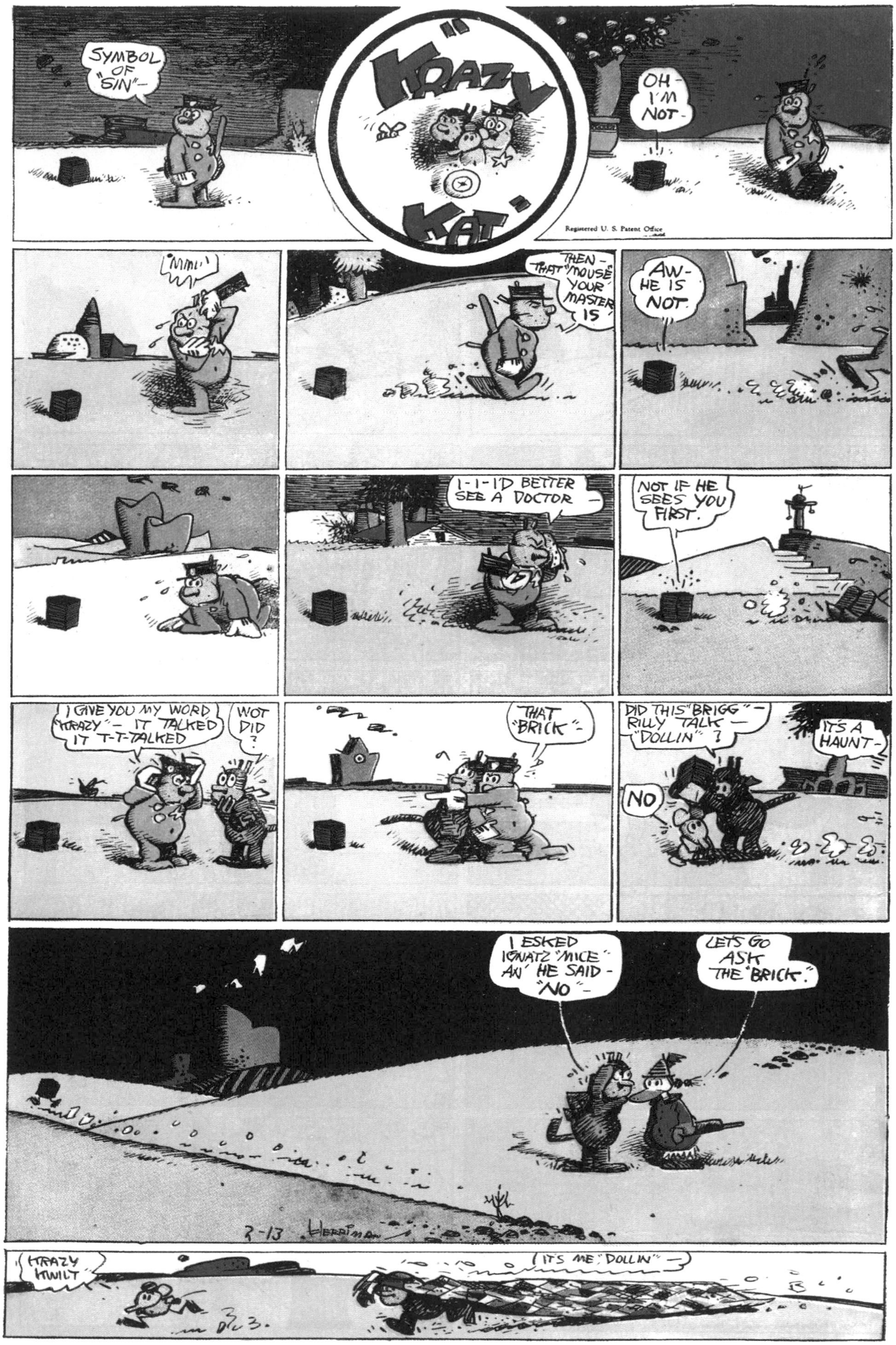

SYMBOL OF "SIN"—
KRAZY KAT
Registered U. S. Patent Office
OH—I'M NOT—
"MMM!"
THEN—THAT "MOUSE" YOUR MASTER IS
AW—HE IS NOT.
I-I-I'D BETTER SEE A DOCTOR—
NOT IF HE SEES YOU FIRST.
I GIVE YOU MY WORD "KRAZY"—IT TALKED IT T-T-TALKED
WOT DID?
"THAT "BRICK"—
DID THIS "BRIGG"—RILLY TALK—"DOLLIN"?
IT'S A HAUNT—
NO
I ESKED IGNATZ "MICE" AN' HE SAID—"NO"—
LET'S GO ASK THE "BRICK".
2-13 HERRIMAN
KRAZY KWILT
IT'S ME "DOLLIN"—

February 13th, 1944.

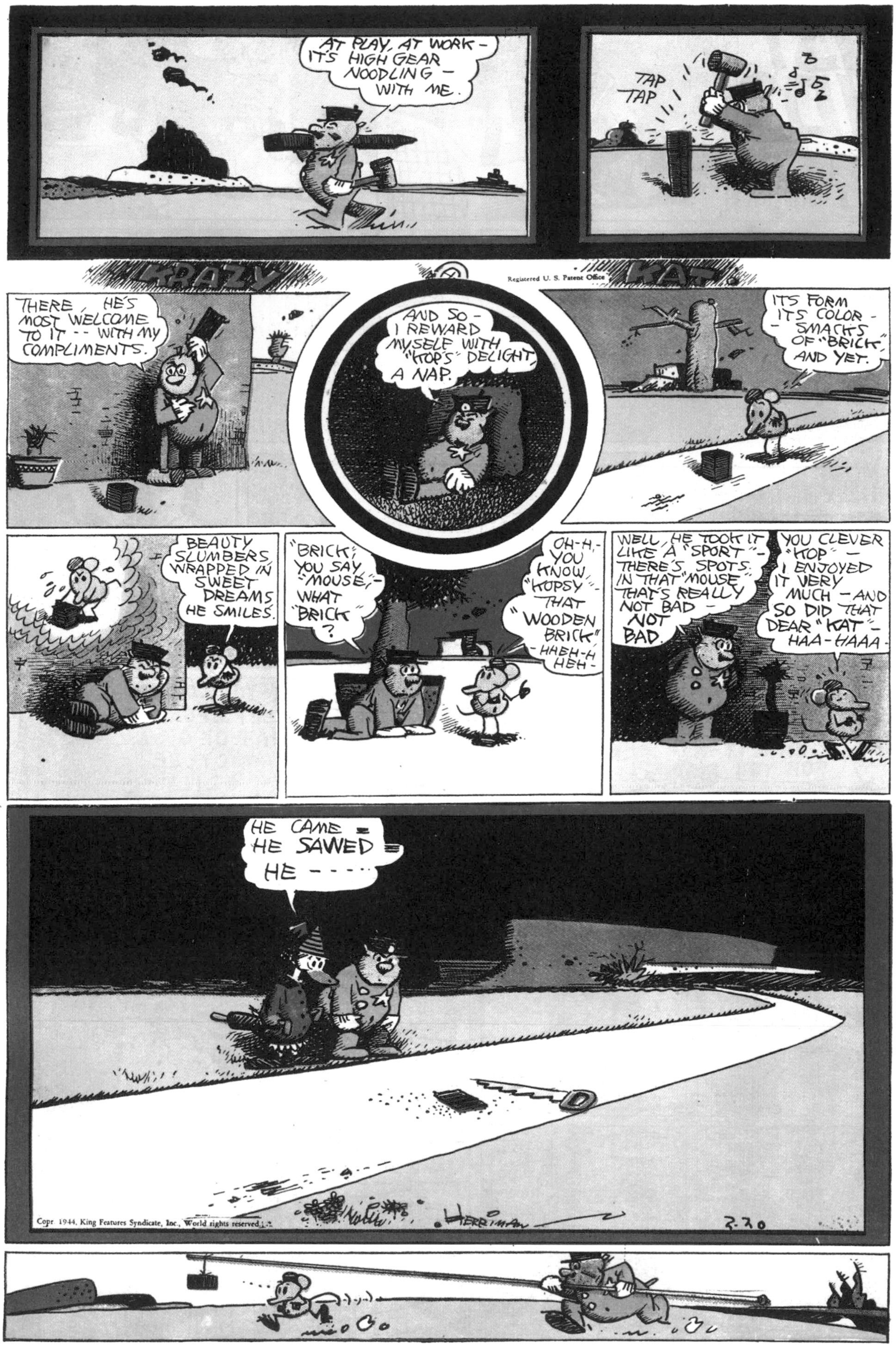
AT PLAY, AT WORK - ITS HIGH GEAR NOODLING - WITH ME.
TAP TAP
KRAZY KAT
Registered U. S. Patent Office
THERE, HE'S MOST WELCOME TO IT -- WITH MY COMPLIMENTS.
AND SO - I REWARD MYSELF WITH "KOP'S" DELIGHT, A NAP.
ITS FORM ITS COLOR - SMACKS OF "BRICK" AND YET.
BEAUTY SLUMBERS, WRAPPED IN SWEET DREAMS HE SMILES.
"BRICK", YOU SAY "MOUSE", - WHAT "BRICK" ?
OH-H, - YOU KNOW, "KOPSY" THAT "WOODEN BRICK" - HAEH-H HEH -
WELL, HE TOOK IT LIKE A "SPORT" - THERE'S "SPOTS" IN THAT "MOUSE" THAT'S REALLY NOT BAD - NOT BAD.
YOU CLEVER "KOP" - I ENJOYED IT VERY MUCH - AND SO DID THAT DEAR "KAT" - HAA-HAAA -
HE CAME = HE SAWED = HE - - - -
Copr 1944, King Features Syndicate, Inc., World rights reserved
HERRIMAN
2-20

February 20th, 1944.

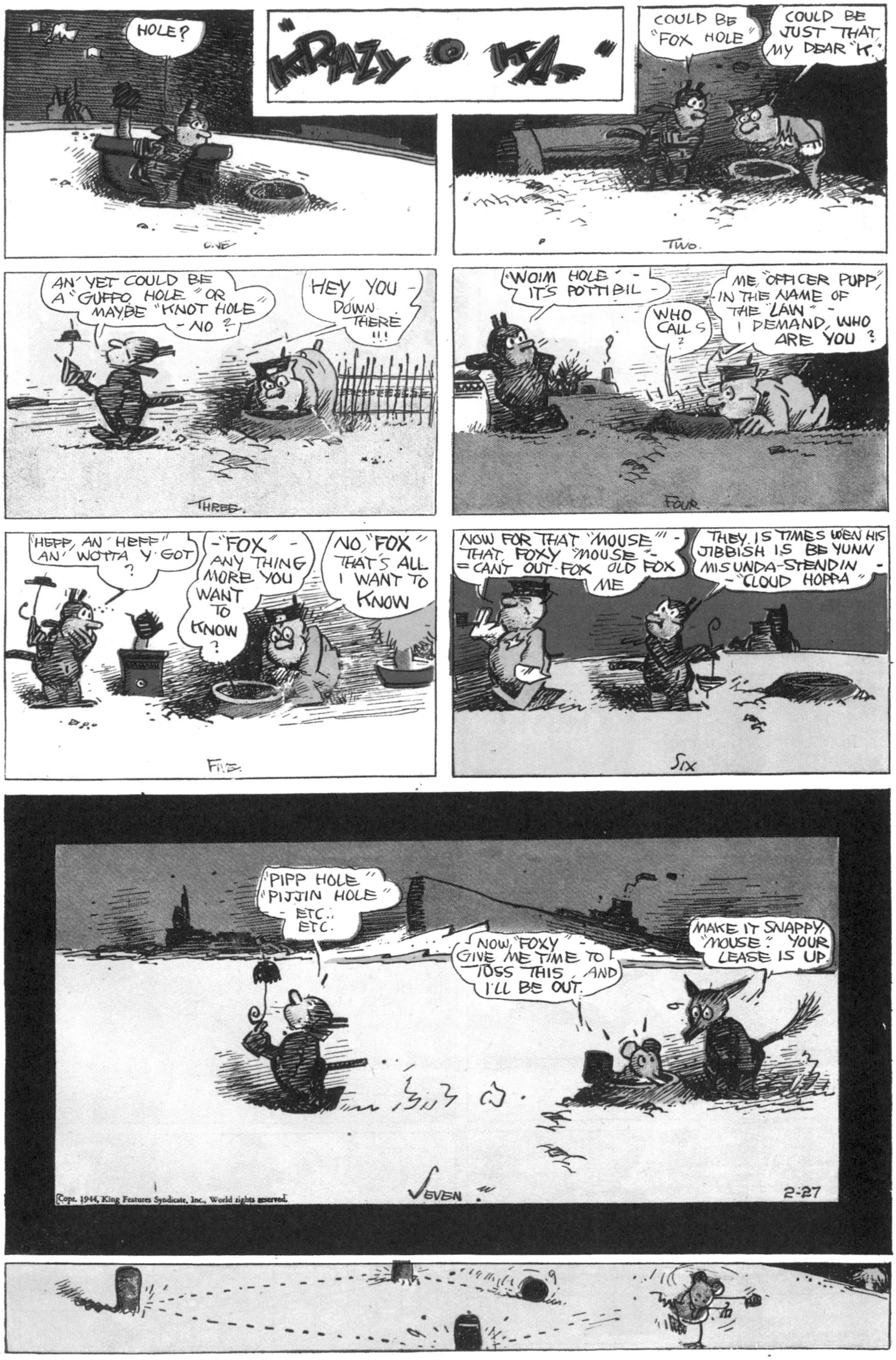
"KRAZY KAT"
HOLE?
ONE
COULD BE "FOX HOLE"
COULD BE JUST THAT MY DEAR "K."
TWO.
AN' YET COULD BE A "GUFFO HOLE" OR MAYBE "KNOT HOLE" - NO?
HEY YOU - DOWN THERE !!!
THREE.
"WOIM HOLE" - IT'S POTTIBIL -
WHO CALLS ?
ME, "OFFICER PUPP", IN THE NAME OF THE "LAW" - I DEMAND, WHO ARE YOU ?
FOUR
"HEFF, AN' HEFF" AN' WOTTA 'Y' GOT ?
- "FOX" - ANY THING MORE YOU WANT TO KNOW ?
NO, "FOX" THAT'S ALL I WANT TO KNOW
FIVE.
NOW FOR THAT "MOUSE" - THAT FOXY "MOUSE" - CAN'T OUT-FOX OLD FOX ME
THEY IS TIMES WEN HIS JIBBISH IS BE-YUNN MISUNDA-STENDIN - "CLOUD HOPPA"
SIX
"PIPP HOLE" "PIJJIN HOLE" - ETC., ETC.
NOW, "FOXY" GIVE ME TIME TO TOSS THIS AND I'LL BE OUT.
MAKE IT SNAPPY, "MOUSE." YOUR LEASE IS UP.
SEVEN.
Copr. 1944, King Features Syndicate, Inc., World rights reserved.
2-27

February 27th, 1944.

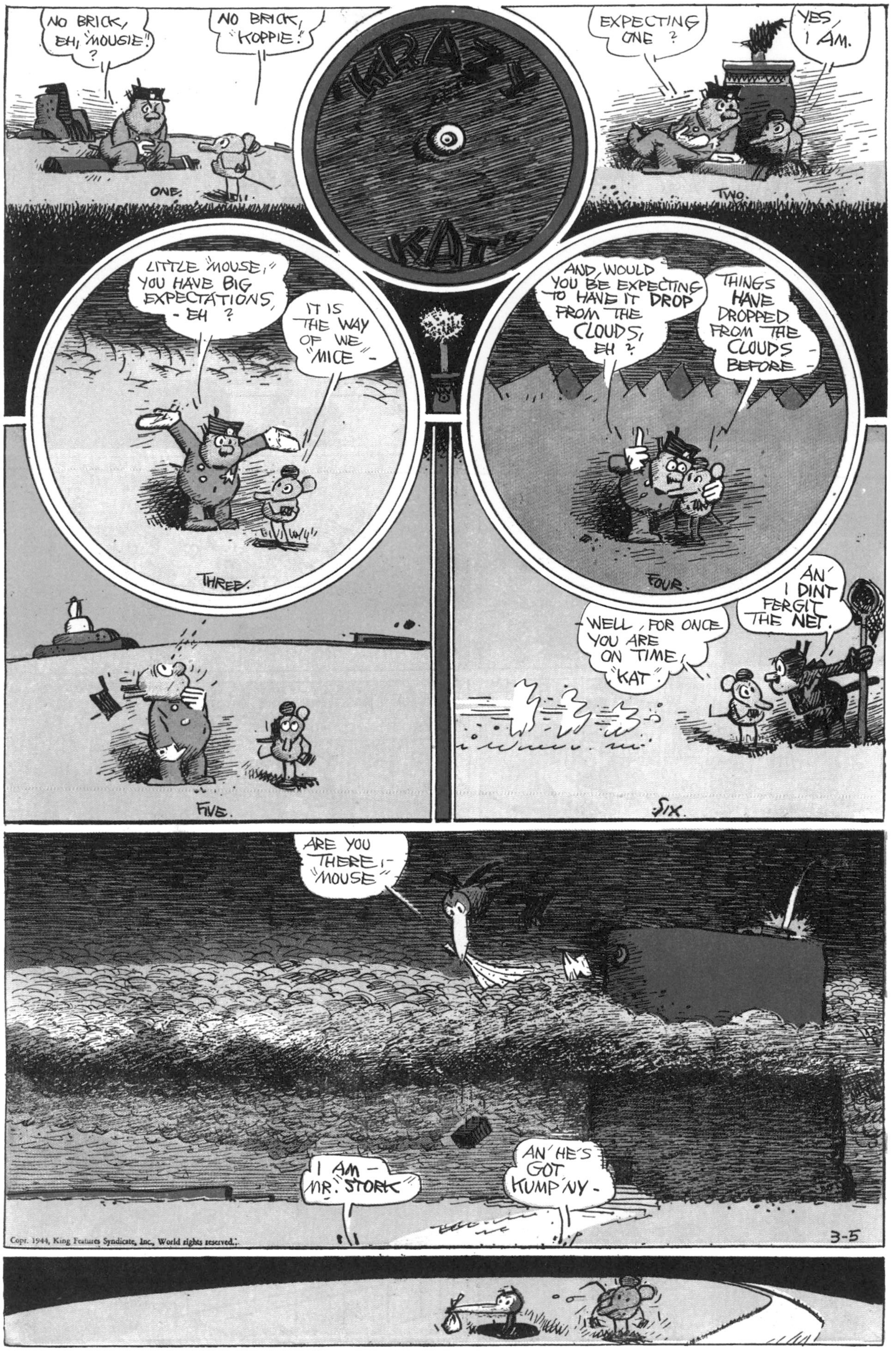

NO BRICK, EH, "MOUSIE"?
NO BRICK, "KOPPIE"
ONE.
"KRAZY KAT"
EXPECTING ONE ?
YES, I AM.
TWO.
LITTLE "MOUSE" YOU HAVE BIG EXPECTATIONS, - EH ?
IT IS THE WAY OF WE "MICE" -
THREE.
AND, WOULD YOU BE EXPECTING TO HAVE IT DROP FROM THE CLOUDS, EH ?
THINGS HAVE DROPPED FROM THE CLOUDS BEFORE
FOUR.
FIVE.
WELL, FOR ONCE YOU ARE ON TIME, "KAT"
AN' I DINT FERGIT THE NET.
SIX.
ARE YOU THERE, - "MOUSE"
I AM - MR. STORK
AN' HE'S GOT KUMP'NY -
Copr. 1944, King Features Syndicate, Inc., World rights reserved.
3-5

March 5th, 1944.

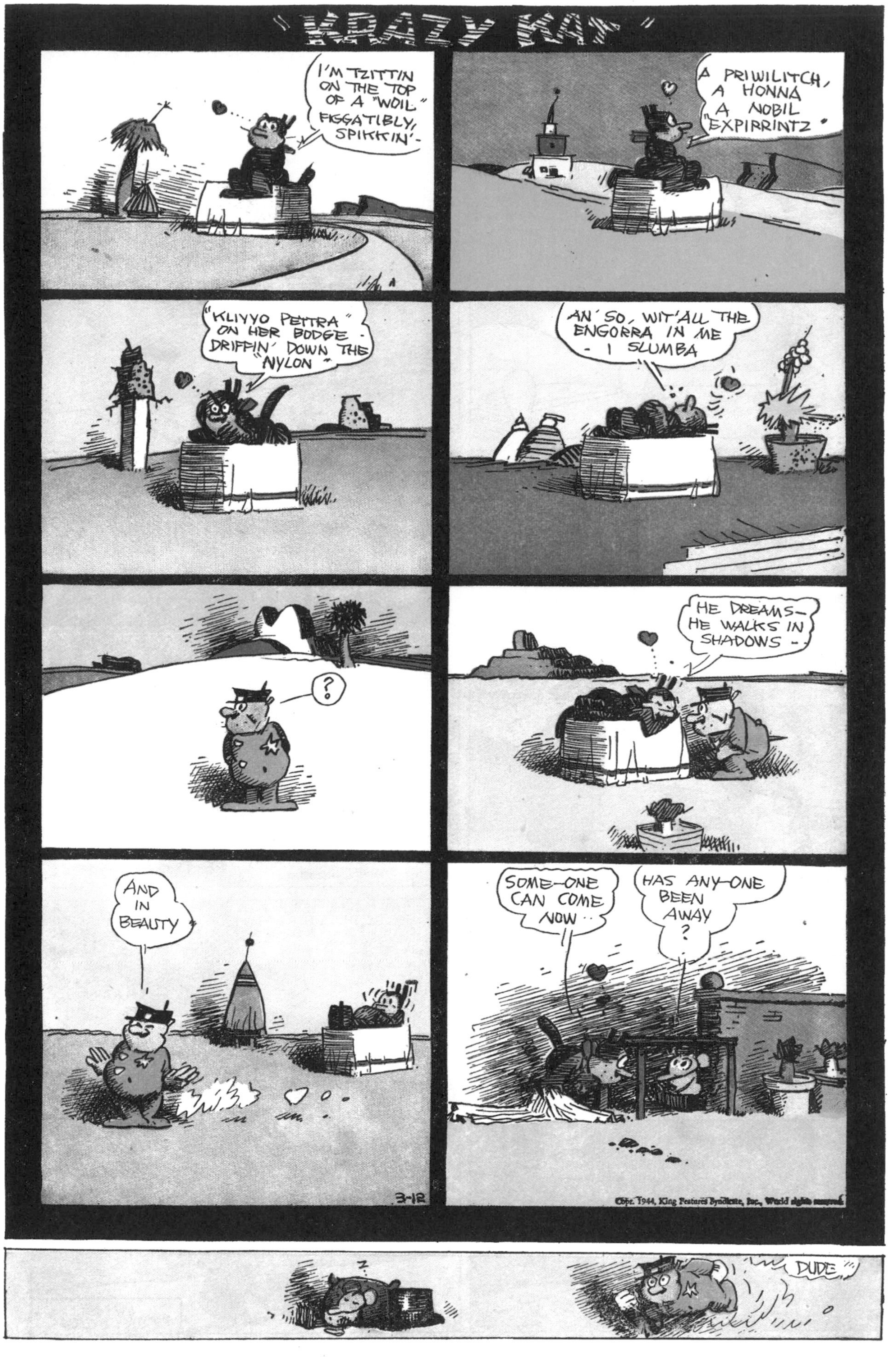
"KRAZY KAT"
I'M TZITTIN ON THE TOP OF A "WOIL" FIGGATIBLY, SPIKKIN' -
A PRIWILITCH, A HONNA A NOBIL "EXPIRRINTZ"
"KLIYYO PETTRA" ON HER BODGE - DRIFFIN' DOWN THE "NYLON"
AN' SO, WIT' ALL THE ENGORRA IN ME - I SLUMBA
?
HE DREAMS - HE WALKS IN SHADOWS -
AND IN BEAUTY
SOME-ONE CAN COME NOW
HAS ANY-ONE BEEN AWAY ?
3-12
©opr. 1944, King Features Syndicate, Inc., World rights reserved.
DUDE

March 12th, 1944.

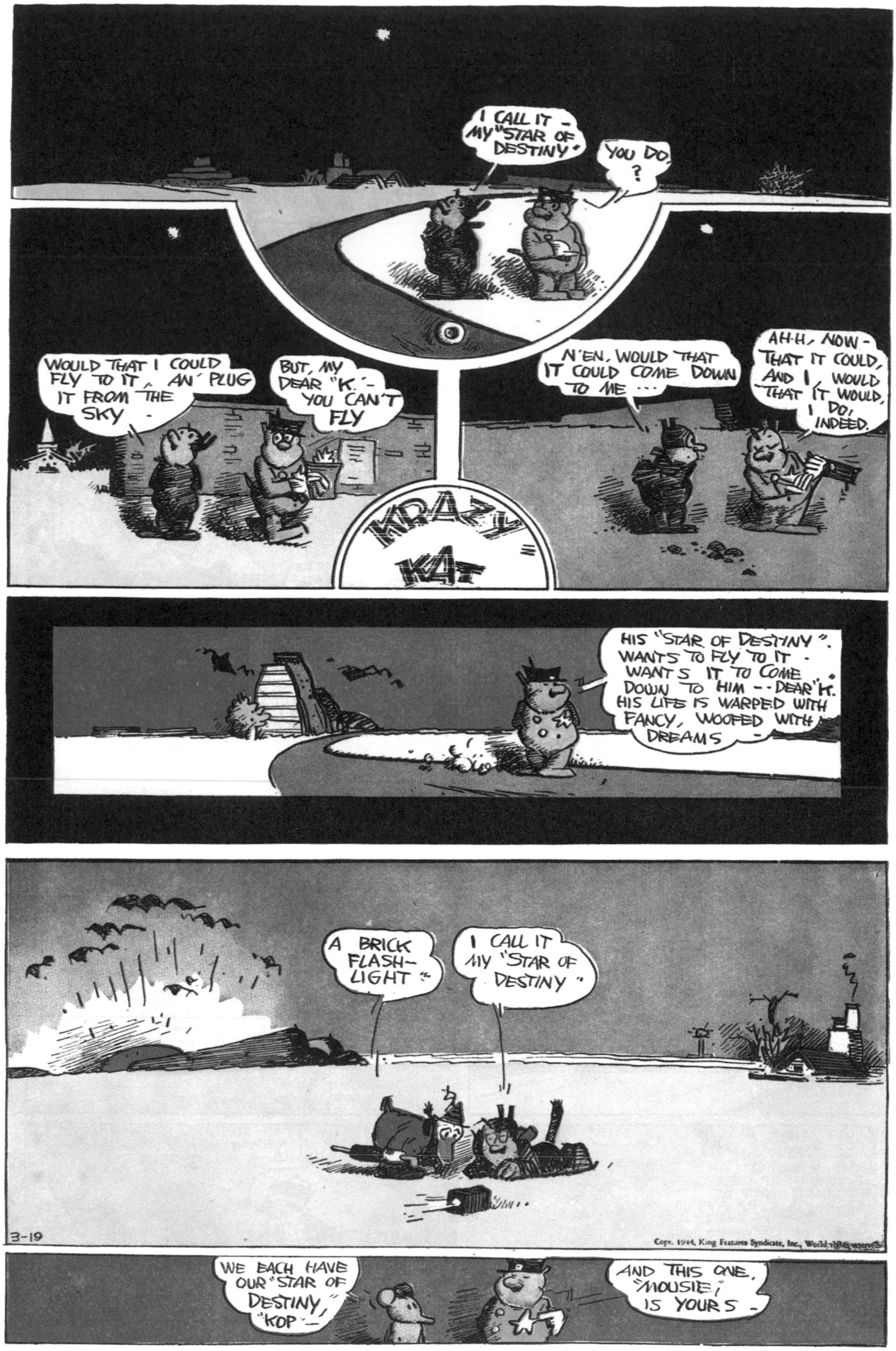
I CALL IT - MY "STAR OF DESTINY"
YOU DO ?
WOULD THAT I COULD FLY TO IT, AN' PLUG IT FROM THE SKY -
BUT, MY DEAR "K." - YOU CAN'T FLY
N'EN, WOULD THAT IT COULD COME DOWN TO ME ...
AH-H, NOW - THAT IT COULD, AND I, WOULD THAT IT WOULD, I DO, INDEED.
KRAZY KAT
HIS "STAR OF DESTINY". WANTS TO FLY TO IT - WANTS IT TO COME DOWN TO HIM -- DEAR "K." HIS LIFE IS WARPED WITH FANCY, WOOFED WITH DREAMS -
A BRICK FLASH-LIGHT
I CALL IT MY "STAR OF DESTINY"
3-19
Copr. 1944, King Features Syndicate, Inc., World rights reserved.
WE EACH HAVE OUR "STAR OF DESTINY," "KOP" -
AND THIS ONE, "MOUSIE," IS YOURS -

March 19th, 1944.

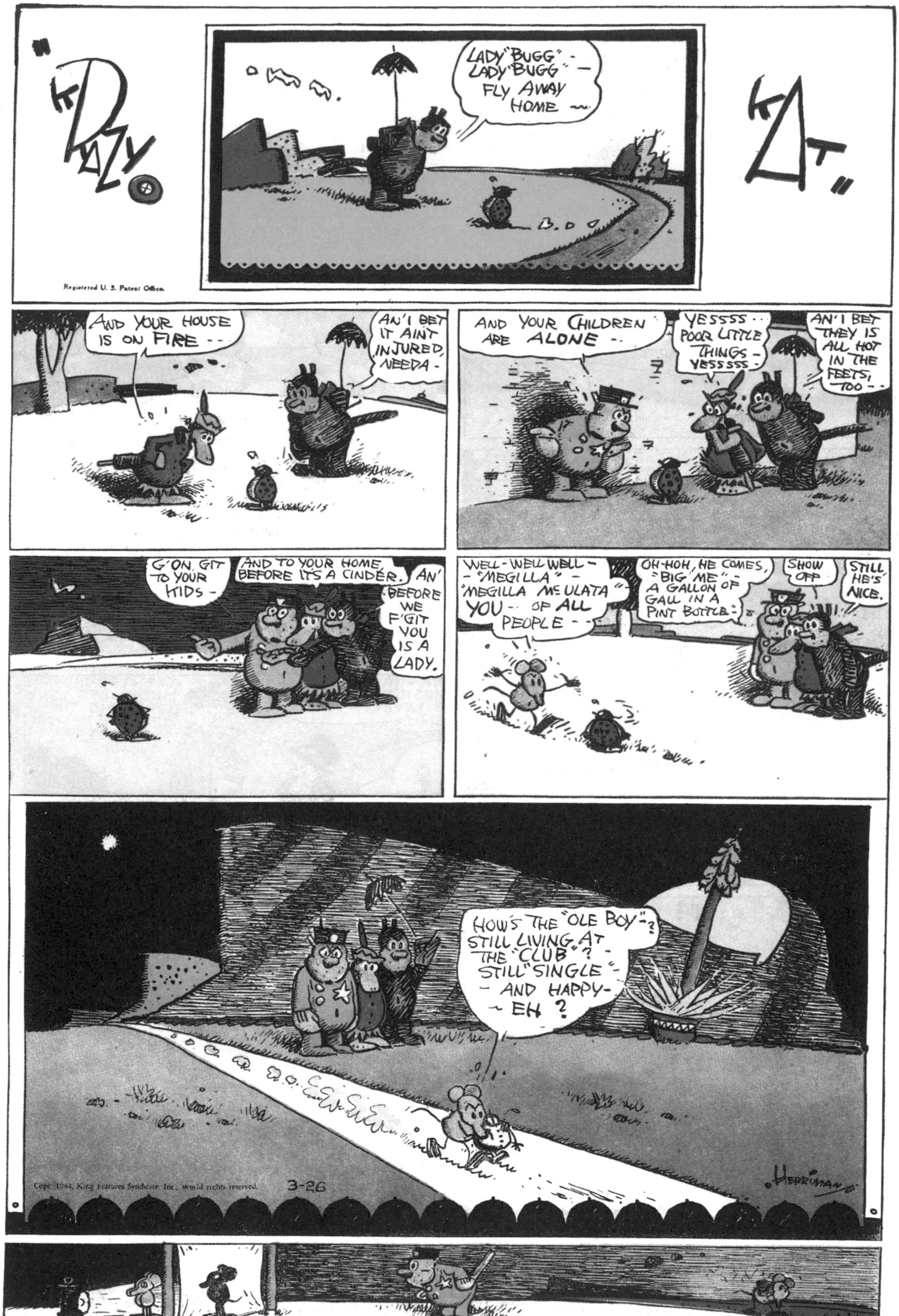
"KRAZY KAT"
Registered U. S. Patent Office.
LADY "BUGG" - LADY "BUGG" - FLY AWAY HOME --
AND YOUR HOUSE IS ON FIRE --
AN' I BET IT AINT INJURED, NEEDA -
AND YOUR CHILDREN ARE ALONE --
YESSSS -- POOR LITTLE THINGS - YESSSSS -
AN' I BET THEY IS ALL HOT IN THE FEETS, TOO -
G'ON, GIT TO YOUR KIDS -
AND TO YOUR HOME, BEFORE ITS A CINDER.
AN' BEFORE WE F'GIT YOU IS A LADY.
WELL - WELL WELL - - "MEGILLA" - "MEGILLA McULATA" - YOU -- OF ALL PEOPLE --
OH-HOH, HE COMES, - "BIG ME" - A GALLON OF GALL IN A PINT BOTTLE -
SHOW OFF
STILL HE'S NICE.
HOW'S THE "OLE BOY" -? STILL LIVING AT THE "CLUB"? - STILL "SINGLE" - - AND HAPPY - - EH ?
Copr. 1944, King Features Syndicate, Inc., World rights reserved.
3-26
HERRIMAN

March 26th, 1944.

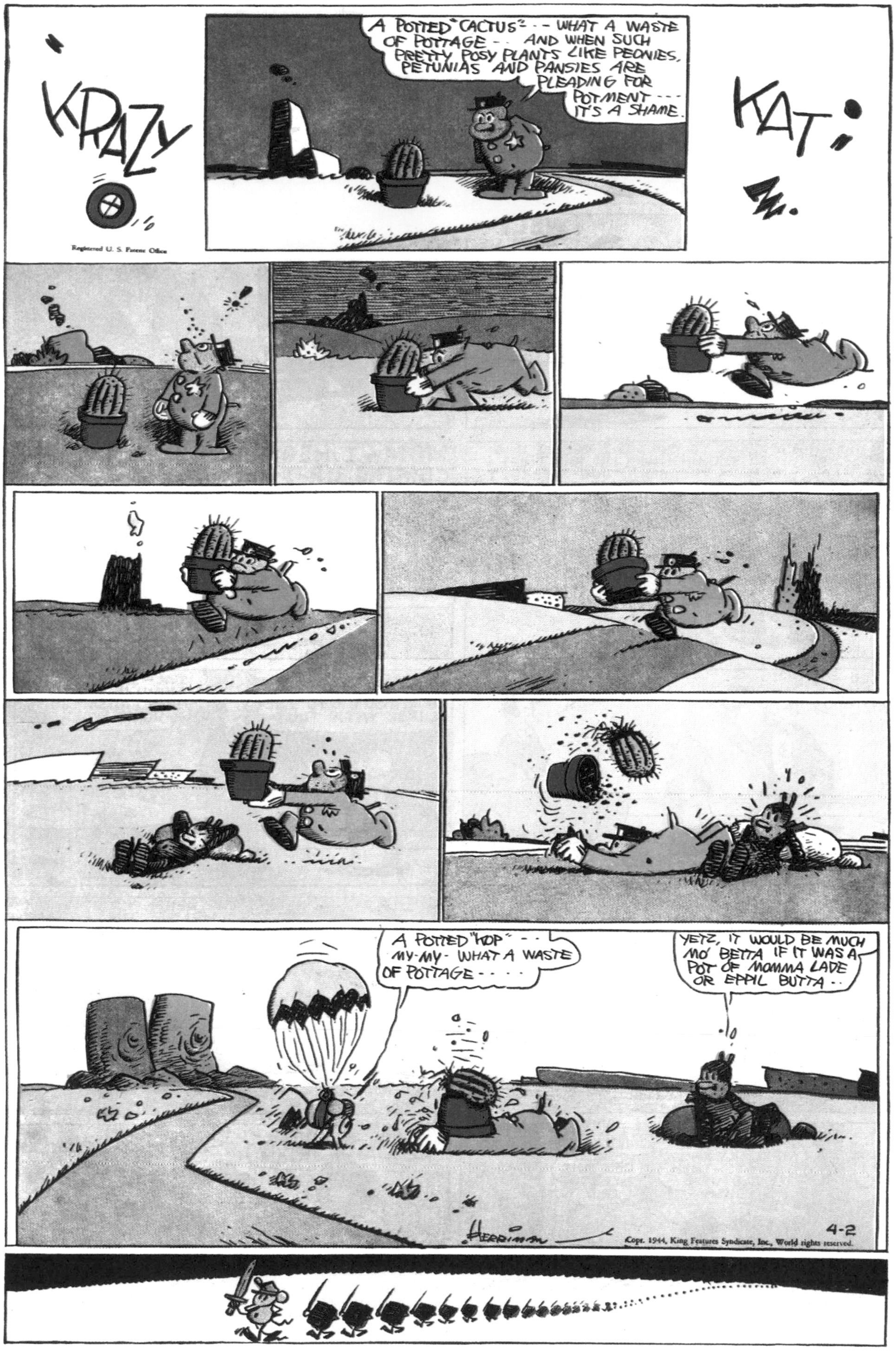
KRAZY KAT
Registered U. S. Patent Office
A POTTED "CACTUS" - - WHAT A WASTE OF POTTAGE - - AND WHEN SUCH PRETTY POSY PLANTS LIKE PEONIES, PETUNIAS AND PANSIES ARE PLEADING FOR POTMENT - - - IT'S A SHAME
A POTTED "KOP" - - MY-MY - WHAT A WASTE OF POTTAGE - - -
YETZ, IT WOULD BE MUCH MO' BETTA IF IT WAS A POT OF MOMMA LADE OR EPPIL BUTTA - -
HERRIMAN
4-2
Copr. 1944, King Features Syndicate, Inc., World rights reserved.

April 2nd, 1944.

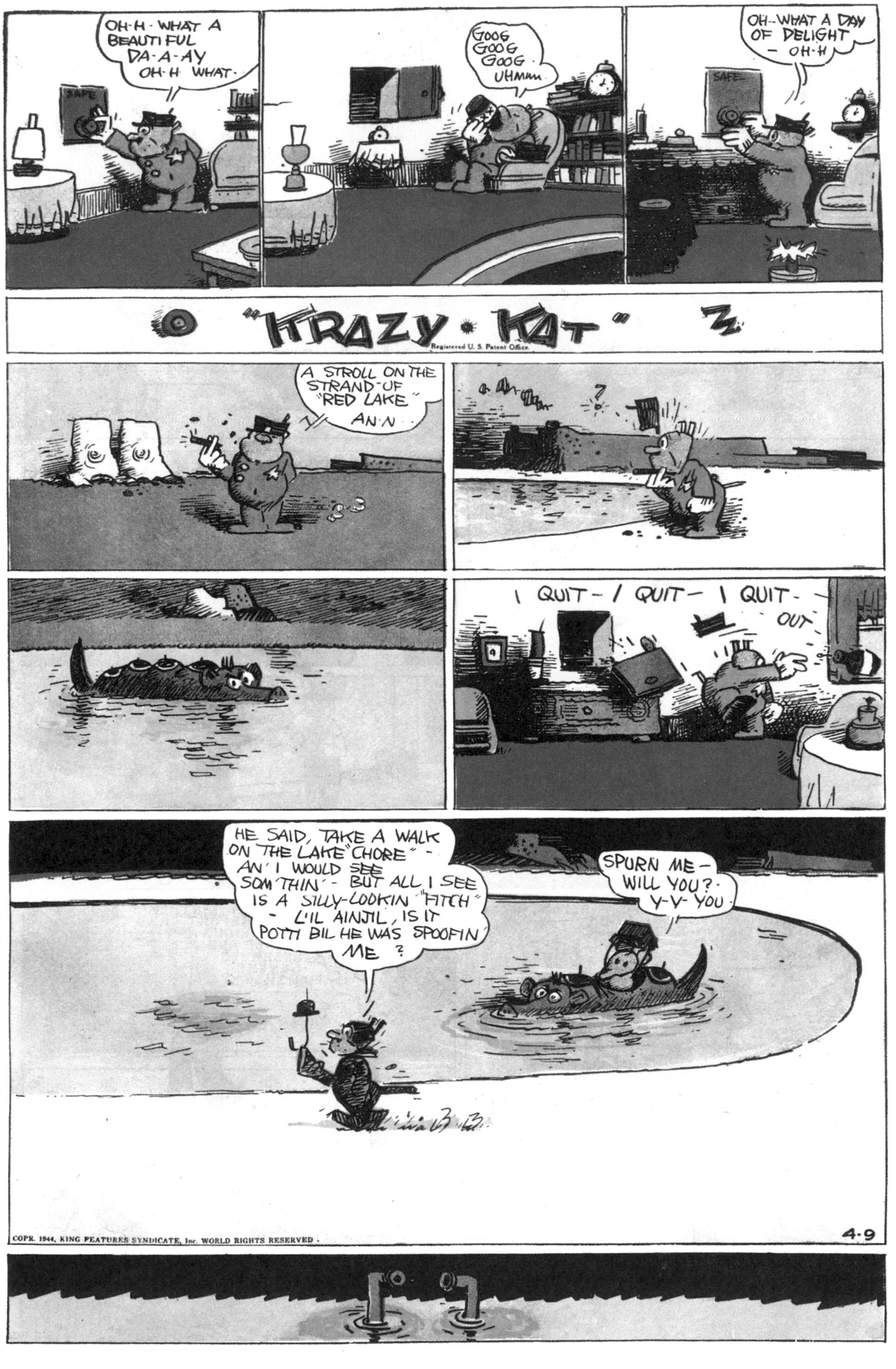
OH-H- WHAT A BEAUTIFUL DA-A-AY OH-H WHAT-
SAFE
GOOG GOOG GOOG UHMMM
OH-WHAT A DAY OF DELIGHT - OH-H
SAFE
"KRAZY KAT"
Registered U. S. Patent Office.
A STROLL ON THE STRAND OF "RED LAKE" AN-N
I QUIT - I QUIT - I QUIT - OUT
HE SAID, TAKE A WALK ON THE LAKE "CHORE" - AN' I WOULD SEE SOM'THIN' - BUT ALL I SEE IS A SILLY-LOOKIN "FITCH" - L'IL AINJIL, IS IT POTTI BIL HE WAS SPOOFIN' ME ?
SPURN ME - WILL YOU? - Y-Y-YOU
COPR. 1944, KING FEATURES SYNDICATE, Inc. WORLD RIGHTS RESERVED.
4-9

April 9th, 1944.

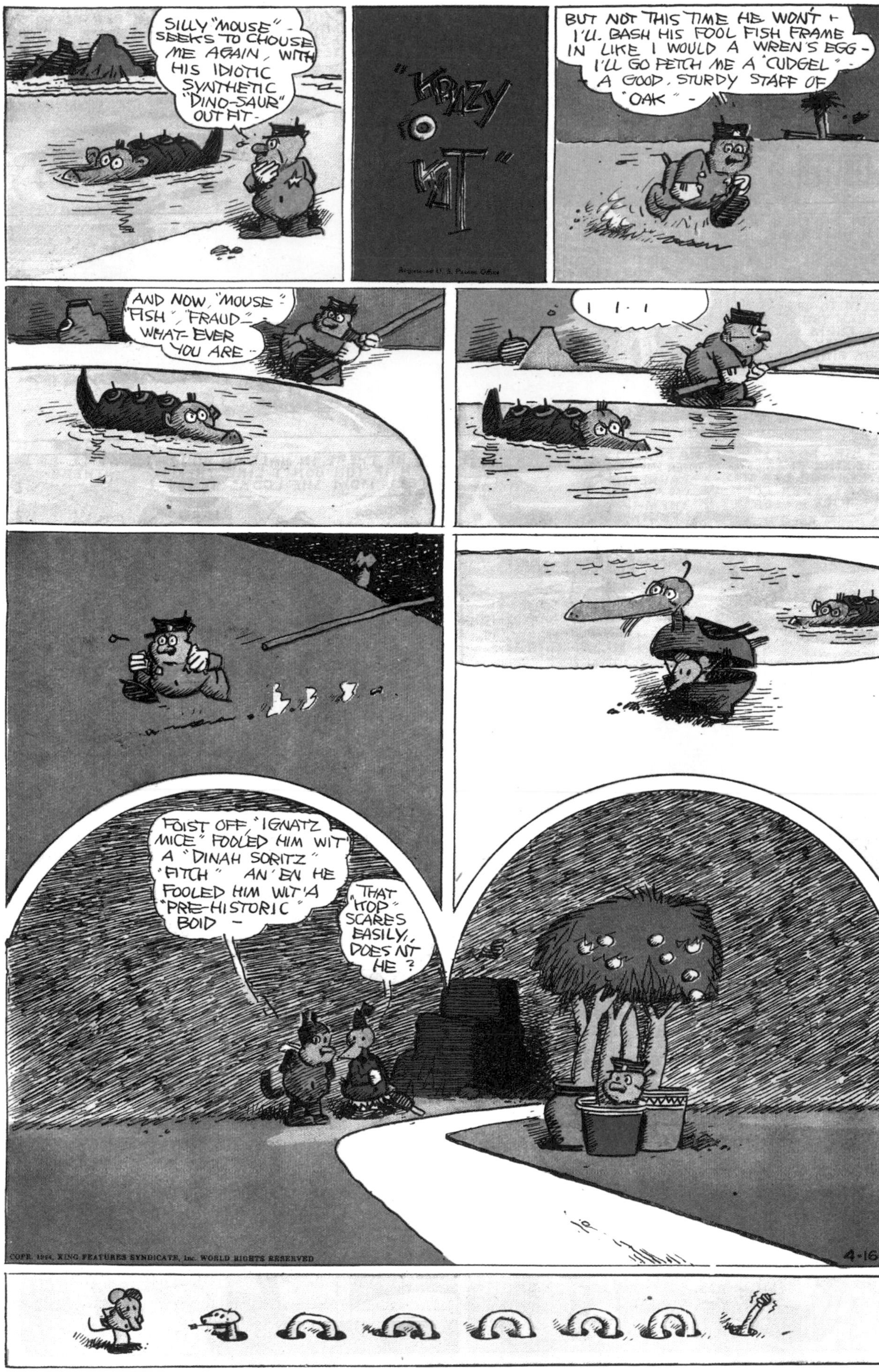
SILLY "MOUSE" - SEEKS TO CHOUSE ME AGAIN, WITH HIS IDIOTIC SYNTHETIC "DINO-SAUR" OUTFIT -
"KRAZY KAT"
BUT NOT THIS TIME HE WON'T - I'LL BASH HIS FOOL FISH FRAME IN LIKE I WOULD A WREN'S EGG - I'LL GO FETCH ME A "CUDGEL" - A GOOD, STURDY STAFF OF "OAK" -
AND NOW, "MOUSE" "FISH" "FRAUD" - WHAT-EVER YOU ARE -
! ! - !
FOIST OFF, "IGNATZ MICE" FOOLED HIM WIT A "DINAH SORITZ" "FITCH" AN' EN HE FOOLED HIM WIT' A "PRE-HISTORIC" BOID -
THAT "KOP" SCARES EASILY, DOES N'T HE ?
COPR. 1944, KING FEATURES SYNDICATE, Inc. WORLD RIGHTS RESERVED
4-16

April 16th, 1944.

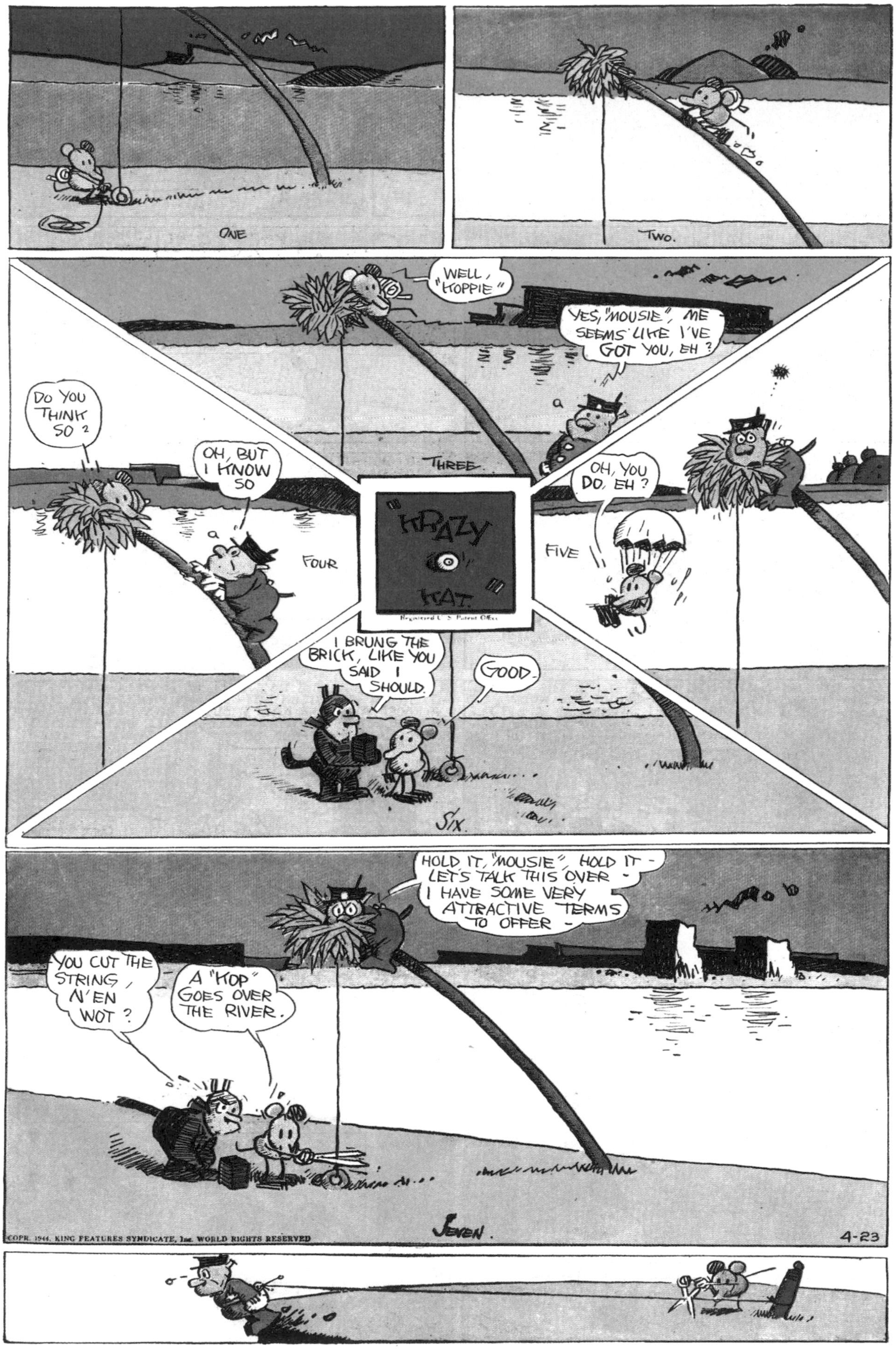

ONE
TWO.
WELL, "KOPPIE"
YES, "MOUSIE", ME SEEMS LIKE I'VE GOT YOU, EH?
THREE
DO YOU THINK SO?
OH, BUT I KNOW SO
FOUR
"KRAZY KAT"
Registered U. S. Patent Office
OH, YOU DO, EH?
FIVE
I BRUNG THE BRICK, LIKE YOU SAID I SHOULD.
GOOD.
SIX
HOLD IT, "MOUSIE", HOLD IT - LET'S TALK THIS OVER - I HAVE SOME VERY ATTRACTIVE TERMS TO OFFER -
YOU CUT THE STRING, N'EN WOT?
A "KOP" GOES OVER THE RIVER.
COPR. 1944, KING FEATURES SYNDICATE, Inc. WORLD RIGHTS RESERVED
SEVEN.
4-23

April 23rd, 1944.

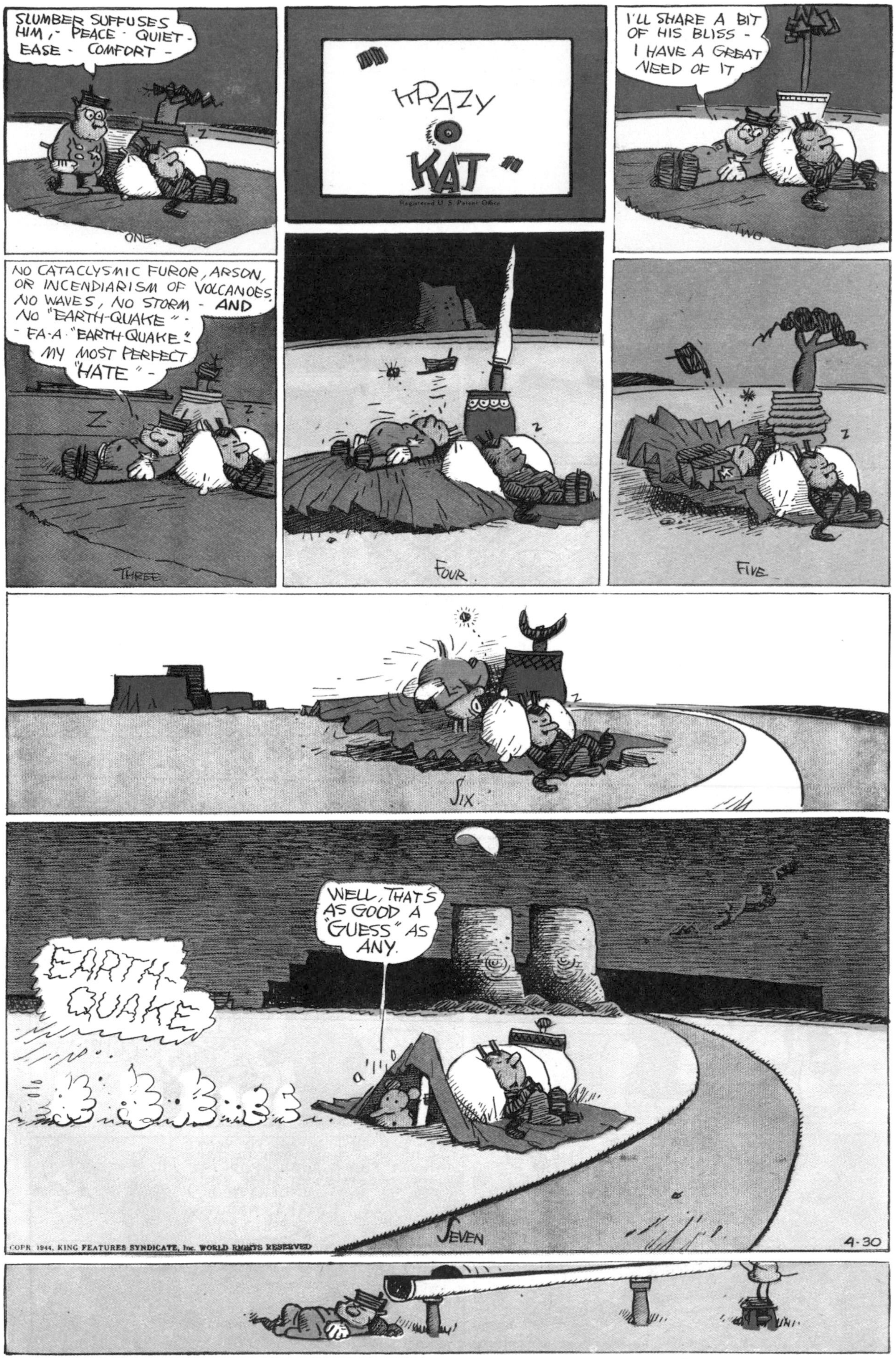
SLUMBER SUFFUSES HIM, - PEACE - QUIET - EASE - COMFORT -
ONE
KRAZY KAT
Registered U. S. Patent Office
I'LL SHARE A BIT OF HIS BLISS - I HAVE A GREAT NEED OF IT
TWO
NO CATACLYSMIC FUROR, ARSON, OR INCENDIARISM OF VOLCANOES, NO WAVES, NO STORM - AND NO "EARTH-QUAKE" - - FA-A "EARTH-QUAKE" MY MOST PERFECT "HATE" -
THREE
FOUR
FIVE
SIX
EARTH-QUAKE
WELL, THAT'S AS GOOD A "GUESS" AS ANY.
SEVEN
COPR. 1944, KING FEATURES SYNDICATE, Inc. WORLD RIGHTS RESERVED
4-30

April 30th, 1944.

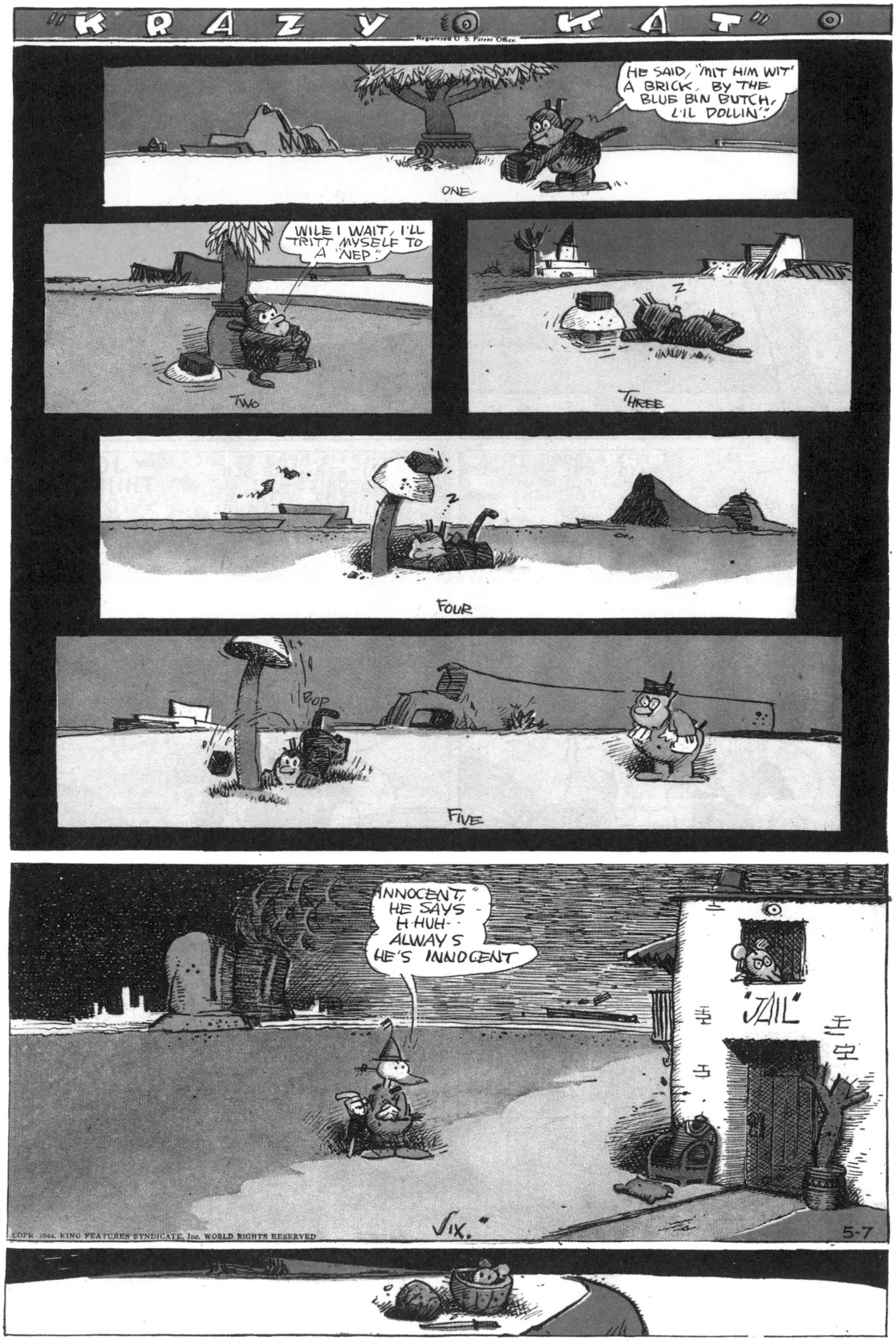
"KRAZY KAT"
Registered U. S. Patent Office.
HE SAID, "HIT HIM WIT' A BRICK, BY THE BLUE BIN BUTCH, L'IL DOLLIN'."
ONE
WILE I WAIT, I'LL TRITT MYSELF TO A 'NEP.'
TWO
Z
THREE
Z
FOUR
BOP
FIVE
"INNOCENT," HE SAYS - H HUH - ALWAY S HE'S INNOCENT
"JAIL"
COPR. 1944, KING FEATURES SYNDICATE, Inc. WORLD RIGHTS RESERVED
SIX."
5-7

May 7th, 1944.

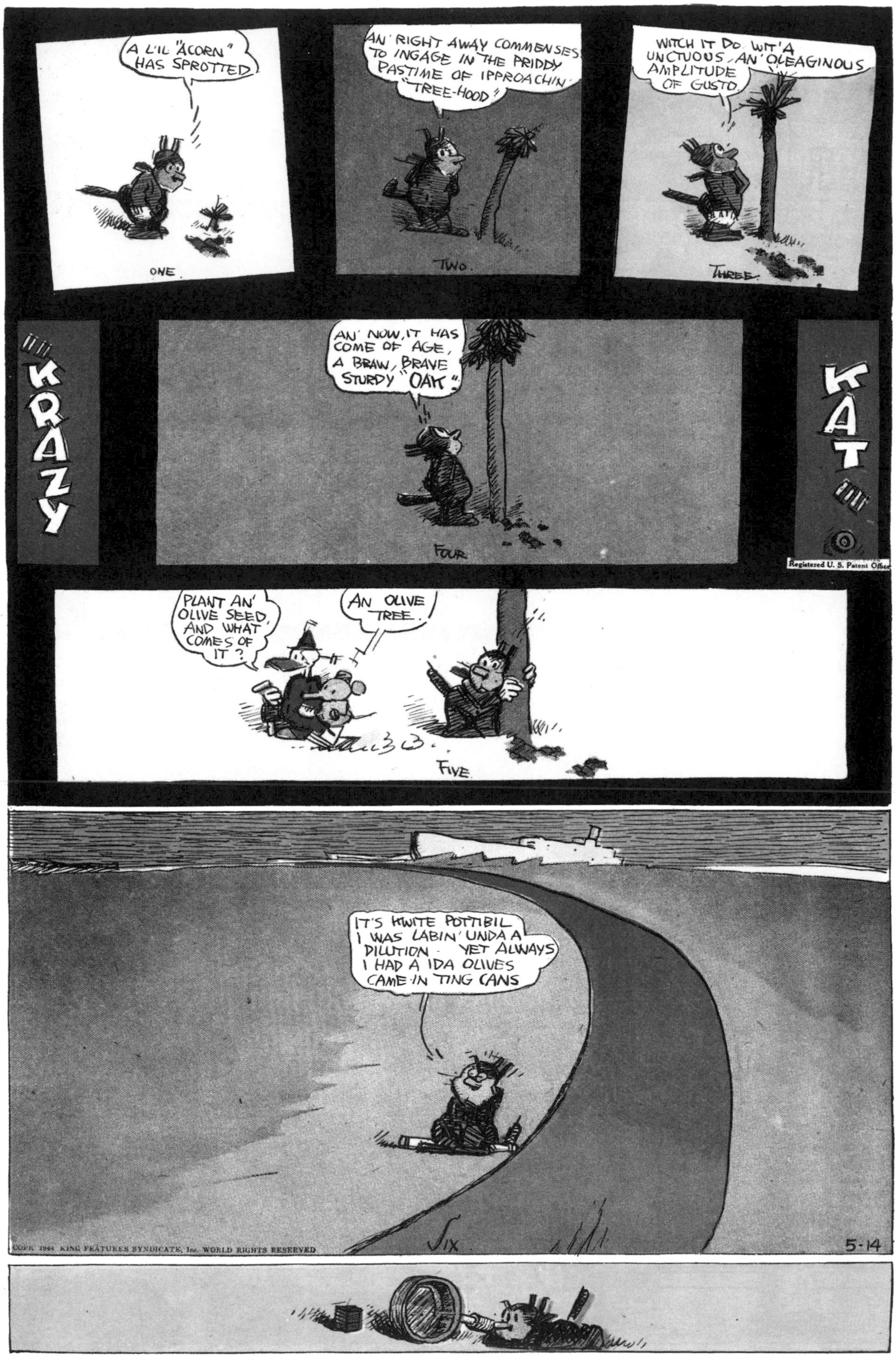

A L'IL "ACORN" HAS SPROTTED.
ONE
AN' RIGHT AWAY COMMENSES TO INGAGE IN THE PRIDDY PASTIME OF IPPROACHIN' "TREE-HOOD".
TWO.
WITCH IT DO, WIT'A UNCTUOUS, AN' OLEAGINOUS AMPLITUDE OF GUSTO.
THREE
KRAZY
AN' NOW, IT HAS COME OF AGE, A BRAW, BRAVE STURDY "OAK".
FOUR
KAT
Registered U. S. Patent Office
PLANT AN' OLIVE SEED, AND WHAT COMES OF IT?
AN OLIVE TREE.
FIVE
IT'S KWITE POTTIBIL I WAS LABIN' UNDA A DILUTION - YET ALWAYS I HAD A IDA OLIVES CAME IN TING CANS
COPR. 1944 KING FEATURES SYNDICATE, Inc. WORLD RIGHTS RESERVED
SIX
5-14

May 14th, 1944.

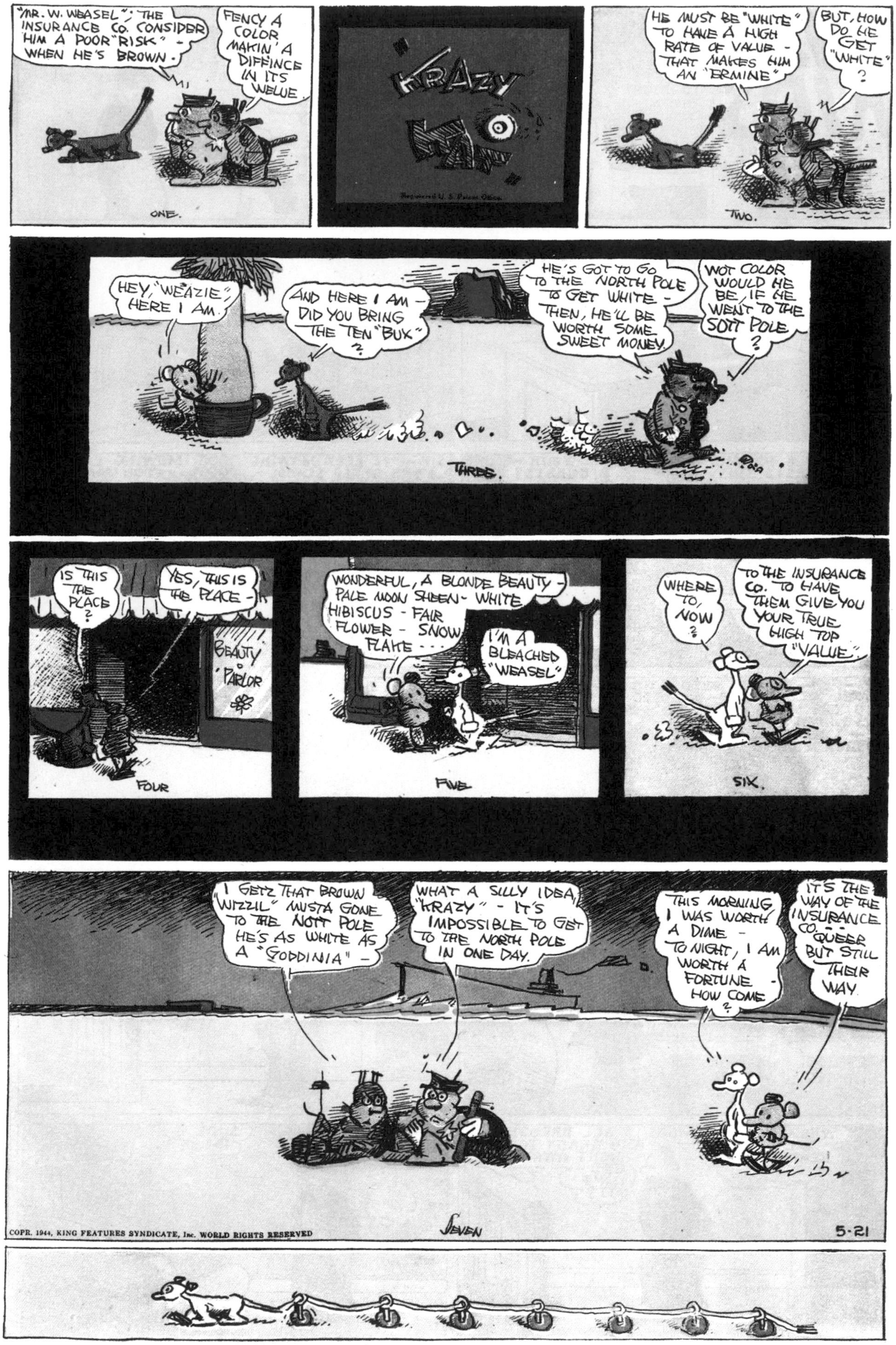
"MR. W. WEASEL", THE INSURANCE CO. CONSIDER HIM A POOR "RISK" - WHEN HE'S BROWN.
FENCY A COLOR MAKIN' A DIFFINCE IN ITS WELUE
ONE.
KRAZY KAT
HE MUST BE "WHITE" TO HAVE A HIGH RATE OF VALUE - THAT MAKES HIM AN "ERMINE"
BUT, HOW DO HE GET "WHITE" ?
TWO.
HEY, "WEAZIE", HERE I AM.
AND HERE I AM - DID YOU BRING THE TEN "BUX" ?
HE'S GOT TO GO TO THE NORTH POLE TO GET WHITE - THEN, HE'LL BE WORTH SOME SWEET MONEY.
WOT COLOR WOULD HE BE, IF HE WENT TO THE SOTT POLE ?
THREE.
IS THIS THE PLACE ?
YES, THIS IS THE PLACE -
BEAUTY PARLOR
FOUR
WONDERFUL, A BLONDE BEAUTY - PALE MOON SHEEN - WHITE HIBISCUS - FAIR FLOWER - SNOW FLAKE - - -
I'M A BLEACHED "WEASEL"
FIVE
WHERE TO, NOW ?
TO THE INSURANCE CO. TO HAVE THEM GIVE YOU YOUR TRUE HIGH TOP "VALUE".
SIX.
I GETZ THAT BROWN "WIZZIL" MUSTA GONE TO THE NOTT POLE HE'S AS WHITE AS A "GODDINIA" -
WHAT A SILLY IDEA, "KRAZY" - IT'S IMPOSSIBLE TO GET TO THE NORTH POLE IN ONE DAY.
THIS MORNING I WAS WORTH A DIME - TO NIGHT, I AM WORTH A FORTUNE - HOW COME ?
IT'S THE WAY OF THE INSURANCE CO. - - - QUEER BUT STILL THEIR WAY.
COPR. 1944, KING FEATURES SYNDICATE, Inc. WORLD RIGHTS RESERVED
SEVEN
5-21

May 21st, 1944.

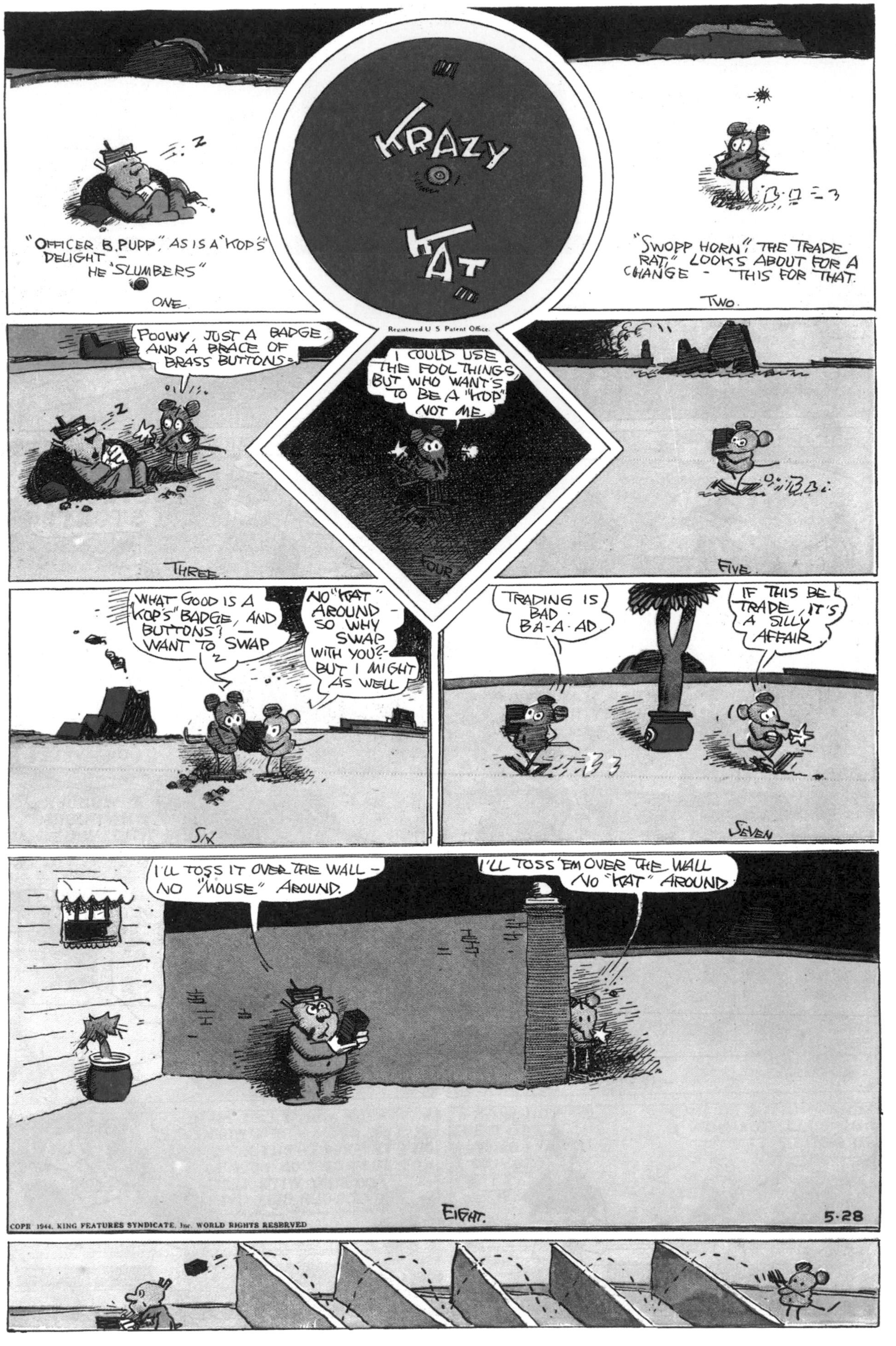
KRAZY KAT
Registered U. S. Patent Office.
"OFFICER B. PUPP," AS IS A "KOP'S" DELIGHT – HE "SLUMBERS"
ONE
"SWOPP HORN," THE TRADE RAT," LOOKS ABOUT FOR A CHANGE – THIS FOR THAT.
TWO
POOWY, JUST A BADGE, AND A BRACE OF BRASS BUTTONS=
THREE
I COULD USE THE FOOL THINGS, BUT WHO WANT'S TO BE A "KOP" NOT ME
FOUR
FIVE
WHAT GOOD IS A "KOP'S" BADGE, AND BUTTONS? – WANT TO SWAP
NO "KAT" AROUND – SO WHY SWAP WITH YOU? – BUT I MIGHT AS WELL
SIX
TRADING IS BAD BA-A-AD
IF THIS BE TRADE, IT'S A SILLY AFFAIR
SEVEN
I'LL TOSS IT OVER THE WALL – NO "MOUSE" AROUND.
I'LL TOSS 'EM OVER THE WALL NO "KAT" AROUND
EIGHT.
5·28
COPR 1944, KING FEATURES SYNDICATE, Inc. WORLD RIGHTS RESERVED

May 28th, 1944.

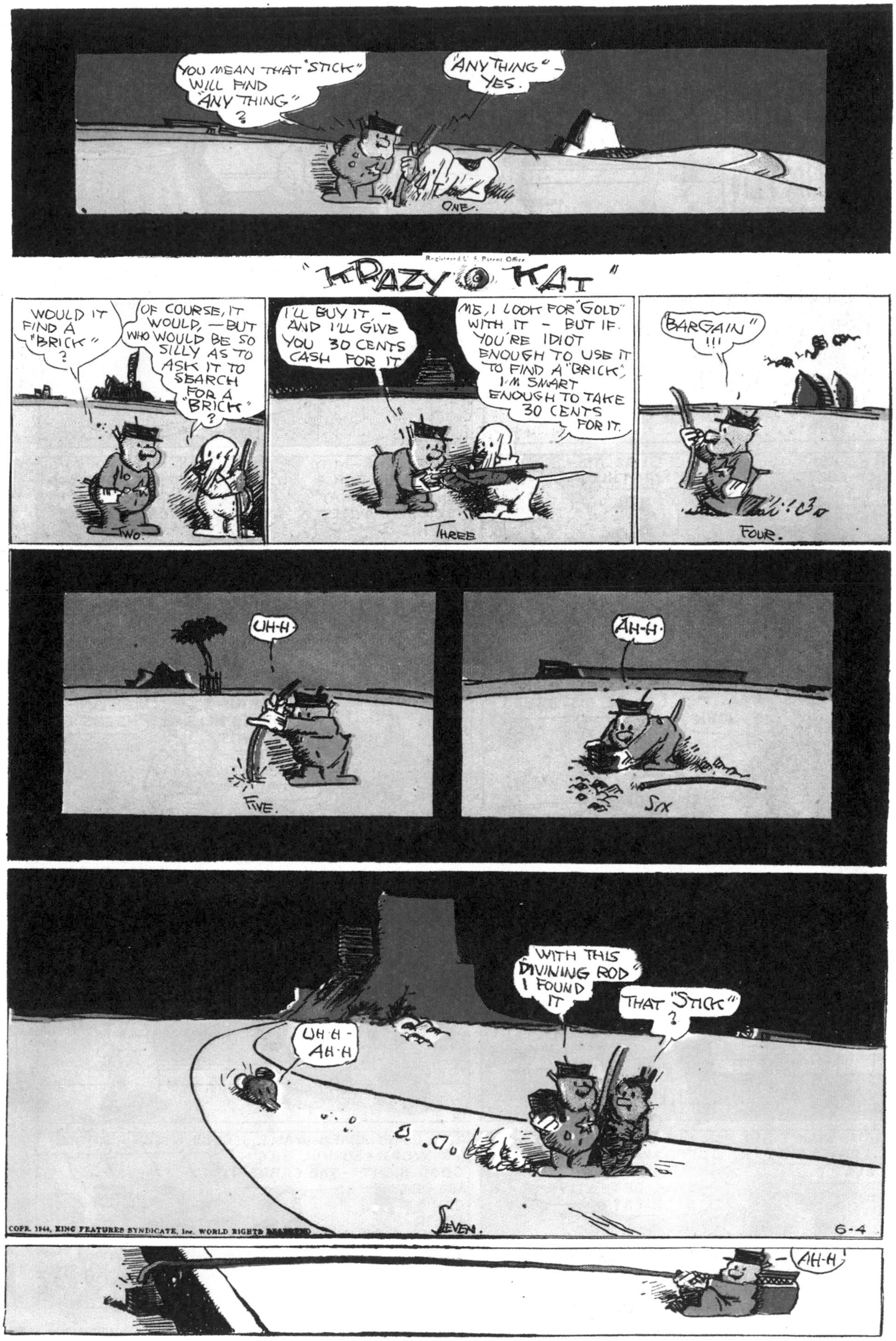
YOU MEAN THAT "STICK" WILL FIND "ANY THING" ?
"ANY THING" — YES.
ONE.
Registered U.S. Patent Office
"KRAZY KAT"
WOULD IT FIND A "BRICK" ?
OF COURSE, IT WOULD, — BUT WHO WOULD BE SO SILLY AS TO ASK IT TO SEARCH FOR A "BRICK" ?
TWO.
I'LL BUY IT — AND I'LL GIVE YOU 30 CENTS CASH FOR IT
ME, I LOOK FOR "GOLD" WITH IT — BUT IF YOU'RE IDIOT ENOUGH TO USE IT TO FIND A "BRICK", I'M SMART ENOUGH TO TAKE 30 CENTS FOR IT.
THREE
"BARGAIN" !!!
FOUR.
UH-H
FIVE.
AH-H
SIX
WITH THIS DIVINING ROD I FOUND IT
THAT "STICK" ?
UH H — AH-H
COPR. 1944, KING FEATURES SYNDICATE, Inc. WORLD RIGHTS RESERVED
SEVEN.
6-4
AH-H

June 4th, 1944.

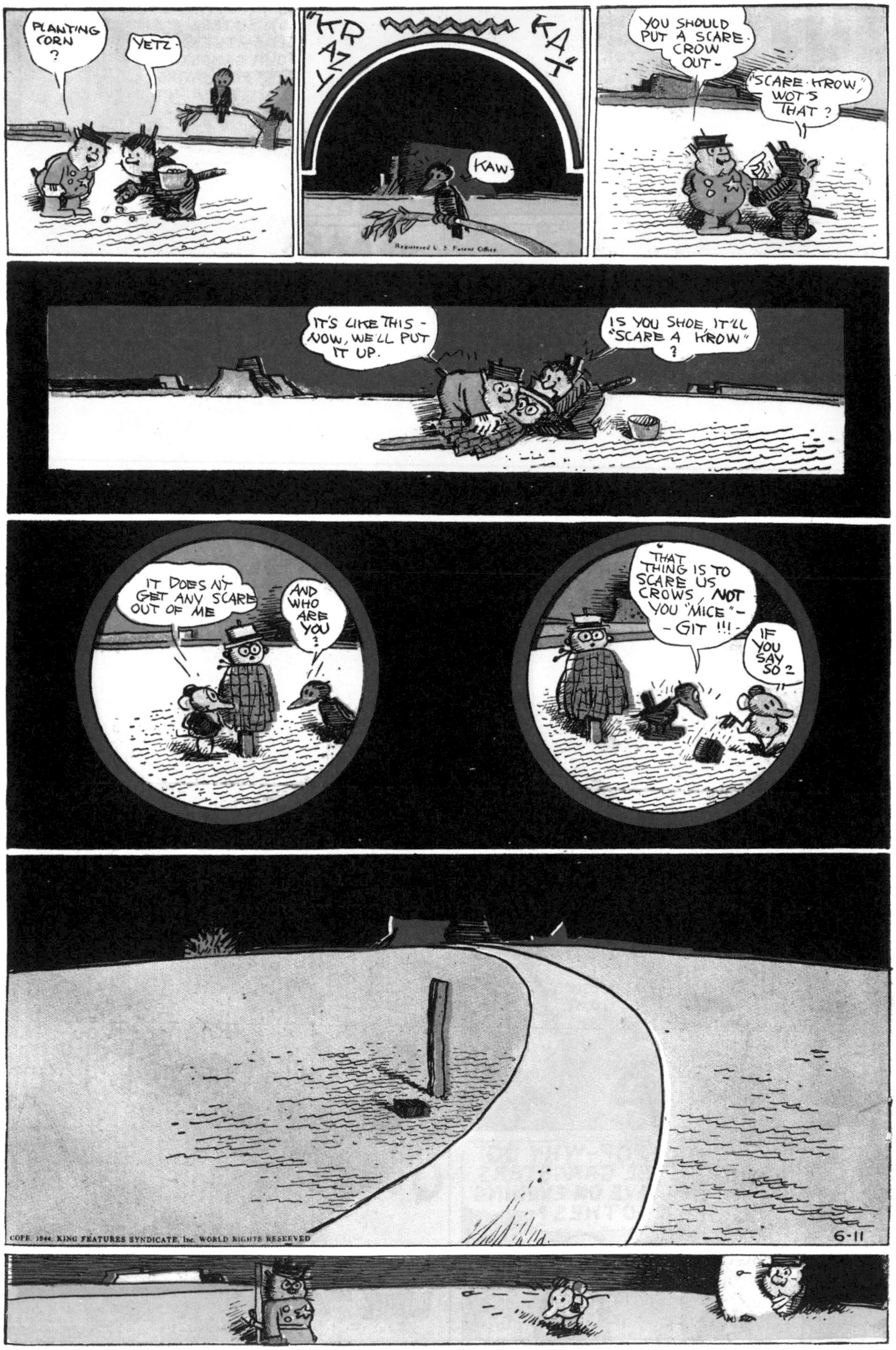
PLANTING CORN ?
YETZ.
"KRAZY KAT"
KAW.
Registered U. S. Patent Office
YOU SHOULD PUT A SCARE. CROW OUT -
"SCARE-KROW," WOT'S THAT ?
IT'S LIKE THIS - NOW, WE'LL PUT IT UP.
IS YOU SHOE, IT'LL "SCARE A KROW" ?
IT DOES N'T GET ANY SCARE OUT OF ME
AND WHO ARE YOU ?
THAT THING IS TO SCARE US CROWS, NOT YOU "MICE" - - GIT !!!
IF YOU SAY SO ?
COPR. 1944, KING FEATURES SYNDICATE, Inc. WORLD RIGHTS RESERVED
6-11

June 11th, 1944.

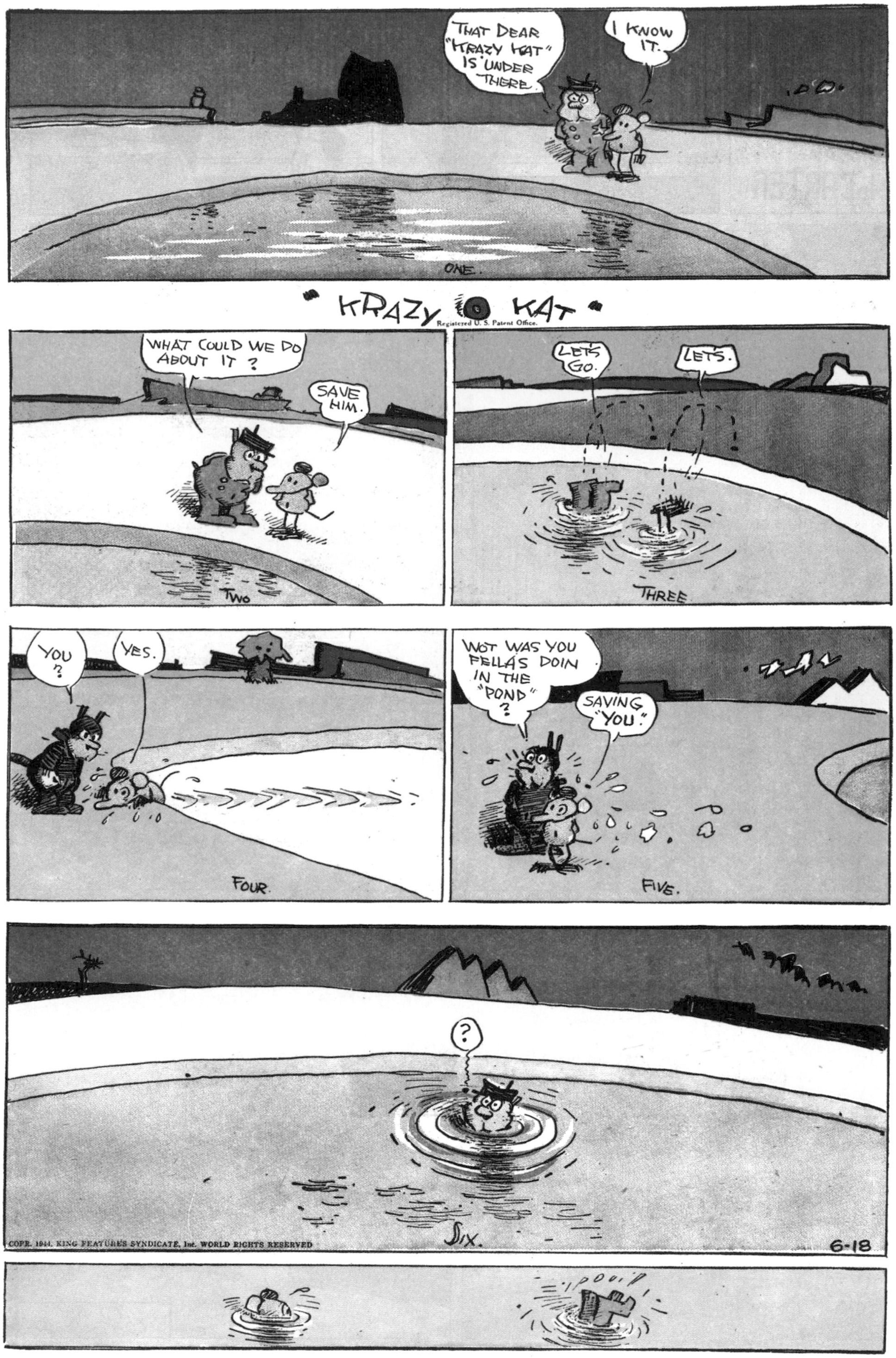
THAT DEAR "KRAZY KAT" IS UNDER THERE.
I KNOW IT.
ONE.
"KRAZY KAT"
Registered U. S. Patent Office.
WHAT COULD WE DO ABOUT IT ?
SAVE HIM.
TWO
LET'S GO.
LETS.
THREE
YOU ?
YES.
FOUR.
WOT WAS YOU FELLA'S DOIN IN THE "POND" ?
SAVING "YOU".
FIVE.
?
COPR. 1944, KING FEATURES SYNDICATE, Inc. WORLD RIGHTS RESERVED
SIX.
6-18

June 18th, 1944.

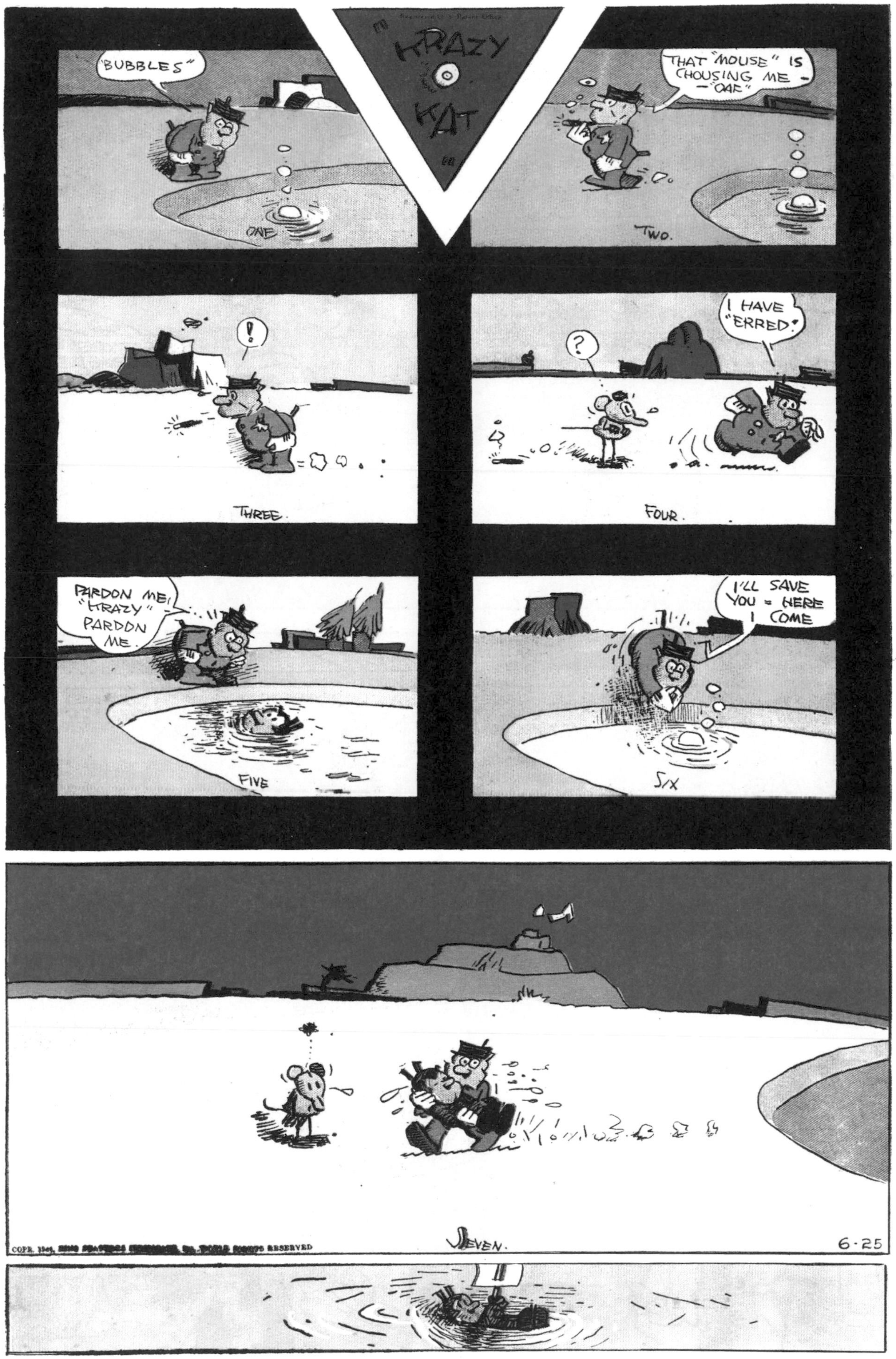
KRAZY KAT
"BUBBLES"
ONE
THAT "MOUSE" IS CHOUSING ME - "OAF"
TWO.
!
THREE.
?
I HAVE "ERRED."
FOUR.
PARDON ME. "KRAZY" PARDON ME.
FIVE
I'LL SAVE YOU - HERE I COME
SIX
SEVEN.
6·25

June 25th, 1944.

WALT DISNEY

May 6, 1944

Dear Miss Herriman:

I am taking this opportunity to express to
you my sorrow at the untimely loss of your
father.

As one of the pioneers in the cartoon business, his contributions to it were so numer-
ous that they may well be never estimated.

His unique style of drawing and his amazing
gallery of characters not only brought a new
type of humor to the American public but made
him a source of inspiration to thousands of
artists.

My staff joins me in paying tribute to his
memory.

Sincerely,

Walt Disney

Miss Mabel Herriman
2217 Maravilla Drive
Hollywood, California

WED:KC

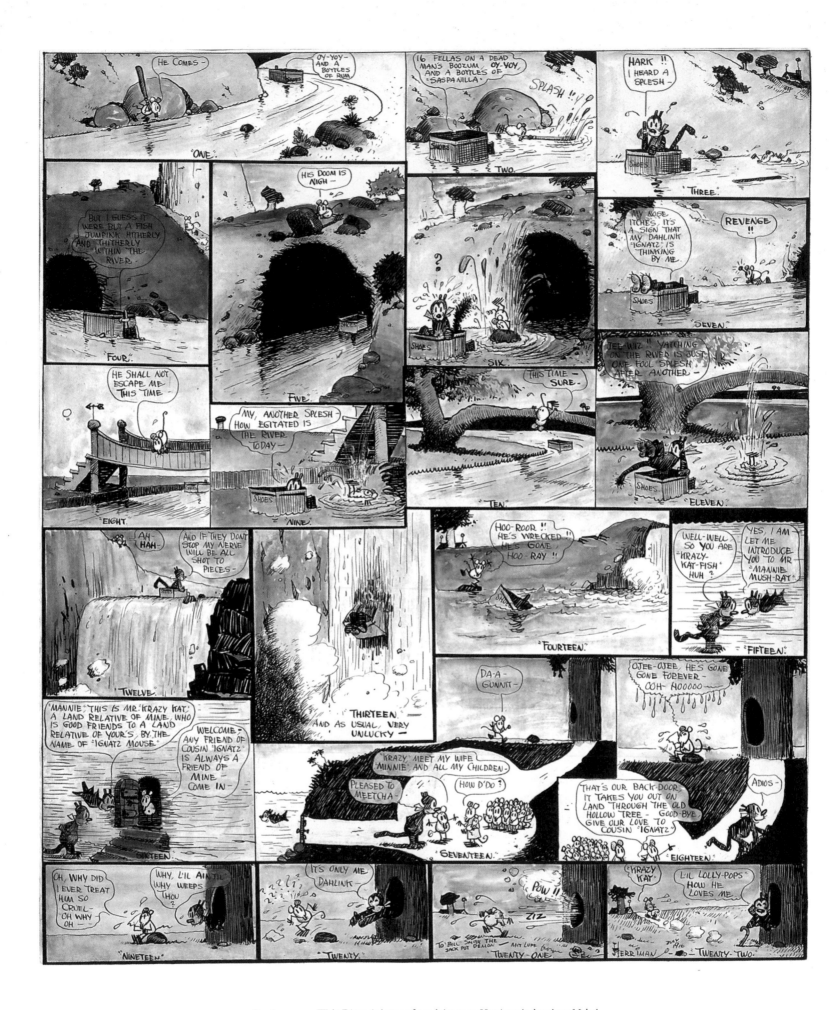

Previous page: Walt Disney's letter of condolence to Herriman's daughter Mabel.
Mabel's rather hastily-written reply, preserved in the Disney archives, reads: "May 9, 1944. Dear Mr. Disney and Staff — I want to thank you for your kind letter of sympathy.
Your expression of tribute and admiration for Dad means a great deal to me at this time. Sincerely, Mabel Herriman."
Courtesy of Geppi's Entertainment Museum.

Above: Hand-colored original drawing for the May 14th, 1916 strip. Courtesy of Peter Merolo.

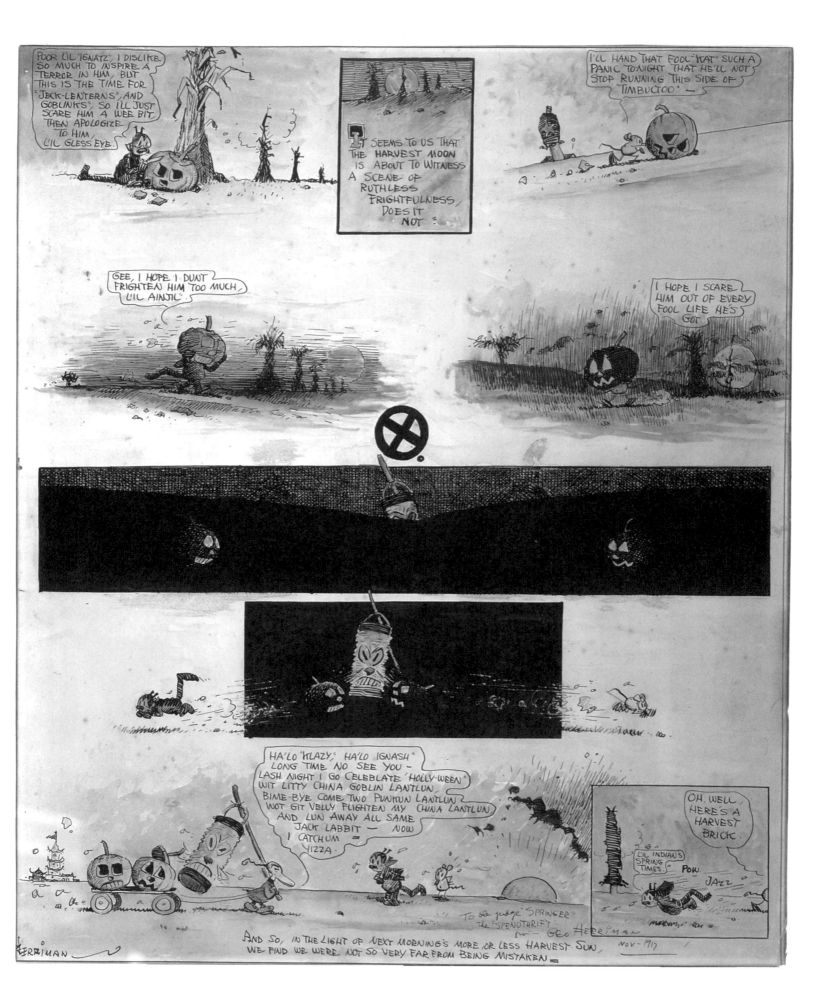

Original hand-colored drawing for strip originally published November 11, 1917, 19" x 22".
Collection of Patrick McDonnell, photo by Jack Abraham.
Special thanks to the Hammer Museum, Los Angeles, CA.

Original hand-colored drawing for strip originally published June 30, 1918, in decorated frame.
Courtesy of Centre National de la Bande Dessinée et de l'Image.

Hand-colored original presentation drawing for Morris Weiss, 1936. Weiss was a comic book artist, assisting Lank Leonard on "Mickey Finn" as well as acting as artist for many teens/girls features in the 1940s and 50s. He also, apparently, collected toys. Courtesy of Ulrich Merkl, current collection of Craig McCracken.

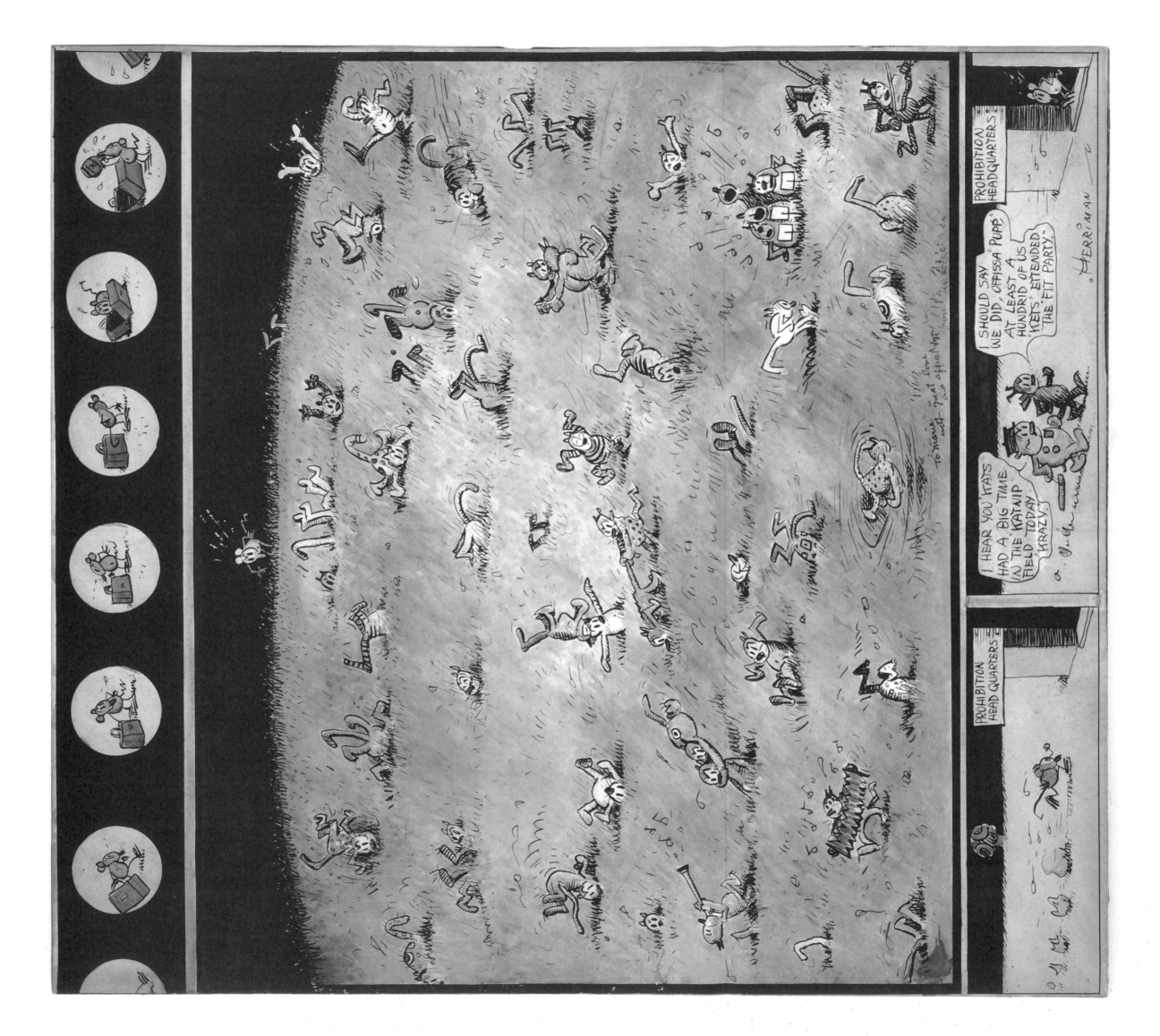

Hand-colored original drawing for the page originally published May 18, 1919. Collection of Craig Englund, photo by Robert Wedemeyer.

Original size 22 x 19 inches. Though already reproduced in our 1939–1940 volume, the editors believe this greatly improved scan warrants republication.

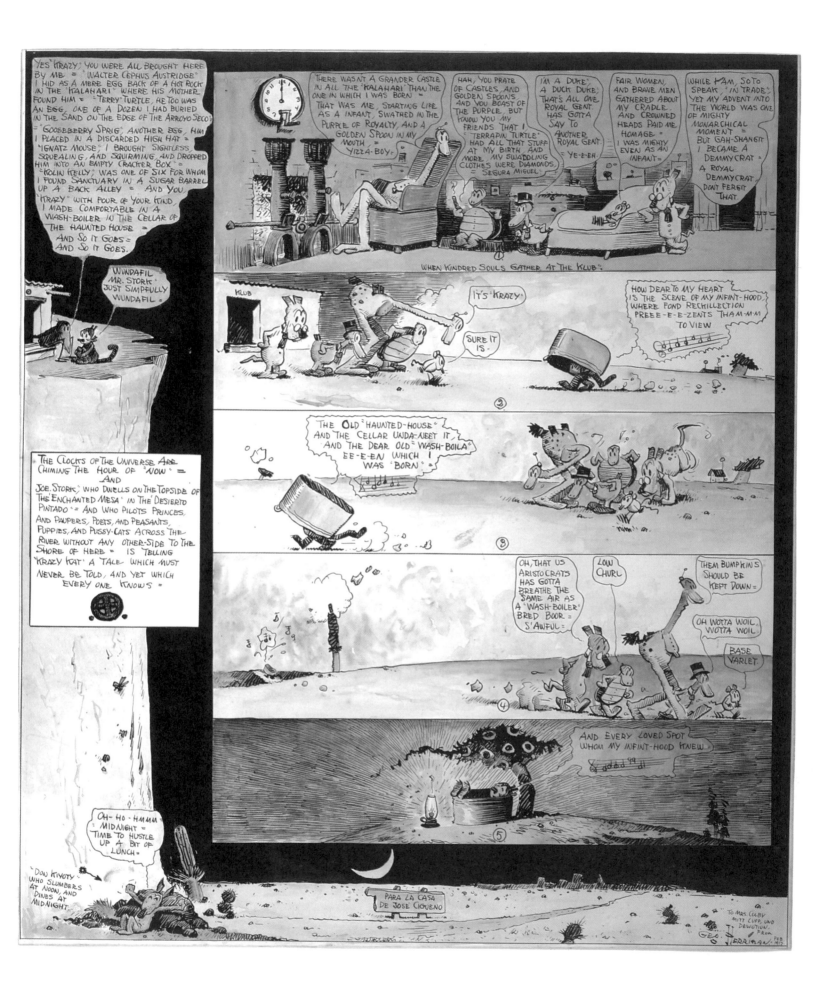

Original hand-colored drawing for strip originally published May 18, 1919, 19" x 22".
Collection of Craig Englund, photo by Robert Wedemeyer.
Special thanks to the Hammer Museum, Los Angeles, CA.

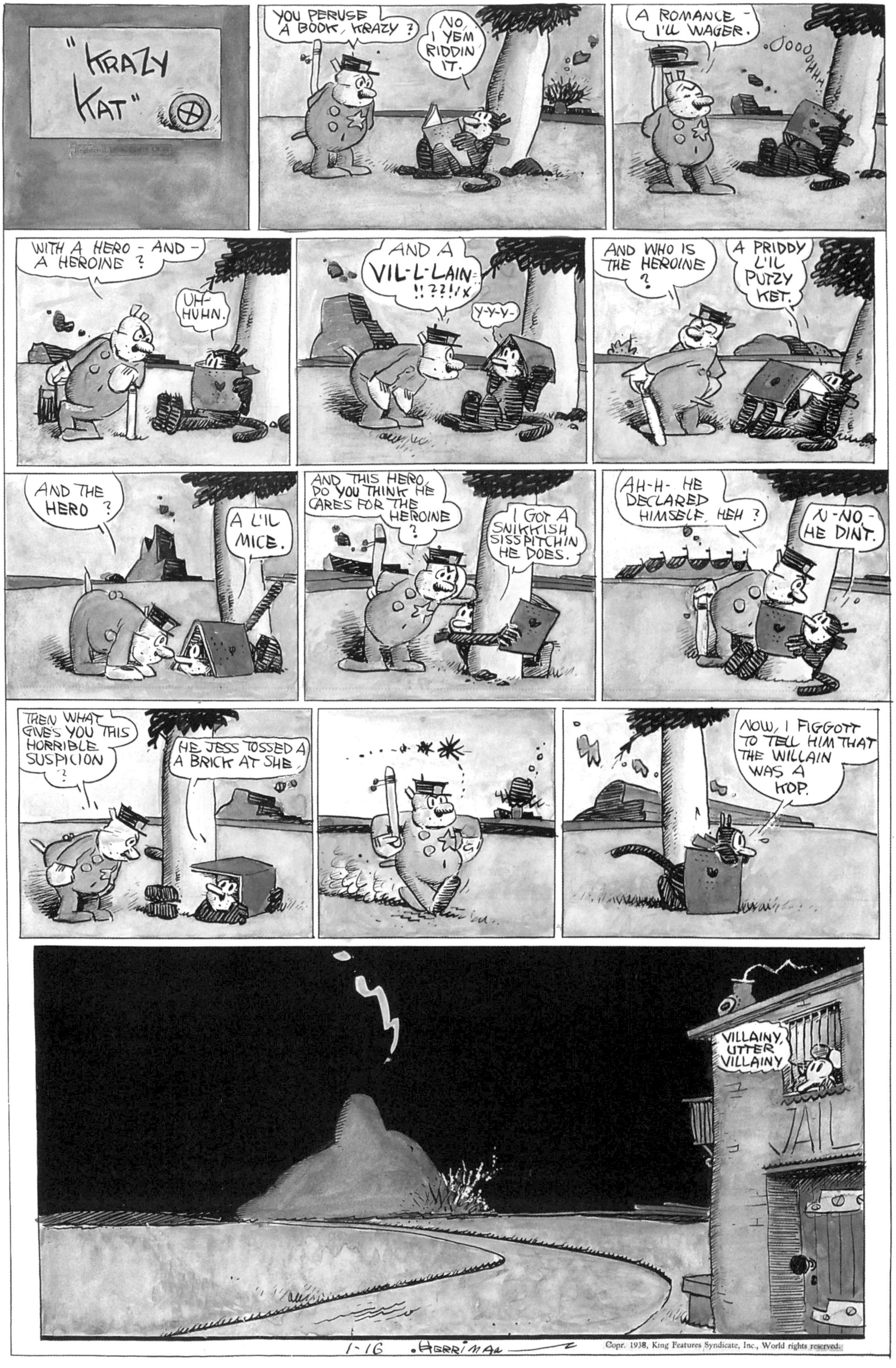
"KRAZY KAT"
YOU PERUSE A BOOK, KRAZY ?
NO, I YEM RIDDIN IT.
A ROMANCE - I'LL WAGER.
OOOOOHHH
WITH A HERO - AND - A HEROINE ?
UH-HUHN.
AND A VIL-L-LAIN !! ??!!X
Y-Y-Y-
AND WHO IS THE HEROINE ?
A PRIDDY L'IL PUTZY KET.
AND THE HERO ?
A L'IL MICE.
AND THIS HERO, DO YOU THINK HE CARES FOR THE HEROINE ?
I GOT A SNIKKISH SISSPITCHIN HE DOES.
AH-H- HE DECLARED HIMSELF, HEH ?
N-NO- HE DINT.
THEN WHAT GIVES YOU THIS HORRIBLE SUSPICION ?
HE JESS TOSSED A A BRICK AT SHE
NOW, I FIGGOTT TO TELL HIM THAT THE WILLAIN WAS A KOP.
VILLAINY, UTTER VILLAINY
JAIL
1-16 HERRIMAN
Copr. 1938, King Features Syndicate, Inc., World rights reserved.

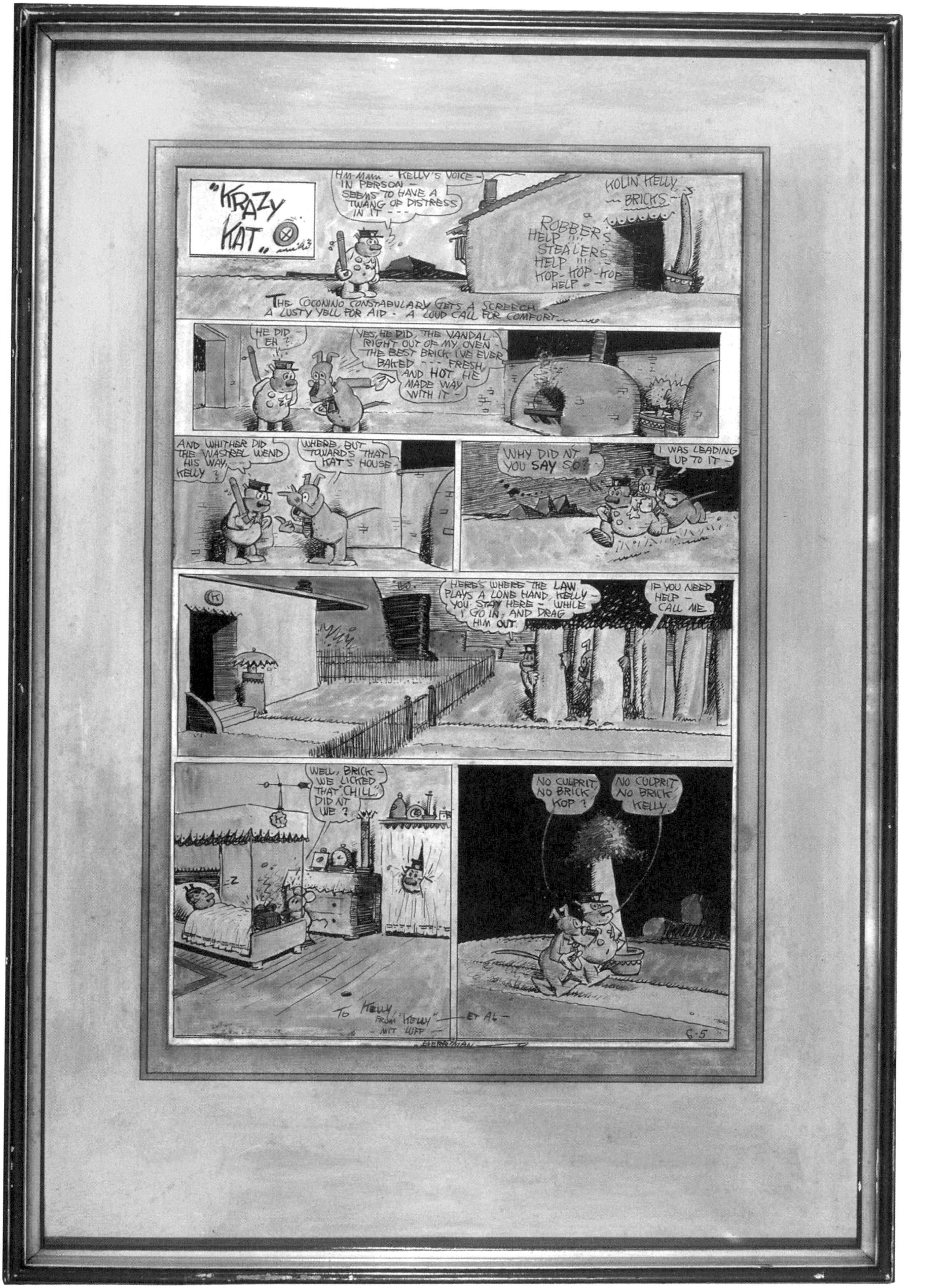
"KRAZY KAT"
HM-MMM - KELLY'S VOICE - IN PERSON - SEEMS TO HAVE A TWANG OF DISTRESS IN IT - - -
KOLIN KELLY - BRICKS -
ROBBERS HELP !!!! STEALERS HELP !!! - KOP - KOP - KOP HELP - -
THE COCONINO CONSTABULARY GETS A SCREECH - A LUSTY YELL FOR AID - A LOUD CALL FOR COMFORT
HE DID - EH ?
YES, HE DID, THE VANDAL - RIGHT OUT OF MY OVEN - THE BEST BRICK I'VE EVER BAKED - - - FRESH, AND HOT HE MADE WAY WITH IT -
AND WHITHER DID THE WASTREL WEND HIS WAY, KELLY ?
WHERE BUT TOWARDS THAT KAT'S HOUSE -
WHY DID N'T YOU SAY SO ?
I WAS LEADING UP TO IT -
HERE'S WHERE THE LAW PLAYS A LONE HAND, KELLY - YOU STAY HERE - WHILE I GO IN, AND DRAG HIM OUT.
IF YOU NEED HELP - CALL ME.
WELL, BRICK - WE LICKED THAT CHILL, DID N'T WE ?
NO CULPRIT, NO BRICK KOP ?
NO CULPRIT, NO BRICK, KELLY.
TO KELLY FROM "KELLY" - ET AL - - MIT LUFF -
6-5

"KOKONINO KOUNTY'S "KROWNING KWANDARY, WHO PUT THE PLUG IN AHINMOLAR MESA'S KAVITY" - WHO DONE IT, EH ? -

TO DOC. DOUGLE FFF PETTY" - THE WILD WEST'S BAA-ADEST TWO GUM DENTIST" - KWIKER ON THE DRAW" - FROM OLE MAN - HERRIMAN - "19●41"

Previous pages: Original hand-colored drawing for strip originally published January 16, 1938. From *America's Great Comic Strip Artists* by Rick Marschall, Abbeville Press, 1989. Original hand-colored drawing for strip originally published June 5, 1938, courtesy of Centre National de la Bande Dessinée et de l'Image.

Above: Herriman created this drawing as a special gift to his dentist. From the Sotheby's June 5, 1998 catalog.

Overleaf: A late Herriman portrait, c. 1940. Courtesy of Rob Stolzer.

The IGNATZ MOUSE DEBAFFLER PAGE.

As our first order of business, we have two items of DeBafflement pertaining to previous volumes.

In our *Krazy + Ignatz* 1939-1940 DeBaffler, we expressed puzzlement as to whose birthday Herriman might be celebrating in the strip published on June 4, 1939. Kat fan Mr. Dan McConnell points out that Herriman's deceased wife Mabel Lillian Bridge was born on June 7th and that therefore she is a likely subject, insofar as June 4th was Sunday closest to that date.

Kat fan Joe Moore suggests that contrary to our caption on page 10-11 of *Krazy + Ignatz* 1941-1942, the likely recipients of this original were not Jean Harlow and Hal Roach but Harlow and Harold "Hal" Rosson, the noted cinematographer to whom Harlow was briefly married in 1933-1934. While "Harlow did work for producer Hal Roach in the late 1920s," Mr. Moore adds, "to the best of my knowledge, they never had anything beyond this professional relationship."

Next, for those of you unable to solve the puzzle on page xxi: Since the drawing shows a six-toed paw, deductive reasoning leads us to conclude that Mike the terrier was a polydactyl (a fancy word that means an animal or human with extra digits — cat lovers are most likely to nod in recognition, but the condition extends to other animals as well) and the fake Latin "sic stoze" simply means… "six toes"! If it's any consolation, this piece sat on the current owner's wall for years before the penny dropped!

Now onto our regularly scheduled DeBaffling for this final volume.—*J.H., B.B., and K.T.*

1/10/1943 and 5/16/1943: Zoot Suits, alluded to in these strips, were a wartime fad, an ostentatious bit of male clothing, popular in the 1930s and 1940s especially with Italian Americans, Hispanics, and African Americans. Wikipedia describes it thus: "A zoot suit has high-waisted, wide-legged, tight-cuffed pegged trousers (called tramas) and a long coat (called the carlango) with wide lapels and wide padded shoulders."

1/24/1943: When reading these strips it's good to keep in mind that America is now at war. Hence the many references to patriotism, victory gardens, fox holes, submarines and European royalty exiled in America. Among the other strips that reference these war themes are: Jan. 31, 1943; Feb. 14, 1943; April 25, 1943; June 20, 1943; July 24, 1943; and Jan. 23, 1944.

3/7/1943: A graphic tribute by Herriman to the bizarre sights in the desert he so reverently relished, including a loncely cactus lifting its imploring hands up to the heavens.

3/14/1943: Look closely at the last panel here — Is it possible Herriman's shifting backgrounds have taken us to a cluster of serene pachyderms at feeding time?

11/14/1943: The song that Krazy sings ("Heddi yoze – merri keeta leenda") is "Adios, Mariquita Linda," a Herriman favorite that he used earlier on July 29, 1941.

2/6/1944: "Flight of the Bumblebee" is a very well-known orchestral interlude composed by Nikolai Rimsky-Korsakov in 1899–1900. A sprightly melody, it lends itself to comic use, so it's not clear what particular "great comedian" Herriman is refering to: possibly Spike Jones, who did a burlesque variation of the song.

2/20/1944: Herriman liked to make jokes based on his schoolboy Latin (see also page xxi). "He came, he sawed, he –" is a take-off of the famous speech by Julius Caesar: "I came, I saw, I conquered."

3/12/1944: When Krazy talks about "'Kliyyo Pettra' on her bodge – driffin' down the 'nylon'" he/she is of course referring to the famous speech in Shakespeare's play *Anthony and Cleopatra*, describing the Egyptian Queen on her barge. See in particular the famous "barge" speech by Enobarbus in Act II, scene ii.

3/26/1944: In case anyone is unfamiliar with the school yard chant that Herriman alludes to here, it goes like this:

Ladybug! Ladybug! Fly away home.
Your house is on fire and your children all gone.
All except one, and that's little Ann,
For she crept under the frying pan.

5/7/1944: Mushrooms, of course, pop up overnight — maybe even faster by the Blue Bean Bush.

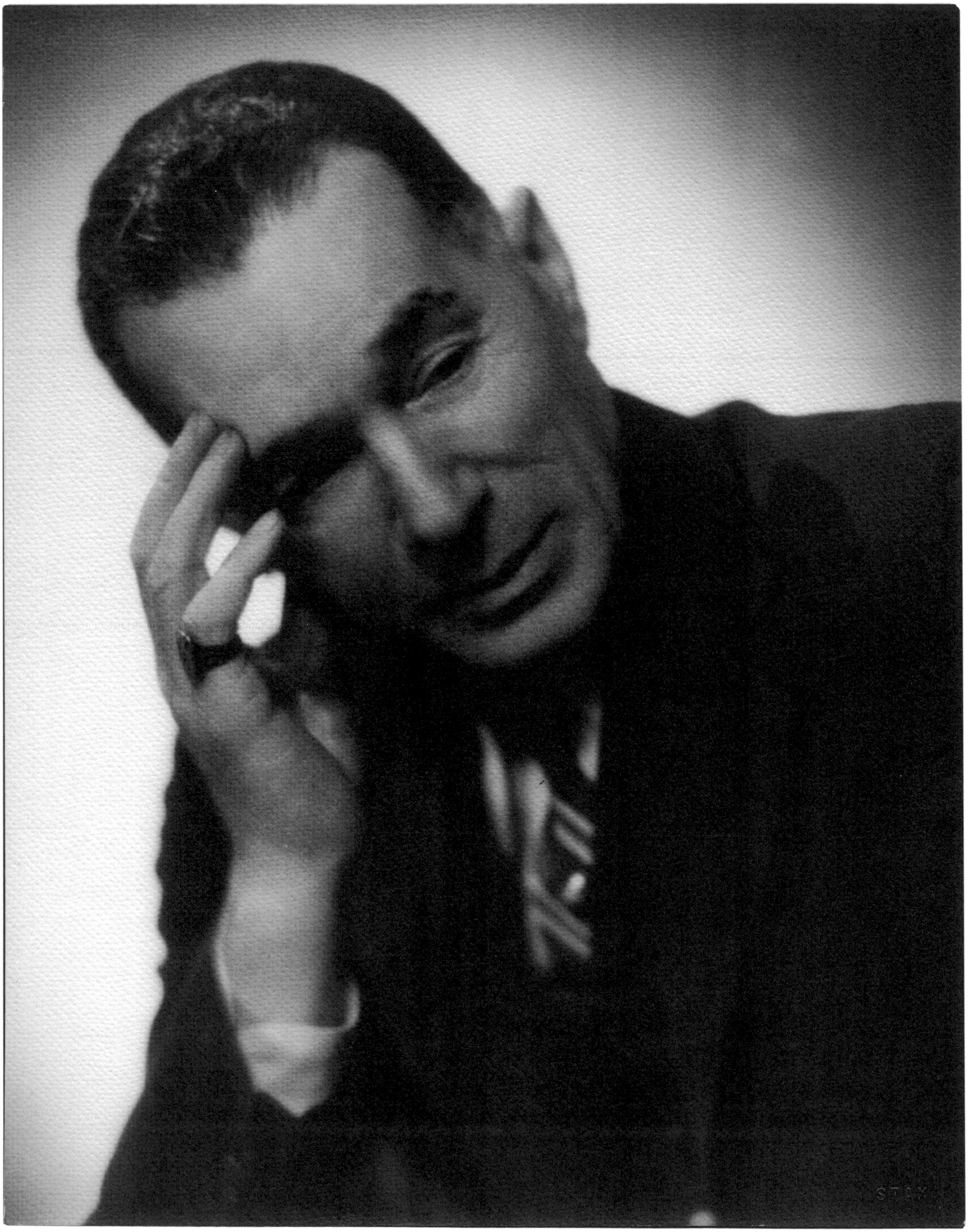

George Joseph Herriman

———————

August 22, 1880
April 25, 1944